TSOSF
©

THE SAVING OF SOULS FOUNDATION, INC.

Instructor Manual

DR. NICOLE SMALL-FLETCHER

Copyright © 2013 by Dr. Nicole Alexandra Small-Fletcher

ISBN: 979-8-9866536-2-4

All rights reserved. No part of this publication may be reproduced, distributed, or transmitted in any form or by any means, including photocopying, recording, or other electronic or mechanical methods, without the prior written permission of the publisher, except in the case of brief quotations embodied in critical reviews and certain other non-commercial uses permitted by copyright law. For permission requests, write to the publisher, addressed "Attention: Permissions Coordinator," at the address below.

Dr. Nicole Small-Fletcher

3200 N. Hiawassee Road, #683286, Orlando, FL 32868

Scripture quotations identified NKJV are from the New King James Version.

Cover design by Nicole Small-Fletcher

Copyright © 2013 Dr. Nicole Alexandra Small-Fletcher. All rights reserved.

PUBLISHING HOUSE

TSOSF

©

THE SAVING OF SOULS FOUNDATION, INC.

Dear Brothers and Sisters in our Lord and Savior, Jesus Christ. The Saving of Souls Foundation has designed the Soul Discipleship Plan for the body of Christ. The plan is designed to help build a strong foundation for a new ministry or church, new believer, or an existing believer. The Soul Discipleship Plan will shape and empower the five-fold ministry and the body of Christ. We do this by going, preaching, baptizing, training, and planting churches through the word of God. We are on a mission to save souls to become disciples who will in turn become disciple makers for the Kingdom of God. We thank you for the opportunity to work with your ministry/church or individually and it will be done, in Jesus Christ name, Amen.

1 John 4:7-8

7 "Loved ones, let us love one another, for love is from God. Everyone who loves is born of God and knows God. 8 The one who does not love does not know God, for God is love".

Sincerely,

Errol & Dr. Nicole Small-Fletcher, Founders

The Saving of Souls Foundation, Inc.

ACKNOWLEDGMENTS

To Father, I consecrate myself unto you as your servant to fulfill my assignment of my purpose and destiny, in the name of Jesus Christ. I dedicate my heart, soul, mind and talents to you, oh God. I dedicate this soul discipleship plan to the kingdom of God and his people. I pray to follow Jesus Christ and follow His example for a consecrated life until death. Empower me to walk in this consecration by your Holy Spirit. Amen.

DISCIPLESHIP PLAN OVERVIEW

Introduction

Welcome to the Soul Discipleship Plan which was designed for the body of Christ to help build a strong foundation for new believers, saved believers, a new ministry and/or a new church. It will teach the new believers and it will preach to the believers. We are on a mission to save souls, shape and empower people with love, teach evangelism and discipleship to fulfill the Great Commission and the Great Commandment of God to become disciples who will in turn become disciple makers for the Kingdom of God. We do this by going, preaching, baptizing, training, and planting churches through the word of God.

The Soul Discipleship Plan is a learning tool to teach about God, Jesus Christ, and the Holy Spirit. It will also teach what God's people were created for and prepare God's people for their assignment and purpose. Romans 11:29 says, "For the gifts and the calling of God are irrevocable". Each one of you is a uniquely gifted person created in the image of God. You are all able to contribute to the community as we unfold your particular gifts.

Discipleship Plan Overview:

You will state one unique thing about yourself and answer each question.

Introduce yourself by answering the questions.

1. Who do you think you are?
_____
_____

2. Who do you desire to become at the end of the journey?
_____
_____

Discipleship

Disciple and Discipleship

A disciple is both a student and a follower. So, discipleship means that a person accepts the way of life that has been taught and demonstrates and applies it in all aspects of his or her life.

SAY: So, what do you think is responsive discipleship?

First, it means a church, school, ministry, mentor, or even your Pastor unwraps your gifts so that you can use your God-given talents to develop your unique potential (Matthew 25:14-30).

Second, disciples learn to share one another's joys and burdens, developing their individuality in order to offer their unique gifts to their neighbors and society (Romans 12:3-8, 15).

Third, those who unwrap your gifts promote Shalom, the biblical peace and justice that helps brokenness and restores relationships (Luke 1:50-53).   In all of these ways, you will learn to respond to God's call in obedient and responsive ways.

The Soul Discipleship Plan will unlock your gifts, prepare you for your Godly assignment and equip you with all the ways of God.

Rules & Expectations

<u>SAY</u>: Let's discuss the rules and expectations in this learning environment.

    Rule #1: Respect for each other.
    Rule #2: Listen to what each person has to say.
    Rule #3: Don't be critical.
    Rule #4: Remain positive.
    Rule #5: Be on time.
    Rule #6: Come with expectation to learn and grow.
    Rule #7: Participate.
    Rule #8: Bring your Bible

Attendance will be taken every time that we meet. The expectation is that everyone will be actively engaged, and the Holy Spirit is here whenever we come together for learning.

Course Contents

The discipleship plan consists of the following goals:

    Goal 1. Circumcision of the Heart
    Goal 2. Gifts of the Spirit
    Goal 3. The Bible
    Goal 4. Weapons of Spiritual Warfare
    Goal 5. Praise & Worship
    Goal 6: Kingdom and Church
    Goal 7. Mission & Missions

> Goal 8. Evangelism
> Goal 9. Discipleship: Disciple to Disciple Others
> Closing: Evaluation

SAY: Daily recite the Books of the Bible. It will sharpen your memorization skills.

Discussion

SAY: So, you have signed up for this soul discipleship plan. Who are you? Why are you here? What are you attempting to accomplish for your soul?

SAY: Are you here because you went to church? Are you here because you believed the good news that God sent Jesus Christ to take your place in death and was buried and is resurrected and alive? Are you here because you confessed that you are a sinner? Are you here because you confessed with your mouth the Lord Jesus and believe in your heart that God raised Jesus from the dead and you will be saved? Are you relying on God's promises?

The Christian walk is a daily lifestyle. A Christian must believe the gospel and the entire Word of God at all times and walk in the light as you receive it (1 Jn. 1:7). Walk by faith (Heb. 10:23-39; Rom. 6:1-23; 8:1-13; Gal. 5:16-26). Read the bible daily, search it, and meditate on it day and night (Ps. 1:1-3; 119:105; 2 Cor. 10:4-7; Eph. 6:10-18; 1 Pet. 2:2). One must be of death to self (Gal. 2:50).

Being crucified with Christ, which means your old nature has been nailed to the cross and you are replacing it with a new nature which is Christ (2 Cor.5:17). Christians must pray daily which includes decreeing and declaring the Word of God, spiritual warfare prayers, and confessing the Word of God (Jn. 16:23-26; Phil. 4:5-6; 1 Pet.5:7). Be stewards of all God entrusts you with. Pay tithes & offerings. Take communion. Be baptized. Baptism and infilling of the Spirit with the evidence of praying in tongues. Operating in your spiritual gift. Praise and worship. Love thy neighbors through action. Do good not evil. Attend church. Seek constantly for the anointing of the Holy Spirit. Be tact. Seek wisdom, knowledge, and understanding. Tame the tongue. Have a zeal to win souls. Testify about the goodness of Jesus Christ and what He has done in your life. Working (Colossians 3:23). Christian work by personal evangelism with all you come in contact with.

The Christian lifestyle is a personal intimate relationship with Jesus Christ.

The Bible tells us all things and answers many questions. It begins with the story of the creation and answers "How did it all begin?". Then there was the fall which answers, "What went wrong?". Then there was the rescue which answers "Is there any hope?". It ends with the restoration which answers, "What will the future hold?".

The discipleship plan focuses on different areas that I believe a Christian should know and understand about the Bible, how to live daily, learn God's plan for your life, and fulfill destiny and purpose on the Earth which is the earth realm. It must all be done with holiness, as God is holy.

CONTENTS

ACKNOWLEDGMENTS ii

DISCIPLESHIP PLAN OVERVIEW iii
    Icebreaker iv
    Discipleship v
    Rules & Expectations vi
    Course Contents vii
    Discussion viii

CHURCH/MINISTRY ACTION PLAN ix
    1. The Layout x
    2. Purpose of Your Church/Ministry Area xi
    3. Process and Programs xii
    4. Church/Ministry Structure xiii
    5. SWOT Analysis xiv
    6. Targeted Completion Date and Significant Person or Persons xv
    7. Targeted Completion Date and Significant Person or Persons, continued xvi
    8. Evaluation of the Church/Ministry xvii
    Information Sheet xviii
    Disciple Attendance xix
    Lesson Plan Template xx

GOAL ONE: CIRCUMCISION OF THE HEART 19
    Lesson Plan   20
    Introduction 21
    Overview 21
    1. The Heart 22
    2. Love… What is Love? 23
    3. Acceptance 24
    4 Forgiveness 24
    5 Sin 25
    6. Salvation 26
    7 Holiness 27
    8 Prayer for Circumcision of the Heart 28
    9 Closing 28

GOAL TWO: GIFTS OF THE SPIRIT 29
    Lesson Plan   33
    Introduction 34
    Overview 35
    1. Understanding the Holy Spirit 35

2. Manifestation Gifts (1 Cor 12:8-10).. 40
3. Nine Gifts of the Holy Spirit (1 Cor 12:7-11)... 41
4.   Ministry Gifts (Eph 4:11).. 42
5.   Motivational Gifts (Romans 12:6-8).. 43
6. Fruit of the Spirit.. 44
7.   Obstacles that Block Gifts.. 46
8. Part of a Whole Body... 46
9. Covenants of the Church... 47
10.   Using Your Spiritual Gifts... 47
12.   Move Forward with Your Gifting... 54
13 Spiritual Growth.. 57
14.   Visionary... 57
15. Life Questionnaire... 58
16. Visual Worksheet.. 62
17.   Write the Vision and Make it Plain.. 63
18. Closing.. 69

GOAL THREE: THE BIBLE.. **71**
Lesson Plan 72
Introduction.. 73

Overview.. 73
1.   The Bible and Its Books.. 73
2.   The Bible and Its Role... 83
3.   God's W o r d 83
4. Genres of the Bible.. 84
5.   Numbers, Colors, Animals, Metals and Elements, Time, Gender and Objects......... 86
6. Bible Study Tools... 92
7.   How to Study the Bible... 93
8.   Activity.. 95
9. Spiritual Growth Through the Bible.. 99
10.   GOD... 99
11.   Jesus.. 103
12. Holy Spirit... 104
13.   Bible Versions and Translations... 105
14.   Interpret the Word of God.. 108
15.   Role of the Holy Spirit.. 125
16.   Living Out the Learned... 127
17 Closing.. 134

GOAL FOUR WEAPONS OF SPIRITUAL WARFARE.................. **136**
Lesson Plan 137
Introduction.. 138
Overview.. 138
1.   Spiritual Warfare.. 139
2. Levels of Spiritual Warfare.. 139
3. Spiritual Attack... 141
4. Angels... 141
5. Satan the Adversary.. 144
6. Blessings and Curses... 147

7. What are our Weapons?.. 153
8. Deliverance... 174
9. Consecration... 176
10. Prayer Session... 177
11. Closing... 177

GOAL FIVE: PRAISE & WORSHIP..179
Lesson Plan 180
Introduction... 181
Overview.. 181
1. Instructions on Praise.. 182
2. Forms of Praise.. 182
3. Instructions on Worship.. 182
4. Expressions of Worship... 184
5. Confessions of Praise & Worship... 184
6. Hebrew Words Relating to Praise & Worship... 184
7. Forms of Worship.. 185
8. Closing.. 193

GOAL SIX: KINGDOM AND CHURCH... 195
Lesson Plan 196
Introduction... 197
Overview.. 197
1. Kingdom of God 198
2. Kingdom of Heaven.. 198
3. Kingdom of God vs Kingdom of Heaven.. 199
4. Creation... 199
5. The Apostolic Church... 200
6. Christians and Christianity... 201
7. Five-Fold Ministry... 203
8. Pastor/Shepherd... 204
9. Role of a Disciple-Making Pastor.. 205
10. Role of the Pastor's Spouse (Male or Female).. 206
11. Role of a Minister, Reverend, Ordained Reverend, Elder, Deacon.......... 206
12. Leaders and Leadership.. 207
13. Leadership of Jesus Christ... 207
14. Baptism... 221
15. Salvation... 222
16. Stewardship.. 223
17. Church Discipline.. 224
18. Teaching... 225
19. Government and Citizenship... 227
20. Relationships.. 228
21. Racial/Class Discrimination... 228
22. Healing.. 229
23. Spiritual Gifts... 230
24. Grace... 231
25. Healthy Body, Healthy Church.. 232
26. Success.. 232

27. Warfare Prayer for the Church 233
28. Closing 234

GOAL SEVEN: MISSION & MISSIONS 236
Lesson Plan 237
Introduction 238
Overview 239
1. Missio Dei 239
2. Mission 240
3. Missions 240
4. Brainstorm Activity 240
5. Closing 241

GOAL EIGHT EVANGELISM 242
Lesson Plan 243
Introduction 244
Overview 244
1. Evangelism 245
2. Preparing for Evangelism 245
3. Evangelist 246
4. Holiness 246
5. Christianity, Cults & Religions 246
6. Questions Lost People Will Ask 248
7. Share Jesus Questions (Witnessing to Others) 250
8. Methods to Evangelize 251
9. Lead them to Christ 254
10. Follow Up 255
11. Assignment 257
12. Closing 258

GOAL NINE: DISCIPLESHIP: DISCIPLES TO DISCIPLE OTHERS 259
Lesson Plan 260
Introduction 261
Overview 261
1. Discipleship 262
2. Disciple(s) 262
3. Making Disciples 264
4. Five Stages 264
5. Family Discipleship 268
6. Local Congregation 270
7. A Child's Heart 271
8. Spiritual Disciplines 272
9. Small Groups 276
10. Closing 278

REFERENCES 281

CHURCH/MINISTRY ACTION PLAN

1. The Layout

Below are the outline teachings of each goal of the Soul Discipleship Plan:

1. Circumcision of the Heart
2. Gifts of the Spirit
3. The Bible
4. Weapons of Spiritual Warfare
5. Praise & Worship
6. Kingdom and Church
7. Mission & Missions
8. Evangelism
9. Discipleship: Disciple to Disciple Others
   Closing & Evaluation

Church/Ministry

We will begin by discussing the Church/Ministry, where it started from, where it is and the vision for where it is going.

Church/Ministry: _____

Location: _____

Start Date: _____ **Calendar Year:** _____

2. Purpose of Your Church/Ministry Area:

The vision of the _____ Church/ Ministry is _____

_____

_____

State how your church/ministry reflects the vision stated.

1_____

2 _____

3 _____

4 _____

The mission of the _____ Church/Ministry is _____

_____

State how your church/ministry reflects the mission stated.

1 _____

2 _____

3 _____

4 _____

3. Process and Programs

Outline the weekly programs within your church/ministry and who is currently responsible to lead, and how these programs help move people through the discipleship process.

Sunday- _____

Monday- _____

Tuesday- _____

Wednesday- _____

Thursday- _____

Friday _____

Saturday- _____

4. Church/Ministry Structure

Outline the foundational structure of your church/ministry including ministers, leaders and volunteers. Write NA, if it does not apply to your ministry or church.

Board: _____

Women's Ministry: _____

Men's Ministry: _____

Intercessors:_____

Youth Ministries:_____

Evangelism: _____

Discipleship: _____

Other: _____

5. SWOT Analysis

Evaluate the conditions of your church/ministry area through a SWOT profile. The SWOT profile will be a tool used in helping you plan goals for the new ministry year. Here is where you identify if the church body of Christ is healthy.

Strengths within the church/ministry

1. _____
2. _____
3. _____
4. _____
5. _____

Weaknesses within the church/ministry

1. _____
2. _____
3. _____
4. _____
5. _____

Opportunities for the future

Unity

Love

Patience

Kindness

Praying for one another

Intercession

Bold and Radical for Jesus Christ

Threats to the health of the church/ministry

Unbelief

Lack of Faith

Strife

Gossip

Envy

Jealousy

Sabotage

6. Targeted Completion Date and Significant Person or Persons

Based on the above, state significant new goals for your area of responsibility, being as objective as possible. The goals should be aligned to your vision and mission. List your goals and the person or persons who will be significant in helping you reaching those goals.

Goal One: _____

Person or Persons: _____

Completion Date: _____

Goal Two: _____

Person or Persons: _____

Completion Date: _____

Goal Three: _____

Person or Persons: _____

Completion Date: _____

Goal Four: _____

Person or Persons: _____

Completion Date: _____

Goal Five: _____

Person or Persons: _____

Completion Date: _____

Goal Six: _____

Person or Persons: _____

Completion Date _____

Goal Seven: _____

Person or Persons: _____

Completion Date _____

Goal Eight: _____

Person or Persons: _____

Completion Date _____

Goal Nine: _____

Person or Persons: _____

Completion Date _____

Explain how each goal will be communicated and executed.

7. Evaluation of the Church/Ministry

The success of the _____ church/ministry will be measured by the presence and anointing power of the Holy Spirit, lives being changed and empowered.

The lack of an efficient strategic plan hinders ministries in reaching the greatest level of ministry effectiveness. By following through with a specified strategic plan, the programs of and church/ministry will reach greater levels of ministry effectiveness. It can be accomplished through the steps of the strategic plan beginning with an external and internal analysis, a clearly defined mission statement, goals and objectives, formulation of specific strategies, concluding with the implementation of the strategy and managed control process.

ATTENDEE SHEET

NAME	Date of Birth	Phone#	Email Address
1.			
2.			
3.			
4.			
5.			
6.			
7.			
8.			
9.			
10.			
11.			
12.			
13.			
14.			
15.			
16.			
17.			
18.			
19.			
20.			

DISCIPLE ATTENDANCE

Room: Instructor:

Time   Course Goal   Week of:

Name	Week 1	Week 2	Week 3	Week 4	Week 5	Week 6	Week 7	Week 8	
1.									
2.									
3.									
4.									
5.									
6.									
7.									
8.									
9.									
10.									
11.									
12.									
13.									
14.									
15.									
16.									
17.									
18.									
19.									
20.									

Soul Discipleship Plan

LESSON PLAN TEMPLATE

Date:	Time:
Curriculum Area:	**Goal /Unit Topic:**
Key enduring understandings, concepts, abilities, and/or values.	
Intended learning outcomes (to know, to do, to create, to value, etc.)	
Assessment Strategies: How will you assess attainment of the intended learning outcome?	
Materials/Preparation:	
Introduction	Setting the Stage: engaging, motivating, experiencing, connecting with prior knowledge, reflecting, conjecturing, posing problems
Guided learning steps	Disclosing: acquiring knowledge/skills, conceptualizing, developing, understanding, integrating
	Practicing, Reinforcing: modelling, giving instruction, checking for understanding, guided practice, independent practice, applying, posing and solving problems
Closure	**Transcending:** *summing up, responding, creating, performing, committing, evaluating*
Modifications: How will you change the lesson to meet the needs of the individual students?	
Personal notes/reminders/homework	
Post-lesson reflections	

GOAL ONE

CIRCUMCISION OF THE HEART

LESSON PLAN

Date & Time:	Curriculum Area: Circumcision of the Heart	Goal /Unit Topic: Goal One

Key enduring understandings, concepts, abilities, and/or values.
Explained in the Introduction

Intended learning outcomes (to know, to do, to create, to value, etc.)
Explained in the Overview

Assessment Strategies: How will you assess attainment of the intended learning outcome?
Questions & Answers, post/pre tests

Materials/Preparation/ Area Setup:
Materials: Poster board, Dry Erase Markers
Preparation: Heart Decorations, Poster board –One for OT and NT with all book listed
Area Setup: For each disciple, place on the desk a TSOSF brochure, blue pen, highlighter, notebook, goal one

Introduction	*Setting the Stage*: engaging, motivating, experiencing, connecting with prior knowledge, reflecting, conjecturing, posing problems
Once the Introduction and Overview have been completed, then move on to the Bible book recitals. It will be recited every time that we meet with the disciples.	

Guided learning steps The learning steps are as follows:	*Disclosing*: acquiring knowledge/skills, conceptualizing, developing, understanding, integrating
1. The Heart 2. Love…What Is Love? 3. Acceptance 4. Forgiveness 5. Sin 6. Salvation 7. Holiness 8. Prayer : Circumcision of the Heart 9. Closing	*Practicing, Reinforcing*: modelling, giving instruction, checking for understanding, guided practice, independent practice, applying, posing and solving problems

Closure	*Transcending*: summing up, responding, creating, performing, committing, evaluating
Prayer, Questions & Answers, Comments	

Modifications	
How will you change the lesson to meet the needs of the individual students?	

Personal notes/reminders/homework/assignments	

Post-lesson reflections	

INTRODUCTION

Our most important part of our body for God is the heart. We are going to start with the heart today. Amen.

A person's life is a reflection of the heart. The heart is the control center for life. The heart determines behavior (Mark 7:21). The basic issue is always what is going on in the heart. All of our behaviors are linked to the attitudes of the heart. People either worship God or they worship idols. People interact with life either of a true covenant of faith or out of an idolatrous covenant of disbelief.

God's Word refers to the heart over 750 times. The Word of God explains that the heart conceals, discerns, instructs, meditates, muses, perceives, plans, plots, ponders, thinks, and weighs.

There are adjectives used in the Bible to describe the heart which are adulterous, anguished, arrogant, astray, bitter, blameless, blighted, broken, calloused, circumcised, contrite, crushed, darkened, deadened, deceitful, deluded, devoted, disloyal, envious, evil, faithful, far off, fearful, foolish, grateful, happy, hard, haughty, humble, mad, malicious, obstinate, perverse, proud, pure, rebellious, rejoicing, responsive, righteous, sick, sincere, sinful, steadfast, troubled, unfeeling, uncircumcised, upright, unsearchable, weary, wicked, wise, and wounded.

Overview

I. Goal Lesson
Goal one teaches about the heart.

II. Goal Objectives
Upon completion of this goal, the disciple will be able to explain:

    a. the makings of the heart and the actions of the heart,
    b. understand heart, love, acceptance, forgiveness, salvation, holiness, and
    c. sin.

III. Bible Book Recitals
Genesis to Revelation

1. The Heart

SAY: Here is where you will talk and learn about the heart. The heart is a person's center for both physical and emotional-intellectual-moral activities. There are eight different uses of the word "Heart".

1. The physical organ- the seat of the physical life; the blood pump (2 Sam. 18:14; 2 Ki. 9:24; Eccl. 12:6; Pr. 14:30)

2. The center of anything (Mt. 12:40)

3. The inner man consisting of soul and spirit (Ps. 51:10; Mt. 5:8; 12:24-25; 15:18-19; 22:37; Rom. 6:17; 1 Pet. 3:4)

4. The conscience (Mk. 8:17; Jn. 12:40; Acts 2:37; Rom.2:5; 1 Jn. 3:20-21)

5. The will (Acts 4:32; 1 Cor. 7:37)

6. The mind, including:

    - Thoughts (Gen. 6:5; Jn.12:40) (the product of mental activity)
    - Imaginations (Gen. 8:21) (forming mental images or concepts of what is not actually present to the senses)
    - Understanding (1 Ki. 3:9,12) (reflective thought; to set together)
    - Wisdom (Ex. 35:35; Pr. 2:10) (knowledge of what is true or right coupled with just judgment as to action; sagacity; discernment, or insight)
    - Blindness (Dt. 28:28; Rom. 12:1) (unable to see; locking the sense of sight)
    - Meditation (Ps. 19:14; Lk. 2:19) (continued or extended thought; reflection)
    - Deceit (Pr. 12:20; Jer. 17:9) (concealment or distortion of the truth for the purpose of misleading; fraud; cheating)
    - Wickedness (Jer. 17:9) (state of being wicked)
    - Doubt (Mk. 9:23; Jas. 4:8) (to be uncertain about; hesitate to believe)
    - Purpose (Acts 11:23) (the reason for which something exists or is done, made, used)

7. The soul, including:

    - Grief (Gen. 6:6; Dt.15:10) (painful regret; keen mental suffering or distress over affliction or loss)
    - Joy and gladness (Dt. 28:47) (emotion of great delight or happiness; keen; elation)
    - Desires (Ps. 37:4) (to wish or long for; crave; want)
    - Sorrow (Pr. 14:10;15:13; Jn. 16:6) (distress caused by loss; affliction; disappointment)
    - Discouragement (Dt. 1:28) (the state of being discouraged)
    - Fear (Dt. 28;65-67) (a distressing emotion caused by impending danger, evil, pain. The feeling or condition of being afraid)

- Comfort (Judg. 19:8) (to soothe, console, or reassure, bring cheer to)
- Pain (Ps. 55:4) (physical suffering or distress, as due to injury, illness, etc.)

8. The spirit, including:

    - Zeal (Ex. 35:21; 26; 36:2) (fervor for a person, object or cause; eager desire or endeavor)
    - Humility (Ps. 34:18; Mt. 11:29) (condition of being humble)
    - Faithfulness (Neh. 9:8) (strict or thorough in the performance of duty, true to one's word, promises, vows, etc.)
    - Hate (Lev. 19:17) (to dislike intensely or passionately; detest)
    - Pride (Dt. 8:14; 17:20) (a higher or inordinate opinion of one's own dignity; importance, merit, or superiority)
    - Foolishness (Pr. 22:15) (resulting from or showing a lack of sense; ill-considered; unwise)
    - Integrity (Gen. 20:5-6; 1 Ki. 2:44; 1 Chr. 29:17) (soundness of moral character; honesty)
    - Immorality (Ps. 22:26:69:32; 1 Pet. 3:4) (immoral quality, character or conduct; wickedness; evilness)

The heart must return to Jehovah, walk before Him, Serve Him, Love Him, Keep His word, Follow Him, Seek Him, Praise Him, Trust in Him, and Believe in Him. (The Dake Annotated Reference Bible-NKJV, Cyclopedic Index, p. 681)

As you continue in the discipleship plan, trust God to help you grow spiritually by revealing heart issues and empowering you to take action. Your actions demonstrate a desire to build God's kingdom. The spiritual heart is the heart that every called child of God must come to have and possess to inherit God's Kingdom.

2. Love... What is Love?

The earthly realm where we reside defines love, according to the merriam-webster dictionary as "*1)*: strong affection for another arising out of kinship or personal ties *maternal love for a child (2)*: attraction based on sexual desire: affection and tenderness felt by lovers *After all these years, they are still very much in love. (3)*: affection based on admiration, benevolence, or common interests *love for his old schoolmates; b*: an assurance of affection".

God's Word says we must love God, neighbors, strangers, salvation, God's name, God's Word, wisdom, good, mercy, truth, peace, enemies, one another-saints, brethren, husbands, wives and children. We must love with all the heart, soul, mind, strength, as one loves himself, exceedingly, as Christ loves, enough to lay down life for others, without hypocrisy, by the Holy Spirit, in sincerity, by service to one another, bearing with one another, with a pure heart, as brethren, not in word but indeed and without fear.

- Love is an action, not a feeling.

- Psalm 85:10 Love and faithfulness meet together.
- Psalm 86:13 For great is your love towards me.
- Psalm 115:1 Because of your love and faithfulness.
- Psalm 117:2 For great is his love towards us.
- Prov. 3:3 Let love and faithfulness never leave.
- Rom. 12:10 Be devoted to one another in love (Love in action).
- Rom. 13:8 For whoever loves others has fulfilled.
- Rom. 13:9 Love your neighbor as yourself.
- Gal. 5: 13 Serve one another humbly in love.
- Gal 5:14 Love your neighbor as yourself.
- 1 John 3:11 We should love another.

SAY: Let Me Explain the Three Types of Love:

1. **Eros love** means desire & longing, erotic love, this is a selfish kind of love as it is associated w/sexual love. Describes appetitive, self-centered love, including sexual desire and physical craving. Does not appear in the New Testament.

2. **Philos love** means brotherly love, fond affection. Christians practice this towards one another. Refers to esteem and affection reflected in the loving concern friends have for one another. Used in the New Testament (John 21:15-17; Titus 2:4)

3. **Agape Love** means the divine love of the love towards his Son Jesus Christ, the human beings and all his believers. This is the best of all three love types. Agape is the love that God commanded all believers to have for everyone whether he or she is a believer or not. Remember that love suffers for a long time (true love puts up with people who would be easier to give up on), love does not envy (if our love is directed toward others, we will rejoice in the blessings they receive rather than desiring those blessings for ourselves), love is not provoked (love is not easily angered or over-sensitive), love does not rejoice in iniquity, but rejoices in the truth (love never gives up, knowing that God can change lives for the better), and finally, love endures all things (love accepts any hardship or rejection, continues unabated to build up and encourage).

Love:

       is longsuffering (Noun: forebearance, patience, to bear with)
       is kind (Noun: serviceable, good, pleasant, gracious)
       is not jealous (moved with envy)
       is not boastful (a vagabond, imposter, any kind of haughty speech which stirs up strife or provokes others)
       is not arrogant (puffed up)
       is not rude (2 Corinthians 11:6, does not behave rudely)
       is not selfish
       is not resentful

    does not think evil (envy)
    rejoices in truth (real, ideal, genuine, sincerity & integrity of character)
    bears all things (believes all things)
    hopes all things (happy anticipation of good)
    endures all things. (1 Cor. 13:1-13)

Love Relationship

List two things below that can enhance your relationship with God and two things that can interfere with your relationship with God.

Enhance	Interfere
1.	1.
2.	2.

This is a personal reflection.

3. Acceptance

Scripture: Ephesians 5:10

The acceptance of each other in Christ has become difficult in the body of Christ. Why is a man or a woman unable to accept others fully? It is difficult because the man or the woman focuses on the outer appearance instead of focusing on the inner actions of the heart.

Acceptance is "the act of taking or receiving something offered" (dictionary.com).

"Do not consider his appearance or his height, for I have rejected him. The Lord does not look at the things man looks at. Man looks at the outward appearance, but the Lord looks at the heart" (1 Sam. 16:7).

4 Forgiveness

<u>SAY</u>: We can forgive, be forgiven, or give forgiveness.

<u>Scripture</u>: Ephesians 1:7 "7 In Him we have redemption through His blood, the forgiveness of sins, according to the riches of His grace".

<u>Question</u>: What is forgiveness?

<u>Answer:</u> *Forgiveness is defined as the willingness to forgive. (www.dictionary.com)*

<u>**Confession of God's Forgiveness**</u>: "I am blessed of the Lord because He has forgiven my transgressions and covered my sins". (Psalms 32:10).

When I repent and cry unto the Lord, He creates a clean heart within me, and renews me with a right spirit (Psalms 51:10). True repentance comes from the heart and then change must follow.

Is there a person(s) you need to forgive, do you need to be forgiven, and have met the two necessary things for forgiveness (Acts 3:19), which is repentance and to be converted? There must be true repentance.

Participant response

_____

_____

_____

Let's pray.

Prayer of Forgiveness: "Father, in Christ Jesus' Name, I lay down at Your feet all present and past unforgiveness, anger, bitterness, or resentment, directed at (name or names). I repent of it and renounce it all and ask You to forgive me for it. I forgive and release them. I repent for anyone who was hurt by it and ask for your forgiveness for that also. I forgive and release myself of all unforgiveness, anger, resentment, and bitterness also. I renounce this and all past sin, and ask You to forgive me, Lord Jesus Christ, I ask all these things in your Holy Name, Amen."

5 Sin

God is holy and will not have sin in His presence. When we choose not to follow God's plan and ways with our actions, words, and attitudes, then we rebel against God Himself. God takes sin seriously. People tend to categorize and minimize sin. A sin is anything that is not of God. We have to make sure there is no sin left in our hearts and in our lives. Disobedience is sin (1 Peter 2:7). There are 370 kinds of sins committed and recorded in Scripture.

Scriptures: John 1:29; Rom 6:23; 1 Pet 2:22

There are two classes of sin:

- Sin of commission: an active sin, doing something that is wrong.
- Sin of omission: passive sin, not doing the right thing (Luke 10:30-37; James 4:17).

SAY: Ask yourself "Do I struggle with sins of commission or omission?" _____

"Why?" _____

Sin affects us by damaging our legal standing before God (Rom. 8:1), damages our relationship with God (Eph. 4:30; Isa. 59:2), damages our relationship with physical surroundings (Gen. 3:16-

19) and damages our relationship with others (Gen. 3:16). The concept of original sin refers to a sin that dwells in our hearts (Mark 7:14-23; Matt. 12:33-37).

The Results of Sin

Gen. 3:7	• The experiential knowledge of evil. • The shame and guilt. • The search for clothing to cover.
Gen. 3:8	• The desire for concealment. • The fear of God's presence. • The loss of fellowship with God.
Gen. 3:12	• The refusal of personal responsibility. • The shifting of blame from self to others.

(The Results of Sin, The Woman's Study Bible, 2006, p. 9)

Pray the prayer found in Psalm 139:23-24 and confess any sins to God and sin no more, seek holiness and righteousness.

6. Salvation

Salvation speaks to three of our most significant needs. Salvation speaks to our need for forgiveness of sins and the gift of the Spirit. People want to avoid the guilt they feel inside, even if they do not use the term sin. Salvation through Christ addresses this need. Salvation also speaks to the image of God in us longing for completion. Only God can fill this need. And finally, salvation speaks to our longing for wholeness and fulfilment in the midst of our fragmentation caused by sin. God knows our deepest needs, and He addresses them through salvation.

Christian Bible study states, "Jesus Christ is the only means of our salvation. The only means of salvation is Jesus Christ (Acts 4:12; John 14:6). He died on the Cross to pay the penalty of our sins (1 Pet. 2:24). He offers each of us a pardon for our sins (Heb. 9:26) and wants us to become children of God (John 1:12). When we put our faith in Christ, it triggers a spiritual chain reaction. We become the temple of the Holy Spirit (1 Cor. 6:19). Our names are written in the Lamb's Book of Life (Rev. 3:5). [1]

We become citizens of heaven (Phil. 3:20-21). We are given eternal life (John 3:16). We are adopted and become children of God (Gal. 4:47). Our sin is forgiven and forgotten (Heb. 8:12). We are credited with righteousness of Christ (Rom. 4:4-5). The evidence of salvation is two-fold. The internal evidence is the direct witness of the Holy Spirit (Rom. 8:16). The external evidence is the fruit of the Spirit (Gal. 5:22-23). We become a new creation (2 Cor. 5:17) and are transformed into

[1] ChristianBibleStudies.com, Theology 101, 2009, p. 56.

the image of Christ (2 Cor. 3:18)."

Mark McCloskey in his outstanding book Tell It Often—Tell It Well, summarized seven pictures of salvation found in the Bible.

1. "**Regeneration**: From Death to Life (2 Cor. 5:17)
2. **Reconciliation**: From Enemy to Friend (Rom. 5:10)
3. **Propitiation**: From Wrath to Mercy (1 John 4:10)
4. **Sanctification**: A Change in Ownership (Acts 26:18)
5. **Redemption**: From Slavery to Freedom (1 Pet. 1:18)
6. **Justification**: From Guilt to Acquittal (Rom. 3:24)
7. **Adoption**: A Change in Families (Gal. 4:4-7)"[2]

7 Holiness

The Christian call is holiness. Peter advocated holy living in his writings. Holy implies sacredness, being consecrated to God, or being worthy of God. A person has to be free from impurity. There can be no limit of moral pollution or spiritual defilement. It may seem impossible to achieve, but sanctification, the process by which we are made holy is "of the Spirit" (1 Peter 1:2). The Holy Spirit of God, who indwells us at the moment of salvation, is able to transform us. By the power of the Holy Spirit we find the ability to "abstain from fleshly lusts which war against the soul (1 Peter 2:11). As we yield ourselves to God, and as we soberly and vigilantly resist the devil (1 Peter 5:9) and all his temptations, we will find that God is able to "perfect, establish, strengthen, and settle" us (1 Peter 5:10).

Tozer describes, "Holy is the way God is. He does not conform to a standard. He is that standard. He is absolutely holy with an infinite, incomprehensible fullness of purity that is incapable of being other than it is. Because He is holy, His attributes are holy; that is, whatever we think of as belonging to God must be thought of as holy".[3]

Tozer tells us what Christians should do, "We must take refuge from God in God. Above all we must believe that God sees us perfect in His Son while he disciplines and chastens and purges us that we may be partakers of his holiness. By faith and obedience, by constant meditation on the holiness of God, by loving righteousness and hating iniquity, by a growing acquaintance with the Spirit of holiness, we can acclimate ourselves to the fellowship of the saints on earth and prepare ourselves for the eternal companionship of God and the saints above".[4]

8 Prayer for Circumcision of the Heart

2 McRaney, The Art of Personal Evangelism, 2003, Chapter 3.
3 Tozer, The Knowledge of The Holy, 2009, 105-106.
4 Ibid, 107.

Scripture: Colossians 2:11 "11 In Him you were also circumcised with the circumcision made without hands, by putting off the body of the sins of the flesh, by the circumcision of Christ".

SAY THIS PRAYER: "Father, show me my heart the way You see it. Reveal to me all that is unholy in me, all unholy actions, behaviors, habits, thoughts, and beliefs; all that keeps me from drawing closer to You and from knowing You to the fullest of intimacy. I desire that our intimacy with each other grow daily and rapidly, moment by moment. I want to know You more and more, Father, Lord Jesus, and Holy Spirit. Do not hide Yourself from me. I yearn for you and my desire is for You to possess me. Apply your knife of the work of the cross to my "flesh" and the soul-life that agrees with it, in a steady and persistent manner. Be relentless, Holy Spirit. Cut out all pride, stubbornness, secret pride, secret sin, presumption, ambition, and all that is of self, self-will self-promotion, self-indulgence, all desires for self-gratification or self-aggrandizement, all ministry rooted in "self" and "self-promotion", all unholy habits and appetites, all sins of the tongue, sins of the heart, sins of the flesh; the lust of the eye, lust of the "flesh", and pride of life. Get me out of the world, Lord, and get the world out of me. Search my heart where I cannot see or realize. Show me what I do not know I am in the natural. Cut out of me all that is unholy and unrighteous in Your eyes. Make me be able to stand before You, O Lord, and not to be appointed to the day of wrath. I cry unto You, Lord, Jesus Christ. I abide in You. I depend and rely on You for all of those things as I take possession of them by your Grace, and by trusting and expectant faith, calling them applied to my life. All in Your Name and for Your Glory, Lord Jesus Christ, Amen".

9 Closing

Reflection in Action by Connection
Answer the questions on the line provided.

Question 1: What is the heart of the believer?
A: _____
Answer: The heart is a person's center for both physical and emotional intellectual moral activities.

Question 2: How can you develop a healthy loving heart? A: _____
Answer: The first step is genuine forgiveness of others that have hurt you.

Question 3: What are the uses of the word "heart"?
A. _____
Answer: physical organ, center of anything, inner man consisting of soul and spirit, the will, the mind, the soul, and the spirit.

Question 4: Which type of love should the believer be operating in?
A: _____

Answer: The agape love.

Question 5: Where does true repentance come from?
A: _____

Answer: True repentance comes from the heart.

SAY: Saint, you learned about the heart, love, acceptance, forgiveness, salvation, and holiness. God opposes those who would do things outwardly while the heart is far from Him. This is why God wants truth in the innermost being. He wants people to be right with Him on the inside, in the heart and spirit and mind, while also doing the right things outwardly. We cannot have one without the other!

Remember God looks at the heart!
As you continue, the Holy Spirit will be doing a new and mighty thing in you. Just trust God! Amen.

GOAL TWO

GIFTS OF THE SPIRIT

LESSON PLAN

Date & Time:	Curriculum Area: Gifts of the Spirit	Goal /Unit Topic: Goal Two

Key enduring understandings, concepts, abilities, and/or values.
Explained in the Introduction

Intended learning outcomes (to know, to do, to create, to value, etc.)
Explained in the Overview

Assessment Strategies: How will you assess attainment of the intended learning outcome?
Questions & Answers, Dialect, Interaction

Materials/Preparation/ Area Setup:
Materials: Poster board, Dry Erase Markers
Preparation: Decorations, Poster board –for Notes or question
Area Setup: For each disciple, place on the desk a TSOSF brochure, blue pen, highlighter, notebook, goal two

Introduction	Setting the Stage: engaging, motivating, experiencing, connecting with prior knowledge, reflecting, conjecturing, posing problems
Once the Introduction and Overview have been completed, then move on to the Bible book recitals. It will be recited every time that you meet with the disciples.	

Guided learning steps The learning steps are as follows:	**Disclosing**: acquiring knowledge/skills, conceptualizing, developing, understanding, integrating
1. Understanding the Holy Spirit	**Practicing, Reinforcing**: modelling, giving instruction, checking for understanding, guided practice, independent practice, applying, posing and solving problems
2. Manifestation Gifts	
3. Nine Gifts of the Holy Spirit	
4. Ministry Gifts	
5. Motivational Gifts	
6. Fruit of the Spirit	
7. Obstacles that Block Gifts	
8. Parts of a Whole Body	
9. Covenants of the Church	
10. Racial/Class Discrimination in the Church	
11. Using Your Spiritual gifts	
12. Activity Spiritual Gifts Inventory	
13. Move Forward with Your Gifting	

Closure	Transcending: summing up, responding, creating, performing, committing, evaluating
Prayer, Questions & Answers, Comments	

Modifications: How will you change the lesson to meet the needs of the individual students?	
Personal notes/reminders/homework/assignments	
Post-lesson reflections	

Goal Two: Gifts of The Spirit

INTRODUCTION

The Holy Spirit gives spiritual gifts, which are Manifestation Gifts, Ministry Gifts, and Motivational Gifts. A spiritual gift is God working through a believer to give divine action, strength and power to accomplish His will in the believer's life so that, as a channel of God's grace, Christ's life, and His kingdom, may continue to be made manifest. Knowing one's spiritual gifts will help you to:

1. Know God's will for your life,
2. Discover your spiritual "*job description*",
3. Take your appropriate place in the Body of Christ,
4. Begin to see yourself as a channel of God's grace,
5. Avoid over-commitment and burn-out,
6. Become more appreciative of what others are called, and anointed, to do, and
7. Be a part of maintaining the true purpose of the Body of Christ.

Overview

I. Goal Lesson:

Goal two teaches about the gifts of the Spirit. As a result, you will be able to explain the manifestation, ministry, and motivational gifts.

II. Goal Objectives

Upon completion of this goal, the disciple will be able to:

    a. Explain the different gifts given by the Holy Spirit.

    b. Know what can block their gifting.
    c. Know the importance of the body of Christ.
    d. Demonstrate seeking their gifting.

III. Bible Book Recitals

Genesis to Revelation

1. Understanding the Holy Spirit

Christianity Today International explains, "The church is the body of Christ (1 Cor. 12:12-27) and has a three-fold purpose: To evangelize the world (Acts 1:8, Mark 16:15-16), to worship God, and to equip for ministry (Eph. 4:11-16; 1 Cor. 12:28; 14:12). The Holy Spirit is the third person of the Trinity. He comes from the Father and is sent by the Son.

Symbols of the Holy Spirit include wind and breath (Gen. 1:2; John 3:8; 20:22; Acts 2:2), water (John 4:10,15; 7:37-39), fire (Matt. 3:11; Luke 3:16; Acts 2:3), oil/anointing (Ex. 29:7; Acts 10:38; 1 John 2:20, 27), a seal (Eph. 1:13-14; 4:30; 2 Cor. 1:22), and a dove (Luke 3:22)."

"The Holy Spirit does five things:

1. Creates (Gen.1:2).
2. Convicts and Calls (John 15:26 and 16:8).
3. Adopts as members of God's family (John 1:12; Romans 8:14-17; and Ephesians 1:4-5).
4. Sanctifies (Spiritual Growth) – Spirit of God works to make us more and more like Christ (Gal. 5:22-23). Holy Spirit also helps us in prayer (Rom. 8:26-27) and illuminates Scripture (John 16:13; 1 Cor. 2:10) for us.
5. Empowers- Power for ministry that flows from the Father through the Son (Acts 1:4, 8; Rom. 15:18-19)."[1]

When you do something which the Holy Spirit does not want you to do, you grieve the Holy Spirit (Ephesians 4:30). It could be a wrong thought, a wrong word or a wrong action. We quench the Holy Spirit when we neglect to do what He commands us to do (1 Thess. 5:19). You must be sensitive to His stirring in your spirit. If you do not respond to His stirring, you quench the gifts that He wants to manifest.

1   Understanding the Holy Spirit

The Holy Spirit is your indwelling counselor and guide. Let's look at the Deity, Personality, Names, and Works of the Holy Spirit.

Deity of the Holy Spirit		
Scripture	What the Bible says	Meaning to Us
Acts 5:3-4	Peter was explaining that believers can allow Stan to manipulate them. Ananias allowed Satan to use his heart to lie to the Holy Spirit.	A lie that damages the family of God incurs greater judgment. He lied to God by not providing for his brothers and sisters as he'd claimed he would do.
2 Corinthians 3:18	Paul is speaking about being made to resemble and reflect Jesus who is "the image of the invisible God" (Col. 1:15	Believers are to be transformed into the same image from glory to glory.
		Sanctification process.
Note: Transformation is not accumulation of information or simply behavior modification. Spiritual transformation is an eternal change that reflects the character of Christ and brings a external change. God accomplishes this through the Holy Spirit by using exposure, openness, and obedience to the Word of God, which grows us from one level of spiritual development to the next.		
Hebrews 9:14	OT sacrifices cleansed the outside, the blood of Christ cleanses our conscience from dead works so we can serve God.	Being clean on the inside can work its way out so that the dead works become good works.
1 Corinthians 2:10	God helps believers understand things that they cannot learn through a natural means.	The Holy Spirit helps us supernaturally to learn, grasp, and apply the deep things of God.

Goal Two: Gifts of the Spirit

1 Understanding the Holy Spirit, continued

Personality of the Holy Spirit		
Scripture	What the Bible says	Meaning to Us
John 16:13-14	"When He, the Spirit of truth, has come, He will guide you into all truth>'	Jesus is telling us that He will reveal these things when the Holy Spirit shall come.
Ephesians 4:30	Do not grieve the Holy Spirit of God.	Do not do the forbidden things described in Ephesians 4:17-5:18.
1 Corinthians 12: 11	One and the same Spirit distributes to each person as he wills.	So, trust him to supply you with the spiritual ability with which you can best serve him and bless others.
Romans 8:26	We don't know the language of prayer like the Father does.	Even in the unknown, the Spirit of God will translate for us.

1 Understanding the Holy Spirit, continued

Assignment: Read each Scripture, write down what the Bible says and its meaning to God's people.

Names of the Holy Spirit

Scripture	What the Bible says	Meaning to Us
Hebrews 10:29	Spiritual disobedience that Israel showed to the Mosaic law and defied God. They were stoned.	The believer who defies God will receive a worse punishment. God is serious about holiness.
John 14:16, 26	Jesus is promising us another helper to abide with us forever.	The Spirit is our helper on earth, and Jesus is our helper in heaven.
Romans 8:15	You have received the Spirit of freedom to break every bondage. You have received the Spirit and nature of God.	Paul mentions here intimacy with God because we have received the rights of heir and can pray, Abba Father, because he is listening.
1 Peter 1: 10-11	The prophets sought the truth about what they were prophesying. The Spirit of Christ was in them and upon them.	They predicted the fulness of grace.

Works of the Holy Spirit

Scripture	What the Bible says	Meaning to the Disciple
Genesis 1:1-3	The original creations of God include the heavens, the earth, and all thongs therein as first brought into being.	It is God's creation of the heavens and the earth.
2 Peter 1:21	The prophets were and still are moved by the Holy Spirit. The Bible's true author is God.	God chose holy men to be His spokesman, men who uttered thoughts given to them by the Holy Spirit.
Luke 1:35	In this passage we see that there was a certain day when God would have a Son and the Son have a Father.	The Holy Spirit welcome upon you.
John 16:8	To convince, to convict, refute, expose, bring to shame the person reproved.	The Holy spirit will convict unbelievers through believers who witness about Christ. Believers are the mouthpiece of God's voice. The Spirit reinforces the truth about sin, righteousness, and judgment.
Titus 3:5	Paul was emphasizing godly living because he did not want anyone to misunderstand or think that good works could contribute to salvation.	The work of the Holy Spirit makes a person new by the cleansing of regeneration (new birth). Here is the new nature to living the Christian life and performing good deeds. The continual process of Christian living is enabled by the Holy Spirit, resulting in growth in character and good works.
Ephesians 1: 13-14	When you believe in Christ as your	The seal or mark of ownership

1 Understanding the Holy Spirit, continued

Assignment: Read each Scripture, write down what the Bible says and its meaning to God's people.

	Savior, you are "in Christ" (v. 13). The Holy Spirit is the down payment of our inheritance until the fulness of the Spirit is received (v.14).	in believer's lives is the Holy Spirit. The guarantee of our inheritance is the Holy Spirit. Christians are the possession of the Lord, bought with the blood of His own Son.
Ephesians 2: 18	The church is a family.	The privilege of entrance.
1 Corinthians 6:19	A Christian's body is a house of worship. God will call everyone to account for how they manage their sexuality.	Christians must renew their bodies as a residence for the Spirit of God.
1 Corinthians 12:13	The Spirit is the agent that brings one into the body Christ by the new birth.	Believers are part of the one body infused by the one God. Christ places each new member of the body in the Holy Spirit for His care and safekeeping.
Romans 8:14	If we walk according to the Spirit as God desires, we prove ourselves to be God's sons.	Those led by the Spirit are God's children, and the sovereign Lord, in turn, is their Father.
Romans 8:16	Being adopted as God's children.	The Holy Spirit bears witness with their spirits.
Romans 8:26-27	We don't know the language of prayer like God does. The Spirit of God translates for us (v.26). In our weakness, we may be simply groaning, but the Spirit translates that into an appeal that is according to the will of God (v.27).	Paul is contrasting between our inability to know how to pray and the effect prayer of the Spirit Himself. The Spirit Himself prays for us. He intercedes on our behalf before the throne of God.
Romans 15:16	Paul understood that he was set apart for a sacred purpose.	Ministering means rendering priestly service. Set apart by the Holy Spirit for God's service.
John 16: 12-14	To carry or bear what is burdensome, not able to understand a matter or receive it calmy.	The Holy Spirit was threefold to them, He would guide them into all truth; He would tell them of the future; He would help them glorify Christ. The Holy Spirit is the source of truth. The Holy Spirit glorifies Christ by declaring Him or making Him known.
1 Corinthians 12: 7-11	The visible manifestations would be the visible healings, miracles, manifest prophecies, tongues, interpretations, & even the giving forth of wisdom, knowledge, and discernments of various kinds.	The believer receives the gifts when the Spirit operates through them to us to accomplish their intended purpose.
Acts 13:4	The Holy Spirit called and now sent them.	The believer is called, and the Holy Spirt sends them out.
Ephesians 5:18	When you come to Christ, you are indwelt by the Spirit, and he will never leave you. But being filled by the Spirit is different. A person filled by the Spirit is under the Spirit's influence.	Not all believers are Spirit-filled, but all have been sealed.
Galatians 5:16-17	Our "walk" is talking about the conduct of our lives (v.16). In the believer, there is a battle between the flesh & the Spirit. Choices will lead to different outcomes. The life of faith is walking by the Spirit.	To overcome the sinful desires of our human nature is to live step-by-step in the power of the Holy Spirit s He works through our spirit.
Galatians 5: 22-23	The fruit of the Spirit provides life and refreshment. The fruit of the Spirit is primarily manifested in our relationships.	The vine, branches, and fruitful harvest.
Philippians 3:3	When you put confidence in yourself about your relationship with God you nullify his work in your life.	True circumcision is worshiping God in the Spirit; rejoicing in Christ; and placing no confidence in any human honor or accomplishment as a means to reach God.

So, now that you understand the Holy Spirit, you also now know who the Holy Spirit is in your life. The Holy Spirit is a person who hears, guides, teaches, instructs, reveals things, and comforts.

The Hoy Spirit in the Godhead is seen throughout the Scriptures:

1.   Matthew 28:19-20
19 Go therefore and make disciples of all the nations, baptizing them in the name of the Father and of the Son and of the Holy Spirit, 20 teaching them to observe all things that I have commanded you; and lo, I am with you always, even to the end of the age." Amen.
The Holy Spirit is essential in the teaching and making of disciples of all nations

2.   Matthew 3:16-17
16 When He had been baptized, Jesus came up immediately from the water; and behold, the heavens were opened to Him, and He saw the Spirit of God descending like a dove and alighting upon Him.
17 And suddenly a voice came from heaven, saying, "This is My beloved Son, in whom I am well pleased."
Here the Son is baptized, Holy Spirit comes a dove, and the Father speaks from heaven. Christ had to come on earth to do the work that the three will be involved in.

3.   2 Corinthians 13:14
14 The grace of the Lord Jesus Christ, and the love of God, and the communion of the Holy Spirit be with you all. Amen.
The Apostle Paul recognizes the Godhead of the Lord Jesus Christ, the love of God , and communion of the Holy Spirit.

4.   John 14:16-17, 26
16. And I will pray the Father, and he shall give you another Comforter, that he may abide with you forever;
17 Even the Spirit of truth; whom the world cannot receive, because it seeth him not, neither knoweth him: but ye know him; for he dwelleth with you, and shall be in you.
26 But the Comforter, which is the Holy Ghost, whom the Father will send in my name, he shall teach you all things, and bring all things to your remembrance, whatsoever I have said unto you.

5.   John 15:26
26 But when the Comforter is come, whom I will send unto you from the Father, even the Spirit of truth, which proceeds from the Father, he shall testify of me.

In these last two scriptures, Jesus, the Son, tells us to recognize the Holy Spirit. It is essential for the believer to become an effective Christian here on the earth.

SAY: Let's move into the next section and learn in detail the manifestation gifts of the Holy Spirit.

2. Manifestation Gifts (1 Cor 12:8-10)

8 for to one is given the word of wisdom through the Spirit, to another the word of knowledge through the same Spirit, 9 to another faith by the same Spirit, to another gifts of healings by the same[a] Spirit, 10 to another the working of miracles, to another prophecy, to another discerning of spirits, to another different kinds of tongues, to another the interpretation of tongues.

Manifestation gifts are the spiritual gifts of the Holy Spirit that are given to the Church to benefit both believers and unbelievers. These gifts represent the work God does through the life of a believer in a given situation to demonstrate His supernatural power.

Power to Speak (Word of Wisdom)	Faith	Interpret Tongues (1 Cor. 12:1-11)	Prophecy	Miracles
Word of Knowledge	Gifts of Healing	Discernment Spirit	Speak Unknown Tongues	

3. Nine Gifts of the Holy Spirit (1 Cor 12:7-11)

7 But the manifestation of the Spirit is given to each one for the profit of all: 8 for to one is given the word of wisdom through the Spirit, to another the word of knowledge through the same Spirit, 9 to another faith by the same Spirit, to another gifts of healings by the same Spirit, 10 to another the working of miracles, to another prophecy, to another discerning of spirits, to another different kinds of tongues, to another the interpretation of tongues. 11 But one and the same Spirit works all these things, distributing to each one individually as He wills.

1. **The Word of Knowledge**: Supernatural knowledge and insight being given directly to you by the Holy Spirit himself. A revelation of the mind of God pertaining to things past and present. We can only know what God permits us to know.

2. **The Word of Wisdom**: A divine answer or solution for a particular event. A revelation of the mind of God pertaining to things in the future. A revelation imparted through hearing the voice of the Holy Spirit.

3. **The Gift of Prophecy**: When you get a direct word from the Lord to usually give to someone else. Supernatural utterance by God to man in a known language. The three operations of this gift are to edify (supplying part of the details to the architectural blueprint our lives), to exhort (to encourage them with the fact that God is walking alongside them, it imparts a blessing) and to comfort the body of Christ (comfort a person, to soothe the pain of missing the mark and encouraging the person to go on with God).

4. **The Gift of Faith**: The supernatural ability imparted by God to receive a miracle. The gift of faith operates in four areas: preservation, provision, proclamation and transportation. This supernatural faith is instantaneously infused into a person to receive a miracle which would be impossible by natural means. (Daniel 6:16; Hebrews 11:33).

5. **The Gift of Healings**: The supernatural ability imparted by God to work a healing on a human being. It is the soul and the body of man that needs healing.

6. **The Working of Miracles**: The supernatural ability imparted by God to work a miracle. The recipient has to be actively involved in working the miracle (Matthew 14:25).

7. **Different Kinds of Tongues**: The gift of various kinds of tongues is a supernatural utterance given by God through human vessels in an unknown language. When it is a message in tongues from God to us, we need the interpretation because we do not understand all languages spoken (1 Cor. 14:5, 27, 28). Praying in tongues is the spiritual development of the spirit man.

8. **The Discerning of Spirits**: The supernatural ability imparted by the Holy Spirit to see into the spiritual world. It is the ability to see spirits, whether they be angels, God or demons. There are three types of visions that can be seen, which are,

The closed vision which is where a person receives the gift of discerning of spirits in a trance-like state. The person is unaware of what is taking place in the physical realm. In the open vision, the spiritual realm is opened to the person while the person is fully conscious of the physical realm. The person sees the spiritual and physical realm simultaneously.

The spiritual vision is the lowest type of vision but the highest type of revelation. It is usually seen with the eyes closed. The three categories of vision are the allegorical, message and plain vision. Allegorical is all that is seen in the vision is symbolic (Dan. 7:4-7; 8:4-8; Acts10:11, 12). The message vision imparts a key message. It carries only one prime message to the recipient (Acts 16:9).

The plain vision is all things, persons, events, environments-must come to pass exactly as seen in the vision (Acts 9:12).

9. **The Interpretation of Tongues**: The supernatural ability given by God to interpret a message in an unknown tongue. The person who interprets the tongue does not understand the tongue, but he receives the interpretation as a message from the Holy Spirit.

SAY: The gifts of the Holy Spirit are related to the ministry gifts.

4. Ministry Gifts (Eph 4:11)

11 And He Himself gave some to be apostles, some prophets, some evangelists, and some pastors and teachers,

These gifts are also known as the five-fold ministry:

Apostles: Doctrine and discipline, an ambassador, one sent forth with orders, the only source of revelation, provide direction and organization for the church. Those sent with a special message for specific purpose.

Evangelists: Preach the Word to the lost. (2 Tim. 4:2-5). Those giving the message of the Good News of Jesus Christ.

Prophets: Spokesman for God. (Eph. 4:11). Must be able to hear the voice of God and bring God's word to the world. Discern and proclaim God's word. Those speaking forth the message of God.

Teachers: Instruct the church in the practical application of God's word. Those who instructs believers in the Word of God.

Pastors/Shepherd: To care for the church family. Those who feeds, or shepherds, believers.

5. Motivational Gifts (Romans 12:6-8)

₆ Having then gifts differing according to the grace that is given to us, let us use them: if prophecy, let us prophesy in proportion to our faith; ₇ or ministry, let us use it in our ministering; he who teaches, in teaching; ₈ he who exhorts, in exhortation; he who gives, with liberality; he who leads, with diligence; he who shows mercy, with cheerfulness.

There are seven motivational spiritual gifts for the body of Christ that must be operating: Let's discuss these in detail.

Service/Servers (help*)*: Possess the measure of faith to enable him to complete God's tasks. The server is available to see a project through to the end and enjoys doing physical work. (Philippians 2:19–22)

Teaching: Possess the measure of faith to instruct in the Word of God. A teacher is particularly concerned with the accuracy of information, especially church doctrine, and is often gifted with research abilities. A teacher should invest time in meditating on the Scriptures. (Luke 1:3–4)

Exhortation/ Exhorters: Possess the measure of faith to find God's solutions to problems. An exhorter is an encourager at heart and is often involved in the ministries of counselling, teaching, and discipling. An exhorter wants to see believers grow to spiritual maturity. (Colossians 1:27–29)

Prophet/Perceivers: Possess the measure of faith to speak the message from God. He or she has a strong sense of right and wrong and speaks out against compromise and evil. (Acts 3:19)

Giving/Givers: Possess the measure of faith that God will supply all needs. A giver is usually good at finding the best buy, noticing overlooked needs, and maintaining a budget. (Matthew 9:9)

Administration/Leaders: Possess the measure of faith that complete difficult projects. An organizer often discerns the talents and abilities of others and knows how those individuals can best serve within a ministry or on a particular project. (Acts 16:15) (Lydia)

Mercy/Compassionate Persons: Possess the measure of faith to help others in love. A mercy-giver is drawn to people in need and seeks to demonstrate compassion, understanding, and love to them. (John 13:34–35)

Motivational gifts shape our personalities. God has a purpose for every believer! We are all ordained to minister! Our responsibility is to recognize our gifts and enter into our God-called gifted ministry.

6. Fruit of the Spirit

The fruit of the spirit should characterize the life of every believer, not just the spiritually mature. Let's read Galatians 5: 22-23 and Ephesians 4:1-3.

Kindness	Love
Gentleness	Peace
Goodness	Self-control
Joy	Reflection of the Character of God
Longsuffering	Faithfulness

SAY: Let's discuss the fruit of the spirit.

1. **Kindness**: Kindness, in both Old and New Testaments, refer to steadfast love expressed in actions. God wants his children to be kind to one another (Eph. 4:32) and expects them to express brotherly kindness even in the midst of trials (2 Cor. 6:6). As a fruit of the Holy Spirit (Gal. 5:22), kindness is a virtue to be added to faith (2 Pet. 1: 5-7). Kindness, not a natural human reaction, must be developed in the believer in order for him/her to minister to others in the name of a loving God.
(The Woman's Study Bible, 2006, Thomas Nelson, Inc., p. 1559)

2. **Gentleness**: Gentleness is necessary for Christian unity. "Gentleness" or "meekness" refers to a humble, submissive attitude that is the opposite of pride. Believers, like their Lord, should pursue gentleness (1 Tim. 6:11) and wear it like a garment (Col. 3:12). A gentle spirit is precious to God. Gentleness is a fruit of the Holy Spirit necessary for godliness (Holy, Christ like living), goodness (kindness toward others), and giftedness (service in the name of Jesus). (The Woman's Study Bible, 2006, Thomas Nelson, Inc, p. 1531)

3. **Goodness**: For the Christian, goodness is not simply the absence of evil; it is righteousness accompanied by acts of kindness. True goodness is difficult to attain. It manifests itself only in a life totally committed to the Lord and is a requirement for effective ministry. Service to others is counted as evidence of the goodness of God at work in the life of a believer (2 Thess. 1:11, 12).
(The Woman's Study Bible, 2006, Thomas Nelson, Inc., p. 1569)

4. **Joy**: The abundance of joy is in direct proportion to the intimacy and steadfastness of a believer's walk with the Lord. The purpose of joy is to provide blessing for the believer. Joy enables you to enjoy all that God has given—health, family, friends, opportunities, and salvation. Abundant joy is a fruit of the Holy Spirit for those who walk in faith.

(The Woman's Study Bible, 2006, Thomas Nelson, Inc, p. 1464)

5. **Longsuffering**: Longsuffering encompasses patience, endurance, steadfastness, and

forbearance. However, Christians can become longsuffering through the power of the Holy Spirit. Believers who walk in the Spirit develop a longsuffering attitude that no circumstance can destroy and patience that no person can defeat (Eph. 4:1-3).

(The Woman's Study Bible, 2006, Thomas Nelson, Inc., p. 732)

6. **Love**: The attributes of love reflect both feelings and loving acts (1 Cor. 13:4-8). True love is characterized as:
    - patience and slow to anger (v.4)
    - kind and gentle to all (v.4)
    - unselfish and giving (v.5)
    - truthful and honest (v.6)
    - hopeful and encouraging (v.7)
    - enduring, without end (v.7)
    - Biblical love is not envious, proud, self-centered, rude, or provoking (vv. 4, 5). Without love, the gifts of the Spirit are deemed worthless and the fruit of the Spirit incomplete (v.8). Christian love is eternal. (The Woman's Study Bible, 2006, Thomas Nelson, Inc., p. 1488)

7. **Peace**: Spiritual peace describes a sense of well-being and fulfilment that comes from God and is dependent on His presence alone (Gal. 5:22). Inner spiritual peace is experienced by any believer who walks in the Spirit despite surrounding turmoil. Though impossible to comprehend fully, true peace is a fruit of the Holy Spirit (Gal. 5:22) and a part of the "Whole armor of God" (Eph. 6:11, 13). The believer receives peace from God as a virtue of holy living and a protection from evil forces. Where the peace of God is present, there is no room for worry. (The Woman's Study Bible, 2006, Thomas Nelson, Inc., p. 1450)

8. **Self-control**: People must practice self-control in order to lead disciplined lives. Divine discipline requires a personal action to receive the Holy Spirit's power. Christian's must learn to discipline both outward behaviors and inward feelings. In order to be godly a disciplined life involves a genuine, personal commitment to obey God's statutes, and frequently it requires lifestyle changes. Scripture teaches that self-control is the crowning fruit of the Holy Spirit (Gal. 5:22).

(The Woman's Study Bible, 2006, Thomas Nelson, Inc., p. 183)

9. **Faithfulness**: The Old and New Testament praise God for his faithfulness and challenges God's people to develop faithfulness in their lives. Believers today are called to faithfulness to God, to self, and to others. A believer is challenged to maintain steadfastness and trust in

God, even amidst trials and suffering. The Lord said, "Be faithful until death, and I will give you the crown of life" (Rev. 2:10). The unfailing faith of a follower of Christ will be rewarded for all eternity. (The Woman's Study Bible, 2006, Thomas Nelson, Inc., p. 1670)

10. **Reflection of the Character of God**: The "fruit" of the Holy Spirit refers to the godly attributes of those who "walk in the Spirit" (Gal. 5:16). The fruit of the Holy Spirit affects the believer's relationship with God, others, and self. The life of Christ is manifested by the fruit of the Spirit; the ministry of Christ is accomplished by the gifts of the Spirit.

7. Obstacles that Block Gifts

Lack of Faith	Lying	Control
Lack of Prayer	Jealousy	Gossip
Sin	Sabotage	

8. Part of a Whole Body

SAY: Let's go to our Memory Verse, I Corinthians 12:12.

Main Point: The Church is a body with many different parts, and you are one part of the body.

Mitchell explains, "First, it is important for us to comprehend that not all members have the same role or function in this body, but each has a different gift in the body, "according to the grace given to us" (Rom. 12:4, 6).

Second, we must not forget the importance of the discernment process in discovering what gifts we have been given by God. Discernment is needed to help a person understand the source of a call, and its content-and to respond appropriately. It is also needed to awaken one who is "deaf" or "blind" or not capable of receiving God's call without the aid of others."[2]

The mission of the church can be separated into three categories:

Outward Mission of Evangelism and Service: "proclamation of the Gospel to unbelievers" (Acts 1:8; Mark 16:15-16; and Matthew 28:19-20). We speak the gospel, but also demonstrate the love and mercy of God through action (Acts 11:29; 2 Cor. 8:4; 1 John 3:17).

Upward Mission of Worship: "dramatic celebration of God" (Col. 3:16; 1 Cor. 10:31).

Inward Mission of Discipleship: Training of people who voluntary submit to the lordship of Christ and who want to become imitators of Him in every thought, word, and deed. (Eph. 4:12-13; Matt. 28:20).

The Holy Spirit gives believers gifts to serve the church. We are to be filled with the Holy Spirit. The church has been given a mission.

SAY: If you do not know your spiritual gifts, ask God to reveal them to you.

---

[2] Webb Mitchell, *Christly Gestures*, 2003, p. 115-116

9. Covenants of the Church

There are also four covenants of the church:
- The membership covenant (Eph. 2:19; Rom. 12:4-5).
- The maturity covenant (2 Pet. 3:18; 1 Tim. 4:7).
- The ministry covenant (1 Pet. 4:10; 1 Cor. 12:5, 27).
- The missions covenant (Acts 1:8; 1 Pet. 3:15).

10. Using Your Spiritual Gifts

Memory Verse: John 15:16

A Christian who stays in fellowship with Christ will bear the fruit of Christ.

We are made to bear fruit. We will be doing a self-discovery process. There are so many people in the church who are not operating in their gifts. So, you are all going to discover your gifts. The nine fruits of the Spirit (Gal. 5:22-23) are the by-product of a Spirit-filled life and evidence of spiritual maturity. The nine gifts of the Spirit are different manifestations of the Spirit to build up the body (1 Cor. 12:1-11). We are instructed to diligently seek the gifts (1 Cor. 12:31; 14:1), but they must be exercised in an orderly way (1 Cor. 14: 26-33), and in the context of love (1 Cor. 13:1-13)

Goal Two: Gifts of the Spirit

11   ACTIVITY: SPIRITUAL GIFTS INVENTORY

Directions: Work through each of the following 110 statements on spiritual gifts. After each, check the appropriate box that best describes to what extent the statement accurately describes you. Do not answer on the basis of what you wish were true or what another says might be true but on the basis of what to your knowledge is true of you.

	Never	Rarely	Some-times	Often	Always
	1	2	3	4	5
1. I enjoy working with others in determining ministry goals and objectives.					
2. I have a strong desire to start or be involved in new ministry.					
3. I delight on telling people about what Christ has done for them.					
4. It bothers me that some people are hurting and discouraged.					
5. I have a strong ability to see what needs to be done and believe that God will do it.					
6. I love to give a significant portion of my resources to God's work.					

7. I have a strong capacity to recognize practical needs and to do something about them.					
8. I have a clear vision for the direction of a ministry.					
9. I feel compassion for those in difficult situations.					
10. I have a strong desire to nurture God's people.					
11. I spend a significant portion of my time each week studying the Bible.					
12. I am motivated to design plans to accomplish ministry goals.					
13. I prefer to create my own ministry problems than to inherit others.					
14. I have a strong attraction to lost people.					
15. I am very concerned that more people are not serving the Lord.					
16. I have a strong capacity to trust God for the difficult things in life.					
17. I am eager to financially support ministries that are accomplishing significant things for God.					
18. I enjoy helping people meet their practical needs.					
19. I find that I have a strong capacity to attract followers in my ministry.					
20. I sympathize with people when they are in the midst of a crisis.					
21. I am at my best when leading and shepherding a small group of believers.					
22. I have a strong insight into the Bible and how it applies to people's lives.					
23. I feel significant when developing budgets to accomplish a good plan.					
24. I am motivated to minister in places where no one else has ministered.					
25. I find that unsaved people enjoy spending time with me.					

26. I have a strong desire to encourage Christians to mature in Christ.					
27. I delight in the truth that God accomplishes things that seem impossible to most people.					
28. God has greatly blessed me with life's provisions to help others.					
29. I enjoy making personal sacrifices to help others.					
30. I prefer leading rather than following people.					
31. I delight extending a helping hand to those in difficulty					

32. I enjoy giving attention to those who are in need of care and concern.					
33. I am motivated to present God's truth to people so that they can better understand the Bible.					
34. I am at my best when creating an organizational structure for a plan.					
35. I am definitely a self-starter with a pioneer spirit.					
36. I derive extreme satisfaction when lost people accept Christ.					
37. I have been effective at inspiring believers to a stronger faith.					
38. I am convinced that God is going to accomplish something special through me and my ministry.					
39. I believe that all that I have belongs to God, and I am willing to use it for his purposes.					
40. I work best when I serve others behind the scenes.					
41. If I am not careful, I have a tendency to dominate people and situations.					
42. I am a born burden bearer.					
43. I have a deep desire to protect Christians from people and beliefs that may harm them.					
	Never	Rarely	Some-times	Often	Always
	1	2	3	4	5
44. I am deeply committed to biblical truth and people's need to know and understand it.					
45. I delight in staffing a particular ministry structure.					
42. I am a born burden bearer.					
43. I have a deep desire to protect Christians from people and beliefs that may harm them.					
44. I am deeply committed to biblical truth and people's need to know and understand it.					
45. I delight in staffing a particular ministry structure.					

46. I am challenged by a big vision to accomplish what some people believe is impossible.					
47. I feel a deep compassion for people who are without Christ.					
48. I have the ability to say the right things to people who are experiencing discouragement.					
49. I am rarely surprised when God turns seeming obstacles into opportunities for ministry.					

50. I feel good when I have the opportunity to give from my abundance to people with genuine needs.					
51. I have a strong capacity to serve people.					
52. I am motivated to be proactive, not passive, in ministry for Christ.					
53. I have the ability to feel the pain of others who are suffering.					
54. I get excited about helping new Christians grow to maturity in Christ.					
55. Whenever I teach a Bible class, the size of the group increases in number.					
56. I am good at using ministry's resources in solving its problems.					
57. I gain deep satisfaction out of creating something out of nothing.					
58. Training and helping others to share their faith is high on my list of priorities.					
59. People who are struggling spiritually or emotionally say that I am an excellent listener.					
60. I delight in trusting God in the most difficult of circumstances.					
	Never	Rarely	Some-times	Often	Always
	1	2	3	4	5
61. I have the capacity to give of myself as well as my possessions to help others.					
62. I am good at doing seemingly insignificant tasks to free people up for their vital ministries.					
63. Most people place a lot of trust in me and my leadership					
64. I have a desire to make a significant difference in the lives of troubled people.					
65. I enjoy being around believers and encouraging them to trust Christ for their circumstances.					
66. I have a desire to search the Bible for truths that apply to my life and the lives of others.					
67. I like monitoring plans that accomplish ministry goals.					
68. I am a risk taker when it comes to developing new ministries.					
69. Over the years, I have prayed much for my non-Christian friends.					
70. I spend a significant amount of time exhorting believers to make Christ Lord of their lives.					

71. I am able to trust God in situations when most others have lost all hope.					
72. Friends worry that some people take advantage of my generosity with my possessions.					
73. I am motivated to accomplish tasks that most people consider insignificant.					
74. People are confident in my ability to help them accomplish their ministry goals.					
75. Suffering people are attracted to me and find me comforting to be around.					
76. I have the ability and courage to confront Christians about sin in their lives.					
77. God has given me an unusual ability to explain deep biblical truths to his people.					
78. I prefer that a ministry's affairs be conducted in an orderly and efficient manner.					
79. I want to accomplish great things for God but in my own way.					
80. I am deeply motivated to address the doubts and questions of lost people.					
81. I have the ability to confront disobedient Christians and see them change.					
	Never	**Rarely**	**Sometimes**	**Often**	**Always**
	1	2	3	4	5
82. I am motivated by people who dream big dreams for God.					
83. People regularly come to me asking for help in meeting their financial needs.					
84. I look for opportunities to serve the practical needs of the ministries.					
85. I am happiest in a ministry when I am able to exert a strong influence on the group.					
86. People close to me believe that I allow "down and outers" to take advantage of me.					
87. Christians often seek me out for counsel regarding important discussions in their lives.					
88. I have a strong desire to study and explain the in-depth truths of the Bible.					
89. I am convinced that paying attention to details is important.					
90. I believe we must create new ministry structures for the new ministries we start.					
91. I fell a strong attraction to evangelistic ministries.					

	Never	Rarely	Some-times	Often	Always
92. I could easily spend much of my time encouraging people in their walk with Christ.					
93. I am frustrated about people who never take risks.					
94. I find it difficult to understand why Christians do not give more to the help people with real needs.					
95. I prefer to remain behind the scenes helping with practical matters.					
96. I have a strong desire to take charge in most situations.					
97. I delight in visiting people in hospitals or nursing homes.					
98. I pray constantly for people who look to me for care.					
99. I have observed that people who sit under my teaching experience changed lives.					
100. I have a strong desire to see people work together to accomplish their goals.					
101. I am convinced that the future of any country lies in starting fresh ministries.					

	Never	Rarely	Some-times	Often	Always
	1	2	3	4	5
102. I get extremely frustrated when I cannot share my faith.					
103. I find great satisfaction in reassuring Christians of their need to walk with Christ.					
104. People are amazed at my ability to trust God to provide in the most difficult situations.					
105. When I give to others, I do not expect anything in return.					
106. I am convinced that no job is too menial if it truly helps people.					
107. In meetings, people look to me for the final opinion regarding the matter.					
108. I believe strongly in giving those who fail a second and third chance.					
109. I enjoy visiting people in their homes.					
110. I am greatly challenged by people's questions about the Bible.					

Instructions for determining your spiritual gifts: Place in the chart below the number that is above the column in the inventory for each of your answers. Then add the numbers horizontally and place the total for each row in the column on the right.

1. _	12._	23._	34._	45._	56._	67._	78._	89._	100.	Admin
2. _	13._	24._	35._	46._	57._	68._	79._	90._	101.	__Apostle
3. _	14._	25._	36._	47._	58._	69._	80._	91._	102.	Evang
4. _	15._	26._	37._	48._	59._	70._	81._	92._	103.	__Encour
5. _	16._	27._	38._	49._	60._	71._	82._	93._	104.	__Faith
6. _	17._	28._	39._	50._	61._	72._	83._	94._	105.	Giving
7. _	18._	29._	40._	51._	62._	73._	84._	95._	106.	Helps
8. _	19._	30._	41._	52._	63._	74._	85._	96._	107.	__Leader
9. _	20._	31._	42._	53._	64._	75._	86._	97._	108.	__Mercy
10._	21._	32._	43._	54._	65._	76._	87._	98._	109.	__Pastor
11.___	22._	33._	44._	55._	66._	77._	88._	99._	110.	__Teach

The gifts are Administration, Apostleship, Evangelism, Encouragement, Faith, Giving, Helps, Leadership, Mercy, Pastor, and Teacher.

SAY: Write the names of your highest-scoring gifts in the spaces under Spiritual Gifts Inventory. Write the names of any other gifts that are not identified in the inventory but are present in your life under Other Spiritual Gifts.

Spiritual Gifts Inventory

1._____

2._____

3._____

4._____

5._____

Other Spiritual Gifts

1._____

2._____

3._____

4._____

5._____

(Retrieved from Being Leaders: The Nature of Authentic Christian Leadership, Audrey Malphurs, 2003, p. 184-190)

12. Move Forward with Your Gifting

First, ask God to reveal your spiritual gifts. Second, ask for the infilling and continuous presence of the Holy Spirit. The question is how do I begin to know what my unique gifting is? In Philippians 2: 13, Paul tells us that "God works in us both to will and to do His good pleasure." If we can begin to understand that we need to be living our lives for God, and not for the approval of others, we will be ready to begin to ascertain His great plan for our lives.

SAY: Ask yourself these questions and respond:

Soul Discipleship Plan

Who am I (identity)? _____

_____

Where am I from (source)? _____

_____

Why am I here (purpose)? _____

_____

What can I do (potential)? _____

Where am I going (destiny)? _____

How has God wired me? _____

What character qualities do I most hope to develop? _____ _____

_____

What are my own priorities in life? _____

_____

What do I hope to accomplish? _____

_____

Having a clear sense of God's purpose for us not only guides our decisions, but also strengthens our resolve against the attacks of Satan, as he attempts to destroy what God is building in our lives.

SAY: Let's do an activity. So, the first list of questions (1-3) is for the things you are good at. Second list (4-5) is for the things you love to do, and the third list (5-6) is the people or causes you have a desire to help with.

SAY: When done, each person will present their mission statement to the group. When presenting, you will be speaking to Jesus Christ.

What have been my greatest moments of happiness and fulfilment?

_____

What activities do I place highest value on?

_____

What are my natural gifts and abilities?
_____

What fascinates me?
_____

What am I passionate about?
_____

How do I best contribute to my community?

Goal Two: Gifts of the Spirit

What group of people do I feel a burden to help?

In conclusion, in Romans 6:23, Paul writes that the greatest gift that we have is Jesus Christ himself.

13 Spiritual Growth

Scripture shows us the relationship between spiritual growth and transformation. Paul explained it in 2 Cor. 3:18. We can read the scriptures and not understand it because of sin barriers in our lives. Sin provides a veil to the face, mind, and heart. Heb. 12: 1-2 helps us to understand and maintain focus on God's glory. As the sin barrier is removed, we must focus on worship, share his truth with others, and then we begin to experience transformation to become Great Commission worshippers.

14. Visionary

Do you have a vision or a strategic plan of what you would like to occur in your life? I am sure you have dreams, ideas, desires and wants that you want to see to be manifested in your life. Life brings us many things that we will not expect but we move forward with faith trusting God to lead us to our destiny of the purpose to fulfill for the Kingdom of God here on earth.

You learned about the gifts of the spirit and how they operate. Do you really know who you are in the Kingdom of God? As you grow and identify your purpose and destiny for the Kingdom of God, you must have a vision.

What is a vision?

A vision is defined on dictionary.com as:

1. the act or power of sensing with the eyes; sight.
2. the act or power of anticipating that which will or may come to be: prophetic vision; the vision of an entrepreneur.
3. an experience in which a personage, thing, or event appears vividly or credibly to the mind, although not actually present, often under the influence of a divine or other agency: a heavenly messenger appearing in a vision.

Biblically, a vision is described in Habakkuk 2:2-4

2 Then the Lord answered me and said:

"Write the vision
And make it plain on tablets,
That he may run who reads it.
3 For the vision is yet for an appointed time;
But at the end it will speak, and it will not lie.
Though it tarries, wait for it;
Because it will surely come,
It will not tarry.
4 "Behold the proud,
His soul is not upright in him;
But the just shall live by his faith.

A vision board allows you to place images and words of who you want to become, what you want to have, where you want to live or vacation, what you want to do, you will work through your life to change it to match those images and desires. It adds clarity to your desires to your desires and feeling to your visions.

15. Life Questionnaire

Okay, let's look back on the past year (_____), today is _____, _____, ____ , _____. Read the below questions and answer:

What was your #1 challenge in _____, and how did it affect you?

_____
_____
_____
_____

If you had goals for _____, what goal did you make the least progress on?

_____
_____
_____
_____
_____

What was your biggest mistake in _____?

_____
_____
_____

What area of your life did you neglect?

_____
_____
_____
_____

What do you desire/want to stop doing now before _____ arrives?

_____
_____
_____
_____
_____
_____

What are you proud of that you achieved this year on your goal list?

_____
_____
_____
_____
_____

What was the most valuable lesson you learned in _____?

_____
_____
_____
_____
_____

If you had goals for _____, what goal did you make the least progress on?

_____
_____
_____
_____
_____

What was your biggest mistake in _____?

_____
_____
_____
_____
_____

Which places do you want to visit in _____?

_____
_____
_____
_____
_____

Which five (5) goals do you want to accomplish in _____?

_____
_____
_____
_____
_____

What should you pay more attention to in _____?

_____
_____
_____
_____
_____

What do you want to start doing in _____?

_____
_____
_____
_____
_____

What do you most want to learn in _____?

_____
_____
_____
_____
_____

_____

What do you want to experience in _____?

_____

_____

_____

16 Visual Worksheet

Category	Like/Dislike
Lifestyle & Entertainment	Like:
	Dislike:
Job, Career, Business	Like:
	Dislike:
Finances	Like:
	Dislike:
Health	Like:
	Dislike:
Family	Like:
	Dislike:
Friends	Like:
	Dislike:
Love & Romance	Like:
	Dislike:
Relationship with God, Jesus, Holy Spirit	Like:
	Dislike:
Personal Growth	Like:
	Dislike:
	Like:
	Dislike:

17. Write the Vision and Make it Plain

You make your vision plain on tablets. So, you have 10 key areas of your life to write out for your vision. Pray, close your eyes and paint a picture in your mind every aspect of your life and how you would like to experience it. When you are done you will put those words into images.

Lifestyle & Entertainment

Imagine your ideal lifestyle with your eyes closed. Where do you live? City, state, country? Is it a house, condo, apartment, mansion? Is it in the city or countryside? What is your everyday routine? How is your free time spent?

_____
_____
_____
_____
_____
_____
_____

Job, Career & Business

Imagine your dream business with your eyes closed. What products & services are offering to the world? Who are your clients and customers? Do you have a home office or a trendy office downtown? What is the impact of your hard work to others?

_____
_____
_____
_____
_____
_____
_____

Finances

Imagine your ideal state of your finances with your eyes closed. How much money are you earning per year? Amount of money in the bank saved up? Student loans paid off? Consumer debt paid off?

_____

_____

_____

_____

_____

_____

_____

Health

Imagine your ideal state of your physical and mental health with your eyes closed. Do you want to lose weight? Are you eating healthy, drinking water and exercising?

_____

_____

_____

_____

_____

_____

_____

Family

Imagine your ideal state of your family and friends with your eyes closed. Are you spending quality time with family? Are you taking family vacations? Are your friends supporting your goals? Are they tolerating you? Are they there for you?

_____

_____

_____

_____

_____

_____

_____

Love & Relationships

Married: Imagine your ideal state of your romantic & sexual relationships with your eyes closed? What type of experiences would you like to share? How about dating, trying new things, making new memories?

_____

_____

_____

_____

_____

_____

_____

Love & Relationships

Single: Imagine your ideal state of your love and marriage to come with your eyes closed? What kind of spouse do you want to attract? What type of experiences would you like to share? What memories would like to make together?

_____

_____

_____

_____

_____

_____

_____

Relationship with God, Jesus, Holy Spirit

Imagine your ideal relationship with the Trinity with your eyes closed? What type of relationship do you want to have with God, Jesus and the Holy Spirit?

How do you want to express your faith?

_____

_____

_____

_____

_____

_____

_____

Personal Growth

Imagine your ideal state of personal growth in your character with your eyes closed? How will achieve Christ like characters of the fruit of the spirit as listed in Gal. 5:22-23?

_____

_____

_____

_____

_____

_____

_____

Education

Imagine your ideal level of education to attain with your eyes closed? What do you want to complete, a college or university degree, a certification, read more books or get coaching?

_____

_____

_____

_____

_____

_____

_____

Now you will create the vision board with the following materials by formatting and placing your items on the board. Take Action for Manifestation of the vision of God.

1. Poster Board
2. Words
3. Images
4. Markers

5. Cut-outs
6. Tape
7. Glue
8. Pictures

18. Closing

Reflection in Action by Connection

Answer the questions on the lines provided.

Question 1: Who should you be thinking like? (Beliefs, Mindset)
A: _____

Answer: As a kingdom citizen.

Question 2: Who should you be acting like? (Practices, Behaviors)
A: _____

Answer: Act like Jesus did by demonstrating the fruit of the Spirit.

Question 3: What should be grafted into your heart? (Emotions)
A: _____
_____

Answer: When Christ saves you and brings you into the vine and his kingdom, the presence and Spirit of God should live
within your heart

Question 4: What difference does the heart make in the way that I live? (Search my heart, O God)
A; _____
_____

Answer: Believe the truth about God in your head and your heart.

Question 5: What is the importance of love in the believer's life? (God, others, and myself)
A: _____

Answer: We must love with all the heart, soul, mind, strength, as one loves himself, exceedingly, as Christ loves, enough to lay down life for others, without hypocrisy, by the Holy Spirit, in sincerity, by service to one another, bearing with one another, with a pure heart, as brethren, not in word but indeed and without fear.

Scripture: [4] For as we have many members in one body, but all the members do not have the same function, [5] so we, *being* many, are one body in Christ, and individually members of one another. [6] Having then gifts differing according to the grace that is given to us, *let us use them*: if prophecy, *let us prophesy* in proportion to our faith. Romans 12:4-6

Answer the questions on the lines provided based on what you have learned.
Question 1: When the Holy spirit takes residences in a man or woman, what should also happen?
A: _____
Answer: God will deposit a spiritual gift or gifts.

Question 2: How can I know God and his will for my life?
A: _____
Answer: Begin with God and His call. God has placed calls on our life that frame who we are and what HE expects us, commands us,
call us to do in this world He has made.

Question 3: What gifts and abilities has God given you to serve others?
A: _____
Answer:

Question 4: What is servanthood?
A; _____
Answer: Using your resources to serve God and others.

Question 5: How can you fulfill God's purposes?
A: _____
Answer: By knowing what the spiritual gift or gifts are that God has given you.

SAY: We are moving into learning about the Bible. Please set a timetable to meet your goals (i.e. monthly, quarterly, etc), have an accountability partner, present it to the Lord and ask him to have his way and wait on his response. Amen.

GOAL THREE

THE BIBLE

LESSON PLAN

Date & Time:	Curriculum Area: The Bible	Goal /Unit Topic: Goal Three
Key enduring understandings, concepts, abilities, and/or values. Explained in the Introduction		
Intended learning outcomes (to know, to do, to create, to value, etc.) Explained in the Overview		
Assessment Strategies: How will you assess attainment of the intended learning outcome? Questions & Answers, Dialect, Interaction, Post/pre tests		
Materials/Preparation/ Area Setup: **Materials**: Poster board, Dry Erase Markers **Preparation**: Decorations, Poster board –One for OT and NT with all book listed **Area Setup**: For each disciple, place on the desk a blue pen, highlighter, notebook, goal three		

Introduction Once the Introduction and Overview have been completed, then move on to the Bible book recitals. It will be recited every time that you meet with the disciples.	***Setting the Stage***: engaging, motivating, experiencing, connecting with prior knowledge, reflecting, conjecturing, posing problems
Guided learning steps The learning steps are as follows:	***Disclosing***: acquiring knowledge/skills, conceptualizing, developing, understanding, integrating ***Practicing, Reinforcing***: modelling, giving instruction, checking for understanding, guided practice, independent practice, applying, posing and solving problems
1. The Bible and its Books 2. The Bible and Its Roles 3. God's Word 4. Genres of the Bible 5. Numbers, Colors, Animals, Metals and Elements, and Objects 6. Bible Study Tools 7. How to Study the Bible 8. Activity 9. Spiritual Growth through the Bible 10. GOD 11. Jesus 12. Holy Spirit 13. Bible Versions and Translations 14. Interpret the Word of God 15. Role of the Holy Spirit 16. Living out the Learned 17. Closing	
Closure Prayer, Questions & Answers, Comments	***Transcending***: summing up, responding, creating, performing, committing, evaluating
Modifications: How will you change the lesson to meet the needs of the individual students?	
Personal notes/reminders/homework/assignments	
Post-lesson reflections	Discussions

INTRODUCTION

The Bible is the greatest book written on the earth. We should be touching the pages of the Bible daily, because it is a lifestyle of a Christian. The Bible directs us on every aspect of our lives. The Bible begins with Genesis telling us of God's creation of the heavens and the earth. The first man was Adam and the first woman was Eve and their fall into sin. It also tells of the other first that occurs such as, judgment, languages, races, and marriage. The fall of humanity into sin is where God had to now create a rescue for all mankind.

Overview

I. Goal Lessons:

Goal three teaches about the Bible, how to study the Bible, and its importance.

II. Goal Objectives:

Upon completion of this goal, the disciple will be able to:

a. explain the purpose of the Bible,
b. study the Bible, and
c. interpret the Scriptures.

III. Bible Book Recitals

Genesis to Revelation

1. The Bible and Its Books

There are 39 books in the Old Testament and there are 27 books in the New Testament, which gives us 66 books. Let's talk about each book and its purpose.

The Background of the Old Testament

Merrill explains, "There are three abiding values of the Old Testament. First, The OT is a rich source of theology and doctrine that is presupposed by the NT and without which Christianity theology would be seriously deficient. Second, mastery of the OT is crucial to an understanding of the New Testament. Indeed, there is not a single teaching in the NT that is not presupposed or at least dimly preshadowed by the Old. To paraphrase the familiar slogan, "The NT is in the Old concealed, and the OT is in the New revealed." Third, the OT offers, by teaching and example, practical principles of belief and behavior for contemporary times."[1]

The Old Testament includes the following books:

Genesis is the first book of the Old Testament written by the prophet Moses. It explains the account of creation, humanity falling into sin, God's plan to bless all nations though Abraham and Sarah, which sets the foundation for the rest of the Bible (p. 1-2).

Exodus is the second book written by Moses. It has two sections, first it portrays God as the Savior and Provider of His people (chs. 1-18). Second, explains the detailed laws and instructions (chs. 19-40) which reveal the very character of God as a Law and as the Holy One. Exodus concludes with instructions about the tabernacle—its construction, furnishing, and service (p. 97-98).

Leviticus is the third book written by Moses. Leviticus is what it says it is, a series of revelations from God about how God's people may approach Him through sacrifice and honor Him in holy living. The purpose was to show the Israelites how they could live in ritual and moral purity. Leviticus reveals the holiness of God and His love for His people in ways found nowhere else in the Bible (p. 173-174).

Numbers is the fourth book of the first five books of the Old Testament, the Pentateuch, written by Moses. Numbers has two basic sections, first census (chs 1-4) numbered the men of war of the first generation of those who had left Egypt. The first generation of Israelites did not trust God and did not thank Him for His provision. The first generation would not inherit the land because they had been faithless. The second generation would succeed, the people of God would inherit the promise of the land of Canaan (p. 225-226).

Deuteronomy is the fifth book written by Moses. Moses challenges Israel to remain faithful to the covenant, reminded them of their past history, and pointed to their future of blessings or curses in the land of Canaan, depending upon their belief and behavior (p. 290-291).

Joshua was written by Joshua. The two most prominent themes in Joshua are the possession of the land and the covenant (p. 350).

Judges was written by the prophet Samuel. Judges was written to show the consequences of disobedience to God and the necessity of summoning a righteous king who would lead the people to God (p. 396).

Ruth was written by the prophet Samuel. The Book of Ruth underscores an overarching theme of the Bible: God desires all to believe in Him, even non-Israelites. This was God's plan from the beginning (p. 441-442).

---

1   Merrill et al., *The World and the Word*, 2011, p. 10-11

1 Samuel was written by the prophet Samuel. The purpose of the First Samuel is to provide an official account of the rise of the monarchy during the time of Samuel and the development of it under Saul and David (p. 449-450).

2 Samuel was written by the prophet Samuel. It recounts the triumphs and defeats of King David. It highlights the character traits that enabled David to succeed—his reliance on God for guidance (2:1), his sincerity (5:1-5), and his courage (5:6, 7). But the book also describes the tragic consequences of David's lust (12:1-23) and pride (24:1-17). Second Samuel covers the period from the death of Saul to the end of David's career. The key to David's successful reign was his relationship with the Lord (p. 505, 506)

1 Kings is the story of one people headed down two different paths. It is a story of good things and bad things, true prophets and false prophets, and of disobedience and loyalty to God. 1 Kings was written by Jeremiah. The purpose was to provide historical information. The author devotes considerable attention to evaluating the kings according to the way they responded to the responsibilities detailed in the Mosaic and Davidic covenants (p. 556, 557).

2 Kings displays both high and low points in the history of Israel and Judah. The books described people without direction, leaders who failed to lead, and a God who was forced to discipline His rebellious people. Second Kings continues the history of the divided kingdom from the point where First Kings ends, with the reigns of Ahaziah in the northern kingdom (853-852 B.C.) and Jehoshaphat in the southern kingdom (872-847 B.C.) (p. 607- 608).

1 Chronicles was written by Ezra. First Chronicles recounts the lineage of the people of God's promise and emphasizes the connection between Perez and King David (2:5-15). God would establish His reign upon the earth through David's royal line (17:7-15; see Gen. 17:7, 8; 2 Sam. 7).

The kings God had promised to Abraham would begin with David and culminate in the One who would reign forever, Jesus (17; 14; see Matt.9:27; 12:23; Mark 10; 47, 48; Luke 18:38). God had given the promise to David, and the faithful remnant inherited that same promise (p. 659, 660).

2 Chronicles was written by Ezra. First Chronicles focuses on the Davidic covenant during David's time, and Second Chronicles continues that theme in the period after David's death. Because of this emphasis on covenant, Second Chronicles makes frequent mention of priests, Levites, the temple, all other elements of Israel's religious life (p. 710).

Ezra was written by Ezra. Together with Nehemiah, Ezra describes the events leading to the return of the Judeans from captivity in Babylon and the discouraging experiences of that small community in the harsh world of the Promised Land. But through every experience God proved Himself faithful (p. 765-766).

Nehemiah was written by Nehemiah. During this period, the Persian emperor Artaxerxes I Longimanus allowed the Jews to return to their land and rebuild Jerusalem. At that time Nehemiah occupied a prominent position in the emperor's court. He was the trusted cupbearer of Artaxerxes

I. The Book of Nehemiah records the restoration of Jerusalem under the leadership of Nehemiah (p. 784, 785).

Esther was written by an unknown author. The Book of Esther has held an important place in the canon due to its strong testimony to God's providence and protection of His people. The narrative demonstrates God's providence and sovereignty in a situation that seemed hopeless (p. 810-811).

Job. There is no consensus about who wrote the Book of Job or when it was written. The Book of Job teaches that it is not wrong for a person to ask the question why, as Job did repeatedly (see ch.3) The Book of Job explores all of the traditional Middle Eastern explanations of the problem of the "righteous sufferer." The book of Job repeatedly emphasizes the sovereignty and omnipotence of God (p. 824-825).

Psalms was written by David. Like the Pentateuch, the first five book of Moses, the Book of Psalms is arranged in five sections: Book I (Ps. 1-41), Book II (Ps. 42-47), Book III (Ps. 73-89), Book IV (Ps. 90-106), and Book V (Ps. 107-150). The categories of the psalms are the royal psalms, psalms of Zion, penitential psalms, wisdom psalms, Torah psalms (subcategory of the wisdom psalms), imprecatory psalms (verb, to invoke or call down (evil or curses) as upon a person), joyful and prophetic Passover psalms and the Hallel psalms (p. 873-874).

Proverbs was written by King Solomon. It passes on a core of knowledge and experience that God says we must have if we are to live successfully. It is to give a course of instruction in wisdom, preparation for life, and the ways of life in God's world. (p. 1030-1031).

Ecclesiastes was written by King Solomon. This is one of the most misunderstood books in the Bible. Christians have tended either to ignore the message of the Book of Ecclesiastes, or to regard it as the testimony of a man living apart from God. This is unfortunate, for the book asks relevant, searching questions about the meaning of life, and it declares the utter futility of an existence without God (p. 1078).

Song of Solomon was written by King Solomon. This unique book is a moving love story about a young country girl and King Solomon. In delicate poetry, the lovers express intense passion and deep longing for each other. In this way, the book celebrates human sexuality within the context of marriage. The Song of Solomon celebrates the beauty and intimacy of married love in a narrative poem. It teaches that a lasting marriage requires dedication, commitment, and strong loyalty between husband and wife (p. 1097).

Isaiah was written by the prophet Isaiah. As a prophet, he spoke God's words. For the most part, these were words of confrontation, exhortation, and warning---words that made him extremely unpopular. But even when he experienced opposition Isaiah continued to stand for the truth (p. 1109).

Jeremiah was written by the prophet Jeremiah. Jeremiah's prayers, confessions, laments, and dialogues reveal the depth of the prophet's understanding of the character of God and the nature of His relationship to people. For Jeremiah, the God of Israel was the incomparable God of all creation, the Lord over nature and history (p. 1220).

Lamentations was written by the prophet Jeremiah. In forceful poetry, Jeremiah expresses his grief over the national tragedy that had unfolded before his eyes: Jerusalem, God's city, had fallen to the Babylonians, Jeremiah's sorrow and tears were not for his own personal loss, however, but for the sinfulness of the Israelites. The Book of Lamentations offers some very practical theological reflections on the purposes and results of suffering (p 1320).

Ezekiel was written by the prophet Ezekiel. Since he was from a priestly family, Ezekiel was a priest as well as a prophet. The Book of Ezekiel stresses the ultimate aim of God's charity and chastisement: that "they shall know that I am the Lord." Ezekiel teaches both individual and corporate responsibility for sin before God (chs. 18; 23) (p. 1332-1333).

Daniel was written by Daniel. Daniel wrote this book with two purposes in mind. First, he wanted to assert that the God of Israel was sovereign, even over the powerful nations that surrounded His people. God's chosen nation had been conquered and dispersed by a mighty empire that did not acknowledge God. Yet Daniel also looked forward to the day when God would restore and reward Israel (p. 1416-1417).

Hosea was written by the prophet Hosea. Hosea began prophesying during a time of general prosperity. The Book of Hosea fluctuates between judgment and salvation. Hosea's purpose was to denounce sin, to warn of impending judgment, and to assure the faithful that God's love would win out in the end. Israel's covenant relationship with God is at the heart of Hosea's message (p. 1445-1446).

Joel was written by the prophet Joel. Joel's prophecy had two purposes. First, Joel wrote to call the nation to repentance (2:12) on the basis of its experience of the recent locust plague. The recent disaster was but a token of a more devastating judgment to come. Yet that judgment could be averted by sincere and humble repentance (2:13.14). Second, the prophecy was intended to comfort the godly with promises of future salvation and blessing (2:28-32; 3:18-21) (p. 1464-1465).

Amos was written by the prophet Amos. He was a Judean sheepherder. The main theme of the Book of Amos is God's passionate concern for justice. Justice is not an abstract issue with God. Instead, justice is relational; it promotes good relations between people and between groups of people. Injustice breaks down good relationships and breeds anger, hostility, and violence. The immediate purpose of Amos's prophetic ministry was to call the leaders of ancient Israel to repent and reform (p. 1473-1474).

Obadiah was written by the minor prophet Obadiah. The Edomite's' pride and presumed self-sufficiency became their downfall. He addressed Edom with an oracle. One purpose of the oracle was to comfort and encourage the surviving Judeans with the message that God had not abandoned them. Judah would be restored to its own land after the judgment of the Exile had been accomplished, and their enemies would be punished (p. 1489).

Jonah was written by Jonah as his own foolish behavior and his final statement of coming to terms with the divine will is a likely possibility. The book of Jonah challenges God's people not to exalt themselves over others. The Book of Jonah is narrative. It is a prophetic parable (p. 1493-1494).

Micah was written by the prophet Micah. The Book of Micah centers on the threat of the Assyrian invasions that occurred throughout this period, beginning around 730 B.C. against Israel and culminating in 701 B.C. against Judah (p. 1500-1501).

Nahum was written by minor prophet Nahum. He was a man of God who was called to preach to Nineveh. The people of the northern kingdom of Israel had been sinning grievously against God and ignoring the warnings of punishment given through God's prophet (p. 1513-1514).

Habakkuk was written by the prophet Habakkuk. Habakkuk was unique among the prophets in that he asked questions of God (p. 1519).

Zephaniah was written by the prophet Zephaniah. The prophet Zephaniah scolded Judah's leaders for countless acts of wickedness (3:1-7). His prophecies against the nations included Philistia (2:4-7), Moab and Ammon (2:8-11), Ethiopia (2:2), and Assyria (2:13-15). These nations were judged because of pride and arrogance against God's people and because of the continuing idolatry (p. 1525).

Haggai was written by the prophet Haggai. Haggai was a prophet to the Jews who had returned from the Exile in Babylon (p. 1531).

Zechariah was written by the prophet Zechariah. Zechariah lived and prophesied during the period following the Babylonian captivity (597-538 B.C). Zechariah's prophecies had two purposes. First, they challenged the returning exiles to turn to the Lord, to be cleansed from their sins and to experience again the Lord's blessing (see 1:3). Second, Zechariah's words comforted and encouraged the people regarding the rebuilding of the temple and God's future work among His people (1;16,17; 2;12; 3:2; 4:9; 6:14,15) (p. 1536-1537).

Malachi was written by the prophet Malachi. This final book of the Old Testament is about the error of forgetting the love of God. When people forget God's love, it affects their attitudes, home, and worship. With God's love and loyalty in doubt, sacred commitments no longer remain sacred. God sends Malachi to rouse the people from their spiritual stupor and to exhort them to return to the living God (p. 1555-1556).

The Background of the New Testament

Lea & Black explain, "Twenty-seven books, known as the New Testament canon, comprise the Christian New Testament. When the New Testament books did begin to circulate, many other writings, such as additional gospels, acts of Christian leaders, additional epistles, and apocalypses appeared. Some groups accepted these additional writings, others rejected them."[2]

Kostenberger explains, "Put succinctly, the word canon comes from the Greek word kanon, which in turn derives from its Hebrew equivalent kaneh and means "rile" or "standard." The term eventually came to refer to the collection of the Christian Scriptures."[3] The background of the New Testament is political and religious.

The New Testament books are as follows:

<u>Matthew</u> was written by Jesus' disciple Matthew. No other Gospel lays such stress on the kingdom; the restoration of the glories of David's kingdom was a burning hope for many Jews at the time. One purpose of Matthew's gospel is to prove to Jewish readers that Jesus is their Messiah and promised King. Another purpose of the book is to outline the characteristics of the Kingdom of God, both for Israel and the church (p. 1573-1574).

<u>Mark</u> was written by Mark. The gospel of Mark is a record of Jesus' actions and achievements. Mark wrote for Gentile Christians, especially Romans. Mark's Gentile readers faced persecution and martyrdom (p. 1636-1637).

<u>Luke</u> was written by Luke. The Gospel of Luke is unique in several ways. It is the only Gospel that has a sequel, which is Acts. Both Luke and Acts include an account of the Ascension, an event that only Luke describes in detail. Second, Luke is the longest of the four Gospels. Third, Luke records a wide variety of miracles, teaching, and parables, making it the fullest portrait of Jesus' ministry (p. 1682-1683). Luke was also a medical doctor and traveling companion of Paul.

<u>John</u> was written by the apostle John. The Gospel of John is a persuasive argument for the deity of Jesus. It concentrates on presenting Jesus as the Word, that is, God [1:1] who became a man [1:14]. Thus John meticulously records the statements and describes the miracles of Jesus that can only be attributed to God Himself. John urges us to trust in Jesus for eternal life (p. 1754-1755).

<u>Acts</u> was also written by Luke. The Book of Acts begins in Jerusalem with the disciples huddled in a room on the day of Pentecost. Then the Holy Spirit came upon them and authorized them to be His witnesses. The rest of Acts describes the ripple effects of that great event (p. 1812-1813).

<u>Romans</u> was written by the apostle Paul to a vibrant church in the city of Rome. His first purpose was to prepare the Romans for his planned journey to Rome and later to Spain. A second purpose involved Paul's understanding that the believers needed to "be established" (1:11). Paul wanted

---

2   Lea & Black, *The New Testament: Its Background and Message*. 2003, p. 69
3   Kostenberger, *The Cradle, the Cross, and the Crown: An Introduction to the New Testament*. 2009, p. 3

to give them a well-instructed faith. The third purpose for the letter was pastoral. Paul wanted to exhort Jewish and Gentile believers to live in harmony (p. 1876-1877).

1 Corinthians was written by the apostle Paul. Corinth was an important city in ancient Greece. First Corinthians is a reply to two letters. Paul wrote First Corinthians to answer both letters and to give some additional instructions. He taught about decorum in worship services (11:2-16), the solemnity of the Lord's Supper (11:17-34), and the place of spiritual gifts (p. 1911-1912).

2 Corinthians was written by the apostle Paul. Second Corinthians is primarily a personal letter, defending Paul's ministry among the Corinthians and appealing to the factions in the church to reconcile themselves to each other. Yet Paul still uses doctrine to address the church's problems. Paul points out that part of the reason for the Corinthians' difficulties and divisions was Satan's opposition to the church (p. 1942-1943).

Galatians was written by the apostle Paul. The ethnic Galatians were Celts who migrated from ancient Europe to Asia Minor in the third century B.C. Paul addresses his letter "to the churches of Galatia" [1:2] and to readers he expressly calls "Galatians" [3:1], but it is not easy to determine what this means precisely. Apparently, Paul became aware of a perversion of the gospel of grace that was actively infecting the Galatian churches (p. 1966-1967).

Ephesians was written by the apostle Paul. Ephesus was the capital of the Roman province of Asia (today part of Turkey). Located at the intersection of several major trade routes, Ephesus was a major vital commercial center of the Roman Empire. Ephesians, like most of Paul's writings, underscores the truth that salvation is by faith alone and not through works or human striving. The whole letter emphasizes the truth that all believers are united in Christ because the church is the one body of Christ (p. 1981-1982).

Philippians was written by the apostle Paul. Named for Philip II of Macedon, the father of Alexander the Great, Philippi was strategically located on a major road, the Egnatian Way that connected the eastern provinces of the Roman Empire to Rome. Thus, Philippi became the leading city of Macedonia. The most prominent theme of the Epistle to the Philippians is joy, specifically the joy of serving Jesus. Another theme of Paul's letter is "partnership in the gospel." (p. 1994-1995)

Colossians was written by the apostle Paul. The city of Colossae was about a hundred miles east of Ephesus, in the valley of the Lycus River. During the Persian Wars of the fifth century B.C., Colossae was a large and strategic city. The circumstances of Colossians and Philemon are the same. Paul is imprisoned, along with others, for preaching the gospel (4:10; Philem. 1:23) (p. 2008-2009).

1 Thessalonians was written by the apostle Paul. Thessalonica was one of the first cities to be evangelized by Paul and Silas when they landed on the continent of Europe. This was a port city and commercial center located in the northwest corner of the Aegean Sea. The Egnatian

Way linking Rome to Byzantium passed through it. The important highway and the thriving port made Thessalonica one of the wealthiest trade centers of the Roman Empire. It was the capital and the largest city of the province of Macedonia, with a population of about 200,000. In first Thessalonians, Paul reviewed some of the basics of the faith and applied those truths to the believers' lives (p. 2020-2021).

2 Thessalonians was written by the apostle Paul. Since the writing of First Thessalonians, reports had come to Paul of continued progress in the Thessalonian church, indicating their faithfulness to the gospel. However doctrinal problems had also arisen. False teachers had begun to tell the believers in Thessalonica that the day of the Lord was already at hand. In Second Thessalonians, Paul stated emphatically that he had never taught that the day of the Lord had already come. To counter false doctrine, Paul gave the Thessalonians a good dose of the truth, explaining to them the emergence of the man of lawlessness and the prevalence of sin during the end times (p. 2031-2032).

1 Timothy was written by the apostle Paul. At the beginning of Paul's second missionary journey, Timothy was chosen by Paul to accompany him and Silas (see Acts 16:3). Paul wrote First Timothy in order to instruct his young protégé on how the church should function and how mature men and women of God should interact in it (p. 2039-2040).

2 Timothy was written by the apostle Paul. The Book of Acts ends with Paul under house arrest in Rome (Acts 28). Paul's primary purpose for writing this letter was to offer final instructions to Timothy regarding the Christian life. Second Timothy has an intensely personal nature and tone.

Paul encourages his close friend to use his spiritual gifts. He writes to strengthen Timothy's loyalty in Christ in the face of suffering and persecution that would come. Paul was well aware that hardships and conflict are a part of Christian ministry (p. 2052-2053).

Titus was written by the apostle Paul. Crete is a large island, approximately 160 miles long and 35 miles wide, in the Mediterranean Sea. The island is located 100 miles southeast of Greece. The Cretans developed a relatively prosperous agriculture and trading economy, creating one of the best –known business centers of the ancient world. It is a key New Testament book for church organization, with its guidelines for elders, pastors, and other believers. Whereas the letters to Timothy emphasize sound doctrine, the letter to Titus emphasizes good works (1:16; 2:7; 14; 3:1, 5, 8, 14) (p. 2063-2064).

Philemon was written by the apostle Paul. Philemon was a slave owner whose home served as the meeting place for a local church. During this period, the Jews practiced slavery according to the provisions of the Law of Moses. The Epistle of Philemon was not written to refute theological error or to teach doctrine. However, into this short letter Paul skilfully weaves the concepts of salvation (vv.10, 16), substitution (v.17), imputation (v.18), and redemption (v.19) (p .2070-2071).

Hebrews was written by the apostle Paul. The Book of Hebrews was written to address the doubts of those who were second-guessing their conversion to Christianity. The author of Hebrews set out to show that Christianity is the true successor to Judaism. He centers his attention on three topics: (1) priesthood, or divine mediation (7:1-28; 10:19-22); (2) sacrifice, or divine redemption (9:11-10; 18), (3) covenant, or divine promises (8:8-13; 9:15-) (p. 2074-2075).

James was written by James. The epistle of James is the "how-to" book of the Christian life (p. 2102-2103).

1 Peter was written by the apostle Peter. Peter wrote to those Christians to encourage them, to explain to them why suffering occurs, and to remind them of their eternal reward at the end of this earthly life. Peter was from Galilee, a region that was bilingual. Peter blended five different themes in this letter (p. 2113-2114).

2 Peter was written by the apostle Peter. Peter addressed his letter "to those who obtained a like precious faith with us", a way of saying "to all believers everywhere." With its emphasis on holy living and its efforts to refute false teachings, Second Peter stresses sanctification. (1:1) (p. 2128-2129).

1 John was written by the apostle John. Gnosticism was a problem that threatened the church in Asia Minor during the second century A.D. Gnosticism was teaching that blended mysticism with Greek dualism (which claimed that the spirit is completely good, but matter is completely evil. Key concepts in the letter include eternal life, knowing God, and abiding in the faith (p. 2137-2138).

2 John was written by the apostle John. Second John is a testimony to the fact that no question consumed more time than "Who is Jesus?" The false teachers who prompted John to write this letter were promoting a heresy about this question. This heresy, called Docetism, was the teaching that Christ did not actually come in the flesh. In other words, Christ did not have a body but only seemed to have a body and suffer and die on the cross (see v.7). John would have none of it. He urged his believers to cling to the truth: Jesus Christ came in the flesh (p. 2150).

3 John was written by the apostle John. Struggles with forces outside the church can be harmful enough but struggles within a church can be devastating. Third John was written in response to one such struggle within a local church. One of the church leaders, Diotrephes, had asserted control over the congregation to such an extent that he was prohibiting representatives of other churches from ministering to his congregation (p. 2153-2154).

The Epistle of Jude. The author is Jude. The primary focus is the faith, the believers, and God. He speaks about the false teachers and their fate. He encourages holiness (p. 2166).

Revelation of Jesus Christ is the last book. The author is John. He took a stand for the Word of God and was exiled to the island of Patmos where he wrote this book. He wrote apocalyptic letters to seven churches from the Lord Jesus. The churches were commended, rebuked and warned, but they were also exhorted to remain faithful in adversity. Revelation's purpose is to comfort and challenge its readers. It affirms God's sovereign control over history and the certainty of His plan for the future (p. 2161-2162).

(From Nelson's NKJV Study Bible, copyright © 1997 by Thomas Nelson, Inc. Used by permission)

2. The Bible and Its Role

Paul told Timothy about the role of the Bible, "All Scripture is God-breathed and is useful for teaching, rebuking, correcting and training in righteousness, so that the man of God may be thoroughly equipped for every good work" (2 Tim. 3;16-17). The Bible enlightens, exposes, and equips.

Paul spoke four words for the role of the Scriptures, which are:

1. **Teaching**: the idea of guidance or instruction. It gives the direction to believers in the path they are to follow.
2. **Rebuking**: it points out one's error. It points out when we are not on the correct path.
3. **Correcting**: involves the concept of returning to the correct path when we stray.
4. **Training**: the idea is to help one stay on track.

Richards explains, "Here, then, is the message and role of the Bible. First, the Bible presents the message of reconciliation thematically from cover to cover. It specifically lays out that message in the New Testament as a fulfillment of the promises of the Old Testament. Second, it provides the means by which a believer can experience daily the reconciled relationship that belongs to the Christian positionally. The Bible is both the story of reconciliation and the tool for experiencing the story firsthand."[4]

Brummelen describes, "In biblical studies, students read and interpret the Bible as God's revelation of His plan of redemption. They practice biblical interpretation, studying the literary forms and cultural background of individual Bible books as well as tracing significant biblical themes. In addition, they apply the biblical message to their personal lives, to their relationships with others, to contemporary issues, and to life in the community."[5]

3. God's Word

SAY: The Dake Annotated Bible explains, "The Bible is God's inspired revelation of the origin and destiny of all things. The Bible is the power of God unto eternal salvation and the source of present help for the body, soul, and spirit. The Bible is God's will or testament to men in all ages, revealing the plan of God for man here and now, and in the next life. The Bible is the record of God's dealings with man in the past, present, and future. As a literary composition, the Bible is the most remarkable book ever made. The Bible is the only book that reveals the mind of God, the state of man, the way of salvation, the doom of sinners, and the happiness of believers. Its doctrines are holy, its precepts binding, its histories true, and its decisions immutable. Men should read it to be wise, believe it to be safe, and practice it to be holy. He should read that it

---
[4] Richards & Bredfelt, *Creative Bible Teaching*, 1998, p 58.
[5] Harro Van Brummelen, *Walking with God in the classroom: Christian approaches to learning and teaching*, 2009, p 88.

might fill his memory, rule his heart, and guide his feet in righteousness and true holiness. He should read it slowly, frequently, prayerfully, meditatively, searchingly, devotionally, and study it constantly, perseveringly, and industriously---through and through, until it becomes a part of his being, generating faith that will move mountains."[6]

4. Genres of the Bible

SAY: Let's learn about the five literary genres of the Bible. In the Old Testament you will encounter narrative, law, poetry, prophecy, and wisdom. In the New Testament you will encounter gospel, history, letters, and prophetic-apocalyptic literature.

Epistles: The New Testament letters follow a logical flow of ideas with the goal of communicating a specific message to a specific audience. Since the epistles were intended to be read in public, it is important to read them in their entirety to discover their structure and how the argument develops. This kind of literature uses a straightforward language to develop an argument. The epistles follow a relatively fixed form containing conventional aspects of Hellenistic letters but with distinctive features: Opening (sender, addressee, greeting).

1. Thanksgiving (prayer for spiritual welfare and remembrance or commendation of the spiritual riches of the addressee).
2. Body.
3. Paraenesis (exhortation).
4. Closing (final greetings and benediction).

Note: Hellinistic means to speak Greek or identity with the Greeks

Narrative: The Bible, especially the Old Testament, is full of stories. The plot is the key element of any story. In order to have a good story, something needs to happen to someone somewhere. Therefore, the plot (action), setting, and characters form the essential elements of biblical narrative. Bible stories are descriptive, not prescriptive because they share the lives of people, including their achievements and mistakes. We can learn from their experiences. They do not, however, provide a model of behavior in every instance.

Several narrative elements guide the proper understanding of this genre:

- Physical, temporal, and cultural settings of the story.
- Characters of the story, with special emphasis on the protagonist.
- Plot conflicts and their resolution.
- Aspects of narrative suspense (how the story arouses curiosity about outcome).
- The protagonist's experience in living as an implied comment about life.
- Narrative unity, coherence, an emphasis.

† Elements of testing and choice in the story.

† Character progress and transformation.

---

[6] Dake Annotated Bible, Cyclopedic Index, 1982, p 563.

† Foils, dramatic irony, and poetic justice.

† The implied assertions about reality, morality, and values.

† Repetition and highlighting as clues to what the story is about.

† Point of view in the story—how the writer gets a reader to share his attitude toward the character and events.

Poetry: Biblical poetry paints images with words to express human experiences. The New Testament includes several poetic sections, and many books in the Old Testament are poetry. The capacity of unfolding the possibilities of images, metaphors, and similes is essential for proper interpretation of the Psalter and other poetic books. Poetry is an emotional and intimate way of communication. Therefore, we need to "feel" the text as we read it to grasp the author's experience.

Hebrew poetry uses parallelism as a structural technique to organize the verses. Parallelism consists of "two or more phrases that express an idea in different words but in similar grammatical form." In most occasions the second line (or verse) relates to the first one in different ways.

For example, it can restate the same truth expressed in the first line (synonymous parallelism); it can contrast the ideas presented on the first line (antithetic parallelism); or it can complement the idea shared on the first line (synthetic parallelism).

Four key questions should guide our reading and interpretation of biblical poetry: What is the overall effect of the poem? What is the structure of the poem? What are the figures of speech of the poem? What are the themes and theology of the poem?

Proverbs: The Bible contains many aphorisms or proverbs, including a complete book that bears that name. Proverbs "are moments of epiphany—high points of human insight." The biblical wisdom literature includes the book of Proverbs. Wisdom in biblical perspective refers to godly living because correct behavior is a manifestation of an accurate understanding of God.

Proverbs, Although proverbs are statements of truth, they should be considered as principles, not promises. Consequently, a proverb presents a general statement of the way life should be, not necessarily the way it will be. "A gentle answer turns away anger, but a harsh word stirs up wrath" (Prov. 15:1). This statement reflects a desired outcome, not a promise that our kind answers will always turn away anger.

Parables: Our Lord Jesus Christ made parables an active ingredient of His teaching. A parable is a short story based on real-life events with the purpose of teaching a central truth. A parable develops only one key truth.

Thus, we need to concentrate on the main focus of the parable instead of spending time on the details of the story. Robertson McQuilkin suggests six basic guidelines for understanding parables: "Begin with the immediate context, identify the central point of emphasis, identify irrelevant details, compare parallel and contrasting passages, and base doctrine on clear literal passages."

Prophetic literature: Fully one-fourth of the biblical text deals with prophetic literature. Although a common aspect of this genre is the prediction of future events, prophetic books also focus on God's messages of judgment, warning, and calling to repentance. The Lord called biblical prophets to proclaim His messages, to "forth-tell" His truths more than just merely foretell the future. Prophetic material is filled with symbols and figurative language. Thus, we need to be careful not to make conclusions about the meaning of the passage before we consider the context and structure of the book.

Yount explains, "Use the following principles when interpreting biblical prophecy:

Compare all related and parallel passages, realize that there may be a long time (hundreds or thousands of years) between the announcement of the prophecy and its fulfilment, distinguish between already fulfilled and yet to be fulfilled prophecy, identify figures of speech and symbolic language and interpret accordingly, and make certain the interpretation does not conflict with other Scripture."[7]

5. Numbers, Colors, Animals, Metals and Elements, Time, Gender and Objects

In the Bible, there are numbers, colors, and animals, metal and elements, time, gender, and objects that help us to understand the design of God's Word. There are times you will be reading the Bible, and you don't understand it because there are things in the word of God that helps you to interpret the Scriptures.

There will be times when you have dreams or visions with people, numbers, colors, animals and other objects. Each one has a meaning that you need to understand.

A. Numbers:

SAY: Let's learn about some numbers that have meaning in the Bible. It is called Biblical numerology, which is the study of individual numbers in Scripture.

One: - Denotes absolute singleness.

Deuteronomy 6:4 "Hear, O Israel: The Lord our God, the Lord is one." (ESV) [8]

➢ Unity (Gen. 2:24); independent existence (Deut. 6:4)[9]

---

[7] Yount, 2008, *The Teaching Ministry of the Church*. Chapter 12, digital.

[8] http://christianity.about.com/od/biblefactsandlists/qt/Bible-Numerology.htm, leads to https://www.thoughtco.com/biblical-numerology-700168, Accessed July 18, 2016.

[9] *The Woman's Study Bible, New Kings James Version*, Nashville: Thomas Nelson, Inc, 2006, p 1683.

Two: - Symbolizes witness and support.

- There were two great lights of creation (Genesis 1:16).
- Two cherubim guarded the Ark of the Covenant (Exodus 25:22).
- Two witnesses establish truth (Matthew 26:60).
- The disciples were sent two by two (Luke 10:1).[10]

➤ An addition—strength, help (Eccl. 4:9-1)[11]

Three - Signifies completion or perfection, and unity. Three is the number of Persons in the Trinity.

- Many significant events in the Bible happened "on the third day" (Hosea 6:2).
- Jonah spent three days and three nights in the belly of the fish (Matthew 12:40).
- Jesus' earthly ministry lasted three years (Luke 13:7).
- John 2:19 Jesus answered them, "Destroy this temple, and in three days I will raise it up." (ESV) [12]

➤ Simplest compound unity; the number for God (Matt. 28:19)[13]

Four - Relates to the earth. The number of creation.

- Earth has four seasons: winter, spring, summer, and fall.
- There are four primary directions: north, south, east, and west.
- Four earthly kingdoms (Daniel 7:3).
- Parable with four types of soil (Matthew 13).[14]

➤ The world with its four seasons and directions (Rev. 7:1)[15]

Five - A number associated with grace.

- Five Levitical offerings (Leviticus 1-5).
- Jesus multiplied five loaves of barely to feed 5,000 (Matthew 14:17).
- The Holy Anointing Oil was pure and consisted of five parts (Exo. 30:23-25).[16]

➤ Mankind with the various five-membered parts of the body (Lev. 14:14-16)[17]

---

[10] http://christianity.about.com/od/biblefactsandlists/qt/Bible-Numerology.htm, leads to https://www. thoughtco.com/biblical-numerology-700168, Accessed July 18, 2016.

[11] *The Woman's Study Bible, New Kings James Version,* Nashville: Thomas Nelson, Inc, 2006, p 1683.

[12] Ibid.

[13] Ibid.

[14] Ibid.

[15] Ibid.

[16] http://christianity.about.com/od/biblefactsandlists/qt/Bible-Numerology.htm, leads to https://www. thoughtco.com/biblical-numerology-700168, Accessed July 18, 2016.

[17] *The Woman's Study Bible, New Kings James Version,* Nashville: Thomas Nelson, Inc, 2006, p 1683.

Six - The number of man.

- Adam and Eve were created on the sixth day (Genesis 1:31).
- Man labors six days only.[18]

➢ Evil, failure; it falls short of the number seven, which represents perfection (Rev. 13:18)[19]

Seven - Refers to the number of God, divine perfection or completeness.

1. God's Word is pure, like silver purified seven times in the fire (Psalm 12:6).
2. Jesus taught Peter to forgive 70 times seven (Matthew 18:22).
3. Seven demons went out from Mary Magdalene, symbolizing total deliverance (Luke 8:2).
4. Seven days in a week, seven colors in the spectrum, there are seven seals, trumpets, parables in Matthew, seven promises to the church.[20]

➢ Perfection or completeness; a number representing earth crowned with heaven (Rev. 1:4)[21]

Eight - Number of new beginnings.

- Eight people on Noah's Ark (2 Pet. 2:5)
- Circumcision on the eighth day (Gen. 17:12)[22]

➢ God made eight covenants with Abraham.

Ten –

➢ Five doubled and thus human completeness (Rev. 2:10)[23]

Twelve

➢ God's perfect manifestation of Himself to the created order (Rev. 21:12).[24]

---

[18] Ibid.
[19] Ibid.
[20] Ibid.
[21] Ibid.
[22] http://christianity.about.com/od/biblefactsandlists/qt/Bible-Numerology.htm, leads to https://www.thoughtco.com/biblical-numerology-700168, Accessed July 18, 2016.
[23] *The Woman's Study Bible, New Kings James Version*, Nashville: Thomas Nelson, Inc, 2006, p 1683.
[24] Ibid.

B. Colors: In the Bible, colors have meaning.

White: Purity; Revelation 3:4,5; 7:14; 19:14	**Blue** = Law; Numbers 15:38-39
Purple: Royalty; Mark 15:17, Judges 8:26	**Red/Scarlet** = Sin/corruption; Isaiah 1:18; Nahum 2:3; Revelation 17:1-4 – Used to describe blood, life and war.
Yellow: Metal of gold (Ps. 69:13)	

The rainbow we often see after rain is biblical, it is not of man and their beliefs. God used a rainbow after the great flood, which Noah saw, as a sign God would never destroy all mankind by using flood waters (Genesis 9:13).

When you have dreams with colors, they also have meanings. In the prophetic, the meanings are[25]:

Black: strength	**Blue**: water - river of God, cleansing life-giving flow of the Holy Spirit, the Word ruler ship, unlimited potential, priesthood (Esther 8:15), tabernacle (Exodus 25:4)
Light Blue: Holy Spirit, the heavens, Gods throne (Ezekiel 10:1)	**Brown**: humanity, humility, good soil
Gold: glory, divinity, refinement, purification (Jeremiah 9:7) (Zechariah 13:9), (Job 23:10) Spirit, priesthood, tabernacle (Exodus 25:3)	**Green**: prosperity, health, growth, prophetic, wealth
Light Green: new life, new beginnings	**Green Emerald**: royalty (Ezekiel 28:13), eternity, faith, heaven (Revelation 21:19)
Orange: fire, proven in fire, power, harvest	**Pink**: love, compassion, the heart of God
Red: blood of Jesus, atonement, grace	**Purple**: royalty, kingship, majesty, sonship, priesthood, tabernacle (Exodus 25:4)
White: purity, holiness, righteousness, triumph, (Revelation 7:9) (Revelation 19:14) the bride of Christ	**Silver**: redemption, wisdom, the soul (Ecclesiastes 12:6), purification (Zechariah 13:9), priesthood, tabernacle (Exodus 25:3)
Yellow: joy, revelation	

---

[25] http://www.pojc.org/colors.pdf, Jaco Kruger, *The prophetic meaning of colors*, Accessed July 18, 2016.

C. Animals: There are animal meanings in the Bible, dreams, and visions.

In the Bible there are meanings for the animals, such as:

Dove: Holy; Spirit Mark 1:10	**Wings**: Speed / Protection / Deliverance Deuteronomy 28:49, Matthew 23:37
Lamb: Jesus/sacrifice John 1:29; 1 Corinthians 5:7	**Serpent** : Satan Revelation 12:9; 20:2

In our dreams and visions, there are meanings for the animals, such as[26]:

Dog: Note type of dog and relationship to dog: biting dog is dissension; hypocrite; attack against God's work; accusation; if a personal pet: something or someone dear to your heart; personal pet that is a wolf: pet sin, or warning you of an attack on the sheep; Judases; watchman as in Elder or prophet as watchdog; returning to sin; false teachers. *(Prov. 26: 11-17; Phil. 3:2; Ez. 3: 17; Gal. 5 15; Ps. 22: 16; Rev. 22: 15; 2 Peter 2: 22; Matt. 7: 6)*
Dove: The Holy Spirit; peace and new life; a sin offering; burnt offering; cleansing; mercy. *(Gen. 8: 8-12; Matt. 3: 16; 10: 16; Lev. 5: 7-14, 14: 21-22; John 1: 32)*
Goat: Carnal, fleshly Christians; unbelief; Christian or group of Christians walking in sin; the cursed, scapegoat or goat of removal showing that our sins have been removed as far as the east is from the west; opposite of lambs; carriers of sin; our need to obtain forgiveness of sin; mixed with sheep, but not called the shepherds own. *(Ex. 25: 4; Matt. 25: 31-46; Lev. 16: 8, 15, 20-22; Ps. 103: 12; Heb. 13: 12)*
Leviathan: See also Crocodile, Alligator, Dragon and Dinosaur: bending; crooked; meandering; snake; monster; devious; distorted; ancient demon; large, evil creature that cannot be tamed with the natural strength of man; principality; evil spirit; ancient demonic control; only the Lord has power over; dragon. *(Is. 27: 1; 51: 9; Job 7: 12; 26: 12-13; 41: 1-10; Ps. 74: 14; 104: 26; Rev. 6: 7; 9: 1-19; 13: 1-18)*

---

[26] http://www.joshuamediaministries.org/dreams/animals, Accessed July 18, 2016.

In the Bible, there are meanings for metals, elements and natural objects.

Bible Universe notes:

Gold = Pure Character Precious and Rare	Isaiah 13:12
Silver = Pure Words & Understanding	Proverbs 2:4, 3:13-14, 10:20, 25:11; Psalms 12:6
Brass, Tin, Iron, Lead, Silver dross = Impure Character	Ezekiel 22:20-21
Water = Holy Spirit / Everlasting Life	John 7:39, 4:14; Rev. 22:17, Eph. 5:26
Waters = Inhabited area/people, nations	Revelation 17:15
Fire = Holy Spirit	Luke 3:16
Tree = Cross; People / Nation	Deut. 21:22-23; Psalm 92:12, 37:35
Seed = Descendants / Jesus	Romans 9:8; Galatians 3:16
Fruit = Works / Actions	Galatians 5:22
Fig Tree = A Nation that should bear fruit	Luke 13:6-9
Vineyard = Church that should bear fruit	Luke 20:9-16
Field = World	Matthew 13:38; John 4:35
Harvest = End of World	Matthew 13:39
Reapers = Angels	Matthew 13:39

E. Time

Let's learn about the hours of the day. Daytime was divided into twelve generally equal sections between sunrise and sundown. The first hour was the first of the daylight period, and the twelfth was the least. As a general rule of thumb, the third hour was approximately 9:00 AM, the sixth hour was noon, the ninth hour about 3:00PM, and the twelfth hour 6:00PM. The night was divided into a series of watches, a watch being the period of time a group of soldiers stood guard before being relieved. In OT times Jews used a system of three watches per night (Judges 7:19. During the Roman Period, N.T. era, there were four watches. The first watch (opse, late) 6:00 to 9:00PM, 2nd watch (mesonyktion, midnight) from 9:00PM to midnight, 3rd watch (proi, early) from midnight to 3:00AM and 4th watch from3:00 to 6:00 AM. All four night watches are mentioned in Mark 13:35.

F. Gender

When God speaks for example "men", he is speaking to the man and woman.

G. Objects

Bible Universe notes: 27

Lamp = Word of God	Psalm 119:105
Oil = Holy Spirit	Zechariah 4:2-6; Revelation 4:5
Sword = Word of God	Ephesians 6:17; Hebrews 4:12
Bread = Word of God	John 6:35, 51, 52, 63
Wine = Blood/Covenant/Doctrines	Luke 5:37
Honey = Happy Life	Ezekiel 20:6, Deuteronomy 8:8-9

Questions

Please write any questions you have and we will discuss later as a group.

_____

_____

_____

_____

_____

6. Bible Study Tools

What is exegesis and hermeneutics?

They are tools to help you interpret the Word of God. The key to good exegesis, and therefore to a more intelligent reading of the Bible, is to learn to read the text carefully and to ask the right questions of the text. Exegesis is an explanation or critical interpretation of a text. It is a systematic study of the Scripture to discover the original, intended meaning. And hermeneutics is a method or principle of interpretation. Hermeneutics ordinarily covers the whole field of interpretation, including exegesis, it is also used in the narrower sense of seeking the contemporary relevance of ancient texts.

Other tools available are Concordances, Maps, Bible dictionaries, Expository Dictionaries, Illustrated Bible Commentaries, Atlases and more.

7. How to Study the Bible

For this discipleship training we will learn about the inductive method to study the Bible. Yount writes, "Always start your study with prayer, to give you insight to understand its intended meaning. There are several ways to study the Bible, but I believe the best way is to follow the inductive method, which will allow us to obtain a more accurate understanding of a Bible passage. **This method includes three steps: observation, interpretation, and application**. Observation answers the question, what does the text say? Interpretation answers the question, what does it mean? Application answers the crucial question, what shall we do?

Step 1: Observation

As you read the word of God you are observing the Word of God. First, when we read the Bible we must ask, Who? What? Where? When? Why? And How?. Ask: Who is talking and who is being talked about? What is the subject? What is before and after the passage? When and where is all of this taking place? What is the purpose of this action? How are the people responding?

Second, is the grammatical structure. In the passage you should be looking for terms, grammatical structure, literary form, and the atmosphere. Look for key words such as nouns and verbs that will define the meaning of the text. Sometimes there is repetition throughout the passage. The grammatical structure of a passage helps us derive meaning from it. The structure helps to determine how the passage was put together.

In the third step, remember Bible passages represent a literary form. It can present arguments around the people, the places, the events, the ideas, and the times. A passage can use the literary genre, for example, cause and effect, comparison, contrast, repetition, problem, and solution, questions

Note:

In the fourth step, you must look at the passage for the tone of the mood and the response it will cause.

<u>SAY</u>: Now let's learn about interpretation of the Bible.

Step 2: Interpretation

The purpose of interpretation is to discover the meaning of the biblical passage as the author intended. To interpret the text.

1. **Interpret the passage literally.** The literal meanings of words are determined in three ways: (1) by their basic definitions, (2) by the way the term is used elsewhere in the Scripture and in other contemporary writings, and (3) by the context in which the word is used.

2. **Interpret the Bible passage considering its immediate context.** The context of a passage

determines the meaning of a particular text. To interpret a passage correctly, we need to consider the paragraph in which it is located, its chapter, its book, and the entire Bible. Some critics argue that the Bible is vague, that we can make the Bible say anything we want. This is true only when readers take verses out of their context. A text out of context becomes a pretext to present ideas contrary to what the Bible is really saying.

3. **Interpret the passage in view of history and culture.** A proper biblical interpretation requires that we pay attention to the geographical, religious, topographical, social, and political factors surrounding the biblical text. The occasion and purpose of each biblical book is central for a proper understanding of the historical context.

4. **Interpret the passage in view of literary form.** As we have discussed, the literary genre of Bible books affects the interpretation of their meaning. The Bible uses six major literary genres: epistles, narrative, poetry, proverbs, parables, and prophecy.

5. **Interpret the passage in view of other parts of Scripture**. The Bible always interprets itself (Scriptura sui ipsius interpres). Thus, we need to pay attention to similar or related passages as we interpret a biblical text. Also, we need to interpret some passages, especially in the Old Testament, according to progressive revelation.

Step 3: Application

Application helps us to change our behavior, attitude, and way of thinking so that we please God and live according to His will. In the Bible we find the parameters for our renovation. The key question we need to ask ourselves when we read a text is, How does God want me to change in light of this passage? Observation and interpretation prepare the way to application, which is the most important aspect of Bible study (Matt. 7:24; Jas. 1:22).

An accurate application of the biblical text has to be practical, personal, and precise. Application is more than good desires and general principles. The dedicated practice of biblical truths in daily experiences, every day, all the time, is a central desire of every serious believer. God speaks to us through His Word, and we should individually respond to His message.

A better application would be able to answer the following: When should I read the Bible? How much? Where do I start? How long? Where? At what time?

God revealed Himself to the biblical authors "progressively throughout history. The most obvious proof is to compare incomplete Jewish theology with the fuller revelation of Christian theology in respect, for example, to such doctrines as the Trinity, Christology, the Holy Spirit, resurrection, and eschatology."

Even though the Bible was written by many authors in different times and places, it presents a thematic unity that brings together all books. The three main Bible themes are creation, fall, and redemption."[28] (Yount, 2008,Chapter 12, Digital)

> 28 Yount, William R., ed. *The Teaching Ministry of the Church*. 2nd ed. Nashville: B&H Publishing Group, 2008. ISBN: 9781943965427. (Chapter 12 -digital).

8. Activity

Fee & Stuart writes, "First, we will read the scripture passage and interpret what the Lord is saying to us. You are going to complete an exercise on discovering the meaning of a scriptural passage. It may be an epistle, narrative, poetry, proverbs, parables, or prophetic literature passage. Remember to identify the book, genre, context, passage, author, audience, purpose and date.

Let's first look at a lament Psalm, which either expresses or presuppose deep trust in Yahweh, help a person to express thoughts, suffering, or disappointment to the Lord.

Most Psalms tend to have the same six elements that appear in one way or another in virtually all of them.

1. *Address*: The psalmist identifies the one to whom the psalm is prayed. This is, of course, the Lord.

2. *Complaint*: The psalmist pours out a complaint honestly and forcefully, identifying what the trouble is and why the Lord's help is being sought.

3. *Trust*: The psalmist immediately expresses trust in God, which serves as the presuppositional basis for his complaint. Moreover, you must trust him to answer your complaint in the way he sees fit, not necessarily as you would wish.

4. *Deliverance*: The psalmist cries out to the God for deliverance from the situation described in the complaint.

5. *Assurance:* The psalmist expresses that assurance that God will deliver. This assurance is somewhat parallel to the expression of trust.

6. *Praise*: The psalmist offers praise, thanking and honoring God for the blessings of the past, present, and/or future."[29]

Let's go the Bible and look at the elements of lament Psalm 3.

Scripture: Psalm 3

1. *Address*: This is the cry" Lord" of verse 1. Note that the address need not be lengthy or fancy. Simple prayers will always do! Note also that the address is repeated twice in verse 7.

2. *Complaint*: This comprises the remainder of verse 1 and all of verse 2 David describes the foes (who can stand in these psalms as personified symbols of virtually any misery or problem) and how bleak his situation seems. Any difficulty can be expressed this way.

3. *Trust*: Here verses 3-6 are all part of the expression of trust in the Lord. Who God is,

---

29 Gordon D. Fee, Douglas Stuart, *How To Read the Bible for All Its Worth*. 2003, p 215-217.

and how he answers prayers, how he keeps his people secure even when their situation is apparently hopeless—all this represents evidence that God is trustworthy.

4. *Deliverance*: In verse 7a ("Arise, Lord! Deliver me; my God!") David expresses his (and our) plea for help. Notice how the direct request for aid is held until this point in the psalm, coming after the expression of trust. This order is not required but is normal. A balance between asking and praising seems to characterize the laments, and this should be instructive to us in our own prayers.

5. *Assurance:* The remainder of verse 7 ("Strike all my...") constitutes the statement of assurance. But remember that this part of the psalm does not promise that God's people will be trouble free. It expresses the assurance that God in his own time will have taken care of our really significant problems according to his plan for us.

6. *Praise*: Verse 8 lauds God for his faithfulness. He is declared to be one who is a deliverer, and in the request for his blessing, he is implicitly declared to be one who blesses."[30]

---

30   Gordon D. Fee, Douglas Stuart, *How To Read the Bible for All Its Worth*. 2003, p 215-217.

Activity: Select a scripture and apply what you have learned using the below format of questions.

| Book: _____ | Scripture: _____ | Date: _____ |

Questions to Ask:

1. What's the context (Writer, location, original audience, setting, etc.?)

_____
_____
_____

2. What are the main points? (How would you describe this to someone?)

_____
_____
_____

3. What are some points from related verses? (Verses before/after, verses listed in the center column, footnotes and concordance section)

_____
_____
_____

4. What action is needed after prayerfully considering this passage? (For example, being obedient in a specific area, claiming a promise given or following a model displayed)

_____
_____
_____

Activity: Select a scripture and apply what you have learned using the below format of questions.

| Book: _____ | Scripture: _____ | Date: _____ |

Questions to Ask:

1. What's the context (Writer, location, original audience, setting, etc.?)

_____

_____

_____

2. What are the main points? (How would you describe this to someone?)

_____

_____

_____

3. What are some points from related verses? (Verses before/after, verses listed in the center column, footnotes and concordance section)

_____

_____

_____

4. What action is needed after prayerfully considering this passage? (For example, being obedient in a specific area, claiming a promise given or following a model displayed)

_____

_____

_____

9. Spiritual Growth through the Bible

Pipes & Lee writes, "As we grow in the word, we grow in God. What does it mean to develop your relationship with Christ? There are six basic disciplines necessary for spiritual growth.

1. Quiet time- starting your days alone with God
2. Lordship
3. Developing a powerful prayer life
4. Personalizing God's Word (decreeing & declaring, confessing God's word)
5. Christian friendship and accountability
6. Developing a ministry—making disciples and using your gifts in your church"[31]

As you grow in the word, you become spiritually disciplined. Spiritual discipline is essential for Christian growth and development. Though at first painful, spiritual discipline resulting from obedience and faith produces abundant blessings (Heb. 12:11). Every believer should seek to become a disciplined in order to grow spiritually. Spiritual discipline is a continual process that helps the believer mature in Christ and know God's will. It is as much an attitude of commitment as it is an activity in holiness. Specific spiritual disciplines may include personal training in Bible study, prayer, worship, fellowship, service, or witnessing, among other godly practices. A conscientious, creative pursuit of these spiritual disciplines should continue throughout a believer's life (Heb. 6:11, 12). Spiritual discipline is essential to deliverance from the power of sin and obedience to God's will. Without spiritual discipline, believers cannot walk with Christ, grow in faith, or receive the heavenly rewards awaiting those who diligently practice spiritual discipline.

(The Woman's Study Bible, NKJV, 2006, Thomas Nelson, Inc., p. 1645)

10. GOD

The Bible tells us from beginning to end who God is. God's attributes are:

God is Eternal. God has no beginning and no ending. He is the only, self-existent being. Eternity is God's signature—it is who He is (is. 63:16). His name, "I Am", expresses clearly His unconditional and independent existence and encompasses the idea of His continuous presence (Ex. 3:14) because He simply "is".

(The Woman's Study Bible, NKJV, 2006, Thomas Nelson, Inc., p. 736)

God is Faithful. "Through the Lord's mercies we are not consumed, because His compassion fail not". Lam. 3:22. God is ever faithful. The root meaning of faithfulness (Heb. 'emunah) is "certainty" and "dependability." Faithfulness describes who God is (1 Cor. 1:19). No matter what you do, God cannot be unfaithful because He cannot deny Himself (2 Tim. 2:13). He is steadfast and trustworthy. He keeps His promises (Heb. 10:23). His faithfulness is experienced in His protection (2 Thess. 3:3), mercy (Ps. 89:2), preservation (1 Thess. 5:23, 24), love (Rom. 8:35-39),

---

[31] Pipes & Lee, *Family to Family: Leaving a Lasting* Legacy, 1999, p. 13.

and discipline (Ps. 89:32, 33); it is revealed in all His promises (Josh 23:14).

(The Woman's Study Bible, NKJV, 2006, Thomas Nelson, Inc., p. 1014)

God is Good. God not only does good; He is the originator of goodness (Gen. 1:31). Goodness is not one of God's part-time activities (Ps. 136:1). He abounds in it (Ex. 34:6). It is the drive behind His blessings and the reason for His compassion, kindness and generosity (Ps. 84:11). God does not give out of obligation, for He is never in anyone's debt. He gives out of His goodness. God's goodness is for this life (Ps. 27:13) as well as eternity (Ps.31:19). It gives hope (Ps. 27:13), leads to repentance (Rom. 2:4), and produces thankfulness (Ps. 136:1).

(The Woman's Study Bible, NKJV, 2006, Thomas Nelson, Inc., p. 686)

God is Grace. Mercy does not give us what we do deserve; grace gives us what we do not deserve. The Lord's grace includes undeserved favor, unexpected acceptance, and unconditional love.

(The Woman's Study Bible, NKJV, 2006, Thomas Nelson, Inc., p. 1528)

God is Holy. The word Holy (Heb. qadosh) means "unique, set apart, unlike all others." Holiness is not what God does but who He is. All God's attributes flow out of his holiness.

That is why He is incapable of the slightest hint of impurity, unrighteousness, untruth, injustice, or questionable use of power (Gen. 18:25). Two consistent responses spring from those who have seen God's holiness: they thirst for more (see Ex. 33:17-23; Ps. 42:1, 2; Phil. 3:10), and they know with certainty that He is God and they are not (Ps. 100:3).

(The Woman's Study Bible, NKJV, 2006, Thomas Nelson, Inc., p. 868)

God Is Immutable. Believers can be sure of God. His character, truth, ways, purposes, love, and promises never vary (Is. 46:9-11). He has never been less than what He is, nor will He be more (Mal. 3:6). God never alters His plans because they are made with complete knowledge and control (Ps. 33:11). What He does in time He planned in eternity He carries out in time (Is. 46:9-11). God does not change because He is bigger than all causes.

(The Woman's Study Bible, NKJV, 2006, Thomas Nelson, Inc., p. 748)

God is Jealous. The relationship between God and His people was designed to be exclusive. Jealousy (heb. qin'ah) denotes "zeal, passion, single-mindedness." To be intertwined in heart and life with the world is the worst kind of adultery (James 4:4, 5). God considers it hatred of Himself (Ex. 20:5) and prostitution with the Evil One (1 Cor. 10:21, 22). The consequence of spiritual adultery is a severed relationship with God (Ps. 78:56-60). The teachings of God's jealousy are given in the context of worship. He alone is God; to worship another is betrayal. God takes His relationship with His people seriously, and so must they take theirs with Him (Ex. 34:10-16).

(The Woman's Study Bible, NKJV, 2006, Thomas Nelson, Inc., p. 228) (Exodus 20:5,6)

God is Judge. God judges. Attempts are made to water down God's judgment, explain it away, or apologize for it, but God's judgment is a manifestation of the reaction of His holiness to evil (Is. 42:8). Judgment is necessary.

(The Woman's Study Bible, NKJV, 2006, Thomas Nelson, Inc., p. 558)

God is Longsuffering. God's judgment is sure (Rev. 19:2, 11). God is called "longsuffering" because He does not execute judgment immediately. He waits (Is. 42:14-16), not to see, what will happen—He knows what will happen, not to see more clearly, He sees perfectly; not to gain More information — He knows everything. God waits because His priority is self-revelation, not judgment. God, for a time, tolerates insults, rejection, and indifference in order to draw people to repentance (Rom.2:4). His longsuffering is linked with His great compassion and becomes active in order to draw us to Himself (2 Pet. 3:9).

(The Woman's Study Bible, NKJV, 2006, Thomas Nelson, Inc., p. 1446)

God is Love. God is the definition of love. God's love is self-starting (1 John 4:10), indestructible (Rom. 8:38, 39), undeserved (Rom. 3:23), compassionate (Is. 49:15), constant (Jer. 31:3), immeasurable (Eph. 3; 18, 19), voluntary (Rom. 5:8), and a gift (John 3:16). He did not begin loving at the Cross, nor will He love us more tomorrow than He does today. There is nothing we can do, think, or say that will change His love because there are no surprises for God He knows us totally and loves us anyway (Ps. 139:1-5).

(The Woman's Study Bible, NKJV, 2006, Thomas Nelson, Inc., p. 1655)

God Is Merciful. Mercy is compassion in action toward sinners who have no claim or right to receive such treatment. God's mercy is great (1 Kin. 3:6), tender (Luke 1:78), and everlasting (Ps. 103:17). Mercy is interwoven with all other attributes of God. His lovingkindness initiates mercy (Eph. 2:4-7); His holiness insures its integrity (Ex. 34:6, 7); His truth guarantees its reliability (Is. 16:5); His power assures its duration (Ps. 89:2); and His faithfulness demands its constancy (Ps. 36:5). The results of mercy are forgiveness (Isa. 55:7), restoration (Ps. 51:2, 10, 11), and praise on the part of those who experience mercy (Ps. 89:1).

(The Woman's Study Bible, NKJV, 2006, Thomas Nelson, Inc., p. 738)

God is Omnipotent. God can do anything, and He gets things done. God is the source of His own power. God uses His power for His children to conquer death, to provide salvation; to complete their transformation; to equip them for service; to protect, provide, and preserve them; and to secure their inheritance (Rom. 8:31). If God were not all-powerful, His mercy would be helpless pity; His justice, an empty threat; His knowledge, useless information; and His love, pure frustration. God reigns without rival (Ps. 86:8-10).

(The Woman's Study Bible, NKJV, 2006, Thomas Nelson, Inc., p. 664)

God is Omnipresent. There is no place without God, no place beyond Him (2 Chr. 6:18), and

He is everywhere simultaneously (Eph. 4:6). Yet God is not bound by, nor dependent upon, any place or anyone (Jer. 23:23, 24). God is always distinct from His creation because He, as the Creator, brought all into existence (Gen. 1:31). His relational presence is experienced only by believers. He indwells His children (1 Cor. 6:19, 20). In "taking up residence", He establishes ownership, provision, love, workmanship, guidance, teaching, and personal friendship (Ps. 139).

(The Woman's Study Bible, NKJV, 2006, Thomas Nelson, Inc., p. 970)

God is Omniscient. God knows everything from eternity past to eternity future simultaneously. He learns from no one, is never surprised, and never forgets (Isa. 46; 9-10). God knows His creation completely. He names the stars (Ps. 147; 4, 5), places the clouds (Job 37:16), tracks activity in the oceans (Job 38:16). Clothes the fields (Matt. 6:28) and is aware of every creature and its activities at all times (Matt. 10:29).

(The Woman's Study Bible, NKJV, 2006, Thomas Nelson, Inc., p. 914)

God is Personal. God is the Ultimate Being. He is a living, speaking, loving, feeling, and seeking God. Though He is spirit (John 4:24), He has intellect (1 Cor. 2:10, 11), will (Dan. 4:35), and emotions (Deut. 4:21, 24), and He communicates with us (Job 22:21, 22; Prov. 2:6). The ultimate communication of God to us is Jesus (John 1:18, 10:30; 12:45; 14:9). Only the God of the Bible is the living God. His greatest glory is found in His creation with whom He is personally and intimately involved, and of whom Christ is the crowning expression.

(The Woman's Study Bible, NKJV, 2006, Thomas Nelson, Inc., p. 126)

God is Righteous. As the ultimate standard for right, God always does the right thing (Ps. 18:30). The idea of righteousness (Heb. tesdeq) is "to be straight". It denotes a right behavior, conforming to an ethical or moral standard. God is the standard of "right"—His ways are right because He is right (Ps. 145:17). God's righteousness is immovable (Ps. 36:5, 6). In other words, His standards are non-negotiable. Setting your own standards about what is right and wrong and is an attempt at being God and as such is doomed to failure. (Rom. 3:10).

God is Righteous, pg. 92 continued

One day you will be clothed and crowned in righteousness (Rev. 19:8). In other words, a day will come when you will always want to live and be able to live the right way.

(The Woman's Study Bible, NKJV, 2006, Thomas Nelson, Inc., p. 266)

God is Sovereign. God alone is accountable to no one and is supreme in power, rank authority, virtues, decrees, and work (Ps. 115:3). Everything depends on God (Col. 1:16, 17), but he depends on nothing. Everything came from Him, but He came from nowhere because He has no beginning and no end (Ps. 90:2). Since all life comes from Him, He rightfully retains ultimate authority (1 Tim. 6:15) and will do what He pleases (Ps. 135:6).

(The Woman's Study Bible, NKJV, 2006, Thomas Nelson, Inc., p. 652)

God is Truth

Every Word God speaks is true (John 17:17). He is unable to speak an untruth (Heb. 6:17, 18), and He is never mistaken. He knows all things as they really are and sees what has happened, is happening, and will happen (Is. 46:9, 10). Since He is responsible for everything, all accurate knowledge comes from Him. He is the standard for all truth; He is that by which all else is measured. The fact that God is Truth is the basis of faith because the opposite of having faith in God is calling God a liar (Rom. 3:4). He is not only dependably accurate, but he is also accurately dependable. (The Woman's Study Bible, 2006, Thomas Nelson, Inc., p. 756)

11. Jesus

SAY: Let's learn about Jesus Christ in the New Testament. The four gospels of Matthew, Mark, Luke and John is where we learn about Jesus from their writings.

Lea & Black writes, "**Homeland**: Jesus spent most his active life in Palestine, a territory of no more than ten thousand square miles, about the size of the state of Vermont. When Jesus was an infant, Joseph took him and Mary to Egypt to escape the wrath of Herod (Matt. 2:13-15)."[32]

Lea & Black writes, "**Teaching Methods of Jesus**: Those who heard Jesus' teaching were gripped by the authority with which he spoke (Mark 1:22). Jesus' best known teaching method was the parable. Using either an extended story or a short, pithy statement, he conveyed spiritual truth by comparing it to familiar facts from daily life. Jesus also used pungent figures of speech to communicate truth. He frequently used the epigram, a terse statement which would grab the attention of his audience like a barb on wire grabs the skin (see Matt. 9:12-13). He also used hyberbole, intentional exaggeration, to communicate this point (see Matt. 5:29-30). Jesus occasionally used arguments in his teaching, but the basis of his arguments centered around the interpretation of Scriptures. Jesus' occasional use of questions and answers stimulated listeners. Usually, his questions dealt with some form of deep human need or spiritual problem. Jesus sometimes used object lesson to communicate concrete to his listeners. Jesus helped his listeners understand and remember his teachings by the use of frequent repetition. Jesus promoted learning by focusing on the performance of a project. In dealing with his disciples, he told them how to minister and what they could expect to encounter. Then he sent them out, allowed them to learn, and concluded this practicum with a reporting session (Luke 9:1-10)."[33]

Lea & Black writes, "**Content of Teachings**: Jesus spoke on moral and theological subjects. He entered it around his own person. Concerning specific doctrinal topics, Jesus taught about the Holy Spirit (John 16:8-11) and emphasized that only one born of the Spirit could enter God's kingdom (John 3:5). He did not teach extensively about the church, but he declared that he had founded it (Matt. 16:18). He promised eternal life and security for those who knew him (John

---

32   Lea & Black, *The New Testament: Its Background and Message*, 2003, p. 87.
33   Lea & Black, , *The New Testament: Its Background and Message* 2003, p. 92-93.

10:28), and he promised a return to bring his followers to a heavenly home with him (John 14:3)"[34].

Lea & Black, writes "**Chronology of Jesus**: Both Matthew and Luke provide information about the birth and death of Jesus. They indicate that Mary gave birth to Jesus by the biotical miracle of the virgin birth."[35]

Before Jesus began his public ministry, three important incidents related to his work took place:

1. the ministry of John the Baptist,
2. the baptism of Jesus, and
3. the temptation of Jesus.

Jesus' early Judean Ministry is in the Gospel of John. During this period Jesus made contacts with those who would later become his committed disciples (John 1:19-42). During this same period he made a detour into Galilee, where he performed the first of his miraculous signs, the wedding at Cana (John 2:1-11). In Jerusalem he cleansed the temple and spoke with Nicodemus (John 2:13-3:21).

Jesus' early Galilean Ministry is in the Gospel of John. There were three chief periods:

1. The first period includes Jesus' work up to the time of choosing the twelve disciples.

2. The second period ends with the withdrawal of Jesus from northern Galilee. It was a time where Jesus continued to teach and perform miracles, and included the development of more intense opposition by the official religious leaders in Jerusalem.

3. In the third period Jesus ministered largely outside of Galilee and returned there only as he travelled toward Jerusalem for the final time. He also manifested his glory in the transfiguration (Luke 9:28-36) and began to prepare his disciples for his death by predictions of his passion (Mark 9:30-32)."[36]

12. Holy Spirit

The Holy Spirit in the Bible and in our lives can be so meaningful. When we read the word of God, the Holy Spirit can mean so many things, for example:

1. **Fire**—zeal and refining power (Lk. 3:16; Isa. 4:3-4; Ps. 104:4; Mal. 3:1-4; Jn. 2:17; Acts 2:3; Mt.3:11)
2. **Dove**—gentleness, harmlessness, and comforting power (Lk. 3:22; Jn. 1:32-33)
3. **Water**—life-giving and infinite power John 7:37-39
4. **Wind**—resurrection power (John 3:8; Acts 2:2; Ezekiel 37:9)

---

34   Ibid, 94.
35   Ibid, 97.
36   Lea & Black, *The New Testament: Its Background and Message,* 2003, p. 98-100.

5. **Oil**—consecration and anointing power (Isa. 61:1-3; Heb. 1:9; James 5:14-16; Ps. 45:7)
6. **Seal**—redemptive and keeping power (Eph. 1:13; 4:30; 1 Pet.1:5)
7. **Guarantee**—ownership and guarantee of power (2 Cor. 1:22; Eph. 1:13-14)
8. **Rain**—life giving and quickening power (Joel 2:23-32; Ps. 1:3; Zech. 10:1; James 5:7; Hos. 6:3; 10:12)
9. **Dew**—refreshing and invigorating power (Ps. 72:6; Hos.14:5)
10. **Gift**—joyful, gracious and liberating power (Acts 2:38-39; 4:31-32; 2 Cor. 3:17-18; Heb. 1:9)

SAY: Let's talk about the role of the Holy Spirit in the Bible. The Holy Spirit is the divine author that used the human author to put the words to paper. The Spirit of God has breathed the character of God into the Scriptures.

13. Bible Versions and Translations

The Bible went through several versions and translations because of the different time periods and the interpretations of the Bible. The first interpreters were the ancient Israelites who studied and later it led to the Hebrew scriptures. The Bible also went through Jewish interpretations. During the history of the Israelites they were exposed to other cultures like Babylon for example and they spoke Aramaic instead of the Hebrew scriptures. In 333 B.C. Alexander the Great obtained the Persian Empire including Palestine. Here is where they imposed the Greek culture on the Jewish community in Alexandria. Hellenistic Judaism flourished, which was integrating Greek philosophy of Plato with Jewish religious beliefs.

Eventually, Greek replaced Hebrew as the common language among Jews outside of Palestine. The Qumran community (the Essenes) went to live at Qumran, the northwestern shore of the Dead Sea. They created the Dead Sea Scrolls and it regarded Judaism centered in Jerusalem as apostate. They formed a monastic community to prepare for the coming of the messianic age. The Bible also went through Rabbinic Judaism which was in Jerusalem and Judea. They obeyed the Torah, in the face of mounting pressure to follow the Greco-Roman culture.

Next came the Apostolic period (A.D. 30-100). The first Christian interpreters which were the Apostles were devout Jews. They regarded Jesus as the promised Messiah of Israel. They used the OT scriptures to support their beliefs and interpreted it as the other Jewish religious groups did. They did not limit themselves to the literal interpretation of the OT prophecies. They used three other interpretive approaches, such as the typological interpretation, the literal-contextual interpretation, and the principle/application method. The apostolic interpretation compared with and departs from the contemporary Jewish interpretive method.

The patristic period (A.D. 100-590) was during the time of Pope Gregory I. The church tradition used their influence on the definition of the church doctrine. There were three periods within the patristic period. The first is the apostolic fathers who used the typological interpretation to relate the OT to the NT focusing on the teachings of Jesus. They used allegory method for the OT. They also used the midrashic interpretive approach that the rabbis and the Qumran used. During the second century many new heretical groups were birthed within the Church. The Gnostics supported their unorthodox views by appealing to the Scriptures and the sayings of Jesus. A new hermeneutical principle came forth known as traditional interpretation in the Church, which is what the traditional interpretation of the Bible is the correct interpretation. They used it to defend the teaching of the Gnostics and the early heretics. The second period was (A.D.150-400) a generation where the interpretation of the OT was to meet the needs of the Christian community. The Christian catechetical school at Alexandria used the allegory, exegetical method of Jewish scholar Philo. Two people also believed in the allegorical method. First, Clement (A.D. 190-203) also taught to read the Bible using the allegorical method. Clement believed that Scripture had two meanings (like a human being it has a body (literal) meaning and a soul (spiritual) meaning hidden behind the literal sense.

Second, Origen (A.D. 185-554) believed the Scripture had three meanings of body, soul, and spirit like a human. He believed the interpreter should move from the events of the passage to find those hidden principles for the Christian living (moral) and the doctrinal truth (spiritual).

There are three main types of Bible translations which are word-for-word, thought-for-thought and paraphrase. Let's discuss some versions and you can then make a decision based on your preference.

Version	Translation
King James Version (KJV) 1611	The translation of the Bible into the current spoken languages of the people in 1611. It establishes sound doctrines. Although both accurate and popular, is increasingly difficult to understand simply because the English language has evolved considerably over the 400 years since its publication.
New King James Version (NKJV) 1982	It updates the language of the King James version, It is great for study.
English Standard Version (ESV) Fall 2001	Uses word-for-word translation, It is highly accurate because it closely reflects the original meaning of the text in clear English.
Holman Christian Standard Bible (HCSB) 2001	It is a combination of word-for-word with dynamic renderings. It is both faithful to the words God inspired. Good for modern readers.
New International Version (NIV) 2005	A meaning to meaning translation. Also helpful in conveying the point of ancient figures of speech—idioms—that would not make sense to us in modern language. Uses more up-to-date language and thus are easier to understand.

New Living Translation (NLT) 1996	A meaning-to-meaning translation.
Good News Bible (GNB)	A meaning-to-meaning translation.
The Living Bible or The Message	Uses more up-to-date language and thus are easier to understand. Paraphrased to make the Bible even easier to read in modern language.
Amplified (Paraphrased)	First published in 1965. An English translation that is revision of the American Standard Bible of 1901. It is designed "to amplify" the text by using additional wording and a system of punctuation and other typographical features to bring out all shades of meaning present in the original texts.
Parallell Bible	It contains two or more versions side by side on the same pages, to be helpful.

Word-for-word means as exactly as possible in English. It is also known as formal equivalence, which attempts to reproduce the Greek and Hebrew as exactly as possible into English. The words, figures of speech, and sometimes even the sentence structure of the original languages are reproduced in a much more limited way.

Thought-for-thought is also known as dynamic equivalent. These bible are more a thought-for-thought philosophy. Greek and Hebrew figures of speech are replaced with modern thought equivalents. Some passages become more interpretations than translations.

Paraphrase means it is really rewordings of the Scriptures that speak in a very earthy, uncommon tongue. The result can be the clearest expression of Scripture but theological biases can creep in. Not good for study or to use as a church Bible.

There is also the aberrational translation which can be an independent religious group that believes they are the only ones on the way to salvation. They translate Scripture by twisting the word of God to fit their theologies. There is a person or organization that believes that they are equally in authority with the Bible.

Types of Bible Translations

Retrieved from https://www.bing.com/images/search?view=detailV2&c-cid=72lQ83qE&id=06F268D6CF933DCD7BED27E193980DA60B58FAE6&thid=OIP.72lQ8 3qEb89zzVNkLZP2hgHaEN&mediaurl=http%3a%2f%2fdeonvsearth.com%2fwp-content%-2fuploads%2f2014%2f03%2ftypes-of-bible-translations1.jpg&exph=511&expw=900&q=types+of+bi-ble+translations&simid=608024000738297213&selectedIndex=0&ajaxhist=0

14. Interpret the Word of God

When we read the Bible, we want to grasp the meaning of the text that God intended. We revere the Bible and treat is as holy because it is the Word of God and because God reveals himself to us through this Word.

Let's go through the journey step-by-step. I decided one day that I have to learn a way to study the Bible and I read the book, "Grasping God's Word which helped me a lot with interpretation. The interpretive journey which is a step by step process, will provide you with a procedure that allows you to take the meaning for the ancient audience and to cross over the river to determine a legitimate meaning for us today.

Step	Journey
1	**Grasping the text in their Town** You ask the question, what did the text mean to the biblical audience? So, you read the text carefully and observe it. See as much as possible in the text, review the grammar and analyze all significant words. Study the historical and literal contexts. You can write the passage if that will help you.
2	**Measuring the width of the river to cross** You ask the question, what are the differences between the biblical audience and us or me? Christians today are separated from the biblical audience by differences in culture, language, situation, time, and often covenant. These differences from a river that hinders us from moving straight from meaning in their context to meaning in ours. The width of the river will vary from passage to passage. Look for significant differences between one situation today and the situation of the biblical audience. Whether Old Testament or New Testament, try to identify unique aspects of the situation of your passage.
3	**Crossing the Principalizing Bridge** Ask the question, what is the theological principal in this text? Look for the theological principle or principles that are reflected in the meaning of the text you identified in step 1. Note the differences from step 2 and then note the similarities between the biblical situation and our own. Now return to the meaning for the biblical audience that you described in step 1 and try to identify a broader theological principle reflected in the text, but also one that relates to the similarities between us and the biblical audience.
4	**Consult the Biblical Map** Ask: How does our theological principle fit with the rest of the Bible? Now enter into the parts-whole spiral. You must reflect back and forth between the text and the teachings of the rest of the Scripture.
5	**Grasping the Text in our Town** Ask: How should individual Christians today live out the theological principles? Here we apply the theological principle in the specific situation of individual Christians in the church today. We have to pace how we respond to that principle in our town. How does it apply to real life situations today? Each of us will grasp and apply the same theological principle in slightly different ways, depending on our current life situation and where we are in relationship with God.

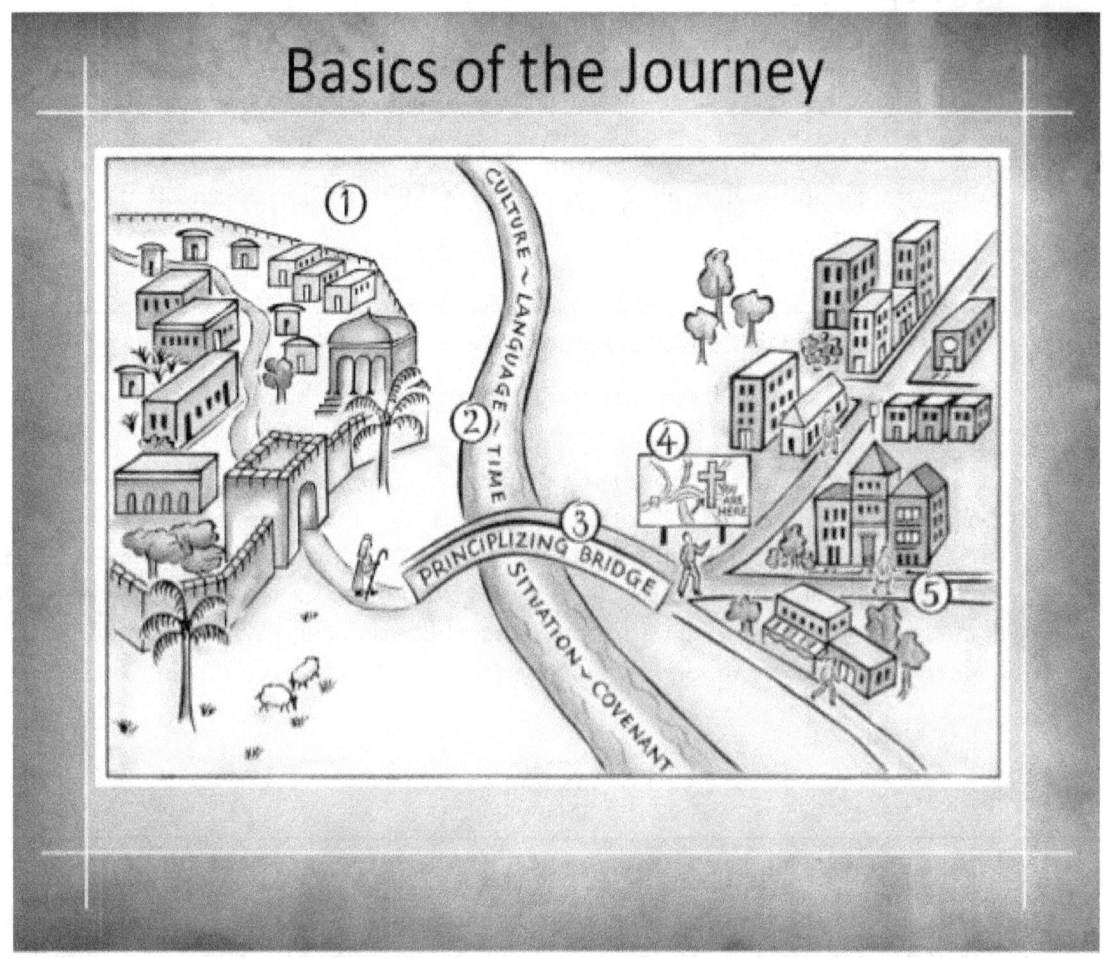

Here is a graphic example of the journey.

Retrieved from: http://tse4.mm.bing.net/th?id=OIP.hNQr1SaDN-FR6Ms8cTmqkgHaFj&w=261&h=196&c=7&qlt=90&o=4&pid=1.7

SAY: Let's move on to How to Read Sentences. The Bible is not boring, we need to learn how to read it with insight and understanding. First, we are able to read the Bible seriously, note as many details as possible. You have to read the text over and over again for you to develop the skill of observing your Bible. We should look for repetition of words, contrasts, comparisons, lists, cause and effects, figures of speech, conjunctions, verbs and pronouns. Always ask, What does the text mean?

In sentences you must look for:

A. Sentences, continued		
1. Repetition of words	Words that repeat. Go to 1 John 2:15-17	
	SAY: Which word is repeated in the first sentence? A: world	
	What about the next sentence? A: yes, world	
	How many times is world in this passage? A: six times	
	Is love repeated? A: yes	
	How many times? A: three times	
	What is the passage about? A: loving the world	
	SAY: Go to 2 Corinthians 1:3-7	
	How many times is "comfort" in the passage? A: four times	
	Who comforts? A: God	
	Where is word "suffering"? A: Verses 5, 6 and 7	
	Who suffers? A: people	
2. Contrasts	They are items, ideas, or individuals that are contrasted with each other.	
	SAY: Let us go to Proverbs 14:31.	
	Which two people do you think are contrasted in this passage?	
	A: The way they treat the poor and the behavior toward them reflected their attitude toward God. One oppresses the poor, and the other is kind to the poor.	
	Let us go to the New Testament scripture Romans 6:23.	
3. Comparisons	Focuses on similarities. Remember to look for items, ideas, or individuals that are compared with each other.	
	SAY: Let us go to Isaiah 40:31.	
	A: Here the renewal of strength from hope in the Lord is compared to the soar of eagles.	

4. Lists	More than two itemized things in a list. SAY: Let us go to Galatians 5:22-23? What is the list? A: Love, joy, peace, longsuffering, kindness, goodness, faithfulness, gentleness, self-control SAY: Let us go to 1 John 2:16. What is the list? A: The lust of the flesh, the lust of the eyes, the pride of life.
5. Cause and effect	The biblical writers wrote a cause and then stated the effect of the cause. SAY: Let us go to Prov. 15:1. What is the cause and effect? A: Cause is "soft/gentle answer", "harsh word" and the effect is "away wrath", "stirs up anger." SAY: Let us go to Rom. 12:1-2. What is the cause and effect? A: Cause is "But be transformed by the renewing of your mind." Effect is "you will be able to test and approve what God's will is". The cause is our transformation through the renewing of our minds. The effect is the ability to discern God's will".
6. Figures of Speech	They plant images to which we can relate emotionally. Images in which words are used. SAY: Let us go to Psalm 119:105. What are the figures of speech? A: "lamp" and "feet/path"
7. Conjunctions	They hold phrases and sentences together. For example, words like "and", "but", "therefore", "since", "because", etc. SAY: Let us go to Rom. 6:23. What is the conjunction? A: "But" indicates a contrast between the wages of sin (death) and the gift of God (eternal life). When you see "therefore", look back in the text and determine what the earlier reason is.

Goal Three: The Bible

8. Verbs	Communicates the action of the sentence. A verb can be past, present, or future tense. Imperative verbs are often God's commands. An active verb is the subject is doing the action. A passive verb is where the subject is acted upon. SAY: Let's go to Col. 3:1 "3 Since, then, you have been raised with Christ, set your hearts on things above, where Christ is, seated at the right hand of God" (NIV) A: "3 Since, then, you have been raised (passive) with Christ, set (active!) your hearts on things above, where Christ is, seated at the right hand of God". SAY: Let's go to Eph. 1:11 "11 In him we were also chosen,[e] having been predestined according to the plan of him who works out everything in conformity with the purpose of his will" A: 11 In him we were also chosen (passive), having been predestined (passive) according to the plan of him who works out (active) everything in conformity with the purpose of his will
9. Pronouns	Pronouns are you, she, her, he, him, and it. Indefinite pronouns identify to whom or what the pronoun refers, such as, anything, everybody, another, each, few, many, none, some, all, any, anybody, everyone, everything, someone, something, most, enough, little, more, either, neither, one, much, such.

Now you will put all of what you have learned about sentences in the scriptures.

Romans 12: 1-2

Therefore, I urge you, brothers and sisters, in view of God's mercy, to offer your bodies as a living sacrifice, holy and pleasing to God—this is your true and proper worship.

2 Do not conform to the pattern of this world, but be transformed by the renewing of your mind.

Then you will be able to test and approve what God's will is—his good, pleasing and perfect will.

SAY: Next is to look for things in paragraphs.

B. Paragraphs

Soul Discipleship Plan

General and specific	Authors will introduce a summary of the main idea. It can start with a general statement and speak to specifics. SAY: Let's go to Gal. 5:16-23. What are the general statements? A: "walk by the spirit" and "gratify the desires of the flesh" What are the specific statements? A: Paul presents the specifics of "desires of the flash" as found in verse 16 in verses 5:19-21. Paul's specifics about "walk in the spirit" is in verses 5:22-23. It can start with the specific and lead to the general. SAY: Let's go to 1 Cor. 13:13. The focus is love. Where are the general statements? A: Verse 13 Where are the specific statements? A: Verses1-12
Questions and Answers	Authors will ask a rhetorical question and then answer it. A rhetorical question is a figure of speech in the form of a question that is asked to make a point rather than to elicit an answer. SAY: Let's go to Rom. 6:1-2. For example, Rom. 6:1, Paul asks and then answers his own question in verse 2. Mark also uses the question-and-answer format.
Dialogue	It overlaps with the question- and answer feature. Ask these questions: Who are the participants? Who is speaking to whom? What is the setting? Are other people around? Are they listening? Are they participating in the dialogue? Is the dialog an argument? A discussion? A lecture? Friendly talk? What is the point? SAY: Go to Habakkuk 1:1-4. It's a dialogue between God and the prophet.

B. Paragraphs, continued	
Purpose/Result statements	Phrases or sentences that describe the reason, the result, of the consequence of some action introduced by result-oriented conjunctions such as "that", "in order that", and "so that". SAY: Go to John 15:16.

104

Means	Brings about the action, result or purpose that is stated. **SAY:** Go to Psalm 119:9.
Conditional Clauses	Clauses that present conditions where an action, consequence, result or reality will occur. The aspect will be introduced by "if". The consequence is the "then" part. **SAY:** Go to 2 Cor. 5:17.
Actions/Roles of People and Actions/ Roles of God	The Bible refers to actions of people and God. Ask what are people doing in the passage or what is God doing in this passage? **SAY:** Go to Ephesians 5:1-2.
Emotional Terms	Look out for emotional overtones. **SAY:** Go to Galatians 4:12-16. 12 I *plead* with you, *brothers and sisters*, become like me, for I became like you. *You did me no wrong.* 13 As you know, it was because of an illness that I first preached the gospel to you, 14 and even though my illness was a trial to you, you did not *treat me with contempt or scorn.* Instead, *you welcomed me* as if I were an angel of God, as if I were Christ Jesus himself. 15 *Where, then, is your blessing of me now?* I can testify that, if you could have done so, *you would have torn out your eyes and given them to me.* 16 Have I now become your *enemy* by telling you the truth?
	SAY: Paul used strong emotional terms to express how he felt.

B. Paragraphs	
Tone	The identification of emotional terms. Determine what the overall tone of the passage is. **SAY:** Go to Col. 3:1-4 and then Gal. 3:1-4. Col. 3:1-4 has a tone of calmness from Paul. He is using an explanatory tone. In Gal. 3:1-4 Paul is scolding the Galatians. What is Jesus' tone in Matthew 23:33-35? Is it calm, gentle, and loving? No. Which one is it? A: Scolding

SAY: Next is to understand discourses.

A discourse are units of connected text that are longer than paragraphs. It can be a smaller episode within a story, for example, David and Goliath, or it can be a longer story itself, for example the David narrative. Here's what to look for:

C. Discourses	
1). Connections between Paragraphs & Episodes	Ask how the paragraph on the episode relates to and connects with other paragraphs/episodes that come before and after what you are studying. **Example**: **Colossians 1:3-8** 3 We give thanks to the God and Father of our Lord Jesus Christ, praying always for you, 4 since we heard of your faith in Christ Jesus and of your love for all the saints; 5 because of the hope which is laid up for you in heaven, of which you heard before in the word of the truth of the gospel, which has come to you, as *it has* also in all the world, and is bringing forth fruit,[a] as *it is* also among you since the day you heard and knew the grace of God in truth; 7 as you also learned from Epaphras, our dear fellow servant, who is a faithful minister of Christ on your behalf, 8 who also declared to us your love in the Spirit. **Colossians 1:9-14** 9 For this reason we also, since the day we heard it, do not cease to pray for you, and to ask that you may be filled with the knowledge of His will in all wisdom and spiritual understanding; 10 that you may walk worthy of the Lord, fully pleasing *Him,* being fruitful in every good work and increasing in the knowledge of God; strengthened with all might, according to His glorious power, for all patience and longsuffering with joy; 12 giving thanks to the Father who has qualified us to be partakers of the inheritance of the saints in the light. 13 He has delivered us from the power of darkness and conveyed *us* into the kingdom of the Son of His love, 14 in whom we have redemption through His blood,[a] the forgiveness of sins.

SAY: So, what do you believe is the connection between these paragraphs?

A: The first paragraph is where Paul and Timothy have heard of the Colossian's faith and love, and that they are thanking God for it. Paul and Timothy desire for them to become mature, know the knowl-edge of God's will, do good works, and to work.

C. Discourses, continued	
2. Major Breaks & Pivots in the Story	There are times when you are reading and it takes a new turn, a major break. The topic will shift from doctrinal to practical discussion. There are also shifts in narratives which are called pivot episodes. **SAY:** A major break can be identified by change in verbs. Let's look at Ephesians 4:1, "I. therefore, the prisoner of t h e Lord, beseech you to walk worthy of the calling with which you were called," (NKJV) **SAY:** Look and list some. They have imperatives, explanatory or descriptive verbs. | Ephesians 1-3	Ephesians 4-6 | |---|---| | Focus on doctrine | Focus on practical living |
3. Interchange	An interchange is used to contrast or compare to stories at the same time. Luke uses an interchange in Acts 7:58; 8:1-3 where Paul is introduced as Saul. Luke then brings back Peter in Acts 8:14-25. Paul is the focus 9:1-30 because of his conversation with Cornelius in Acts 10:1-11, 18. Paul comes back in Acts 11:19-30, and it ends with Peter's escape from prison in Acts 12:1-19. Luke is comparing Peter and Paul.
4. Chiasm	Chiasm was used by the Old Testament authors. A chiasm is a list of items, ideas, or events where the first item parallels the last item, the second item parallels the next to the last forth, and it continues on.
5. Inclusion	A passage that has the same or similar word, theme, event, or statement at the beginning and at the end, which is also known as "bracketing" or framing".

Assignment: Read Nehemiah 1:1-11 and make as many observations as you are able to:

1 It came to pass in the month of Chislev, in the twentieth year, as I was in Shushan[a] the citadel,2 that Hanani one of my brethren came with men from Judah; and I asked them concerning the Jews who had escaped, who had survived the captivity, and concerning Jerusalem. 3 And they said to me, "The survivors who are left from the captivity in the province are **there in great distress and reproach. The wall of Jerusalem** is also broken down, and its gates are burned with fire."

4 So it was, when I heard these words, that I sat down and wept, and mourned for many days; I was fasting and praying before the God of heaven.

5 And I said: "I pray, Lord God of heaven, O great and awesome God, You who keep Your covenant and mercy with those who love You[b] and observe Your[c] commandments,6 please let Your ear be attentive and Your eyes open, that You may hear the prayer of Your servant which I pray before You now, day and night, for the children of Israel Your servants, and confess the sins of the children of Israel which we have sinned against You. Both my father's house and I

have sinned. 7 We have acted very corruptly against You, and have not kept the commandments, the statutes, nor the ordinances which You commanded Your servant Moses. 8 Remember, I pray, the word that You commanded Your servant Moses, saying, 'If **you are unfaithful, I will scatter you among the nations;**[d] 9 but if you return to Me, and keep My commandments and do them, though some of you were cast out to the farthest part of the heavens, yet I will gather them from there, and bring them to the place which I have chosen as a dwelling for My name.'[e] 10 Now these are Your servants and Your people, whom You have redeemed by Your great power, and by Your strong hand. 11 O Lord, I pray, please let Your ear be attentive to the prayer of Your servant, and to the prayer of Your servants who desire to fear Your name; and let Your servant prosper this day, I pray, and grant him mercy in the sight of this man." We have acted very corruptly against You, and have not kept the commandments, the statutes, nor the ordinances which You commanded Your servant Moses.

8 Remember, I pray, the word that You commanded Your servant Moses, saying, 'If **you are unfaithful, I will scatter you among the nations;**[d] 9 but if you return to Me, and keep My commandments and do them, though some of you were cast out to the farthest part of the heavens, yet I will gather them from there, and bring them to the place which I have chosen as a dwelling for My name.'[e] 10 Now these are Your servants and Your people, whom You have redeemed by Your great power, and by Your strong hand. 11 O Lord, I pray, please let Your ear be attentive to the prayer of Your servant, and to the prayer of Your servants who desire to fear Your name; and let Your servant prosper this day, I pray, and grant him mercy in the sight of this man."

SAY: There are two types of context, which is literary and historical context. Let's learn about them.

The historical-cultural context is background. It tells us what God was saying to those people. It is anything that is outside of the text which will help you to understand the text. We have to also know who the biblical writer was, their background, where they came from, when I was written, the relationship to the people, and why the writer wrote.

A lot of background you will find is historical, social, geographical, religious, political, and economic. As you understand the context through the history and culture you will realize God was speaking to people with life issues and he is also speaking to us.

The literal context is the context within a book.

You can use the following tools to assist you, such as:

Bible handbooks (general articles about the Bible and the world of the Bible). The OT & NT introductions & surveys provide background information for each book the Bible and its contents. Commentaries provide detailed information of the historical-cultural context of the book. They shed light on background matters of the passage. The background commentaries provided information arranged in a verse-by-verse format. Bible atlases helps you to learn the people, places, and events. Bible dictionaries and encyclopaedias cover bible topics alphabetically. OT &

NT histories lets you locate by a keyword in the index.

Assignment: Look up Haggai in the Bible and go to the Introduction and read what the author(s) has to say by way of Introduction (e.g., author, date, audience, situation, purpose). Use what you have learned to write a one-to two-page description of the historical setting of this prophetic book.

SAY: What do you think people bring when they read the Bible?

A: Preunderstanding. We can bring preunderstanding, which is consciously and unconsciously preconceived notions and understanding. It can come from good and bad influences, Christian music, jokes, art, nonbiblical literature, culture. There are times you can be reading text and then start to search for details to fit our agenda. If it does not fit what we are looking for, we skip it or ignore it. Familiarity can make you believe you know all about the text. Culture is an example of preunderstanding. It can come from family and heritage. We must identify in ourselves any cultural influences. Our preunderstanding must change each time we study the word of God.

B: Foundational beliefs. Do not change each time we read the Bible. It is the overall view of the Bible. For example: "The bible is the Word of God, The Bible is trustworthy and true."

SAY: We going to discuss the literary context. Remember context determines meaning. Literary context is a particular from a passage takes with the words, sentences and paragraphs surrounding the passage being read or studied. The form it takes is called the literary genre. We discussed the genres earlier.

SAY: What are the different genres of the OT?

In the OT it is the narrative, law, poetry, prophecy and wisdom.

Write your answer: _____

What are the different genres of the NT?

Parables, riddles, sermons, epistles or letters, gospels.

Write your answer: _____

Literary genre helps us to know when reading the word of God, the author's choice of genre, so we know the rules we use to understand the words. Knowing the rules will help you <u>not</u> to misread the Bible.

The surrounding context is the texts that surround the passage being studied.

SAY: For example, the surrounding context of Rom. 12:1-2 is the first eleven chapters of Romans and Romans 12:3.

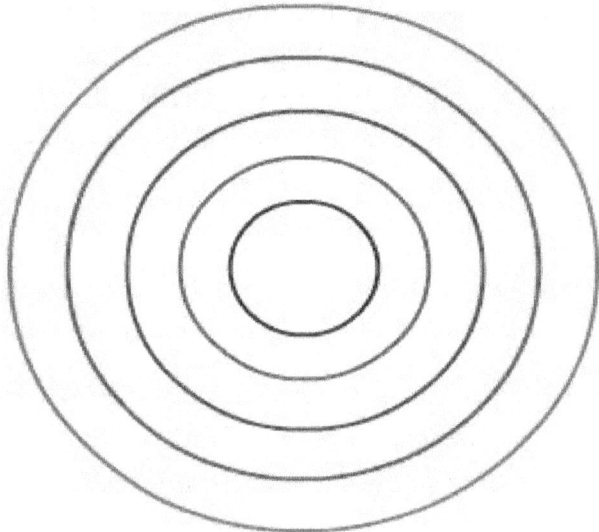

SAY Let's label the surrounding context surrounding a passage. The middle is passage, then immediate context, then rest of larger section, then rest of book, and then rest of Bible.[37]

SAY Let's go to 1 Peter 5:7. The immediate context is verses 5-9 to which describes what comes immediately before and after your passage. What is being revealed in this passage?

A: *Humbling ourselves before God means that we entrust our concerns and troubles to God. God loves us and will not let us down.*

Remember, we must not ignore the surrounding context. For example, let's go to Matthew 18:20 which is talking about church discipline. In verses 15-17, it is made clear that the congregation as a whole must follow God's guidelines for corporate discipline and they will have his blessings.

The surrounding context helps to answer how these sentences, which are the parts come together in the Bible to communicate the larger message (the whole message). Amen.

The surrounding context will answer:

1. What is the unit's role or function or purpose in the book?
2. What would happen if we removed this section from the book?
3. Why did the author include this section?

When you begin to contradict the literary context, literary genre and the surrounding text, you will use normal language and our own interpretation which is not valid.

SAY Turn to the book of Philemon 4-7 in your Bible. To find the surrounding context of any

---

37   Retrieved from https://tse2.mm.bing.net/th?id=OIP.NqZlp4Jct9bkzOR1lGQcHgHaH-H&pid=15.1&P=0&w=173&h=167

passage, you must:

(1) Determine: how the book is divided into paragraphs or sections. Below are how the Bible translations divide the book and the chapter into smaller units.

NIV	KJV	ESV
1-3	1-3	1-3
4-7	4-7	4-7
8-11	8-25	8-16
12-16		17-20
17-21		21-22
22		23-25
23-25		

(2) The main of each section must be summarized.

Summarize the point of the whole section, for example:

vv. 1-3	Paul states the letter senders/recipients and a greeting.
vv. 4-7	Paul is thanking God for Philemon's faith and love. Paul intercedes for him.
vv. 8-16	Paul appeals to Philemon for Onesimus and shows him God's providence in this situation.
vv. 17-20	Paul urges Philemon to take in Onesimus as if he was expecting Paul.
vv. 21	Paul is confident that Philemon will do more than what he is requesting.
vv. 22	Paul hopes to visit Philemon in person.
vv. 23-24	Paul greets his fellow workers.
vv. 25	Paul closes with a benediction of grace.

(3) Explain how this passage relates to the surrounding sections.

Now take a look at how the passage fits into is surroundings. Remember to look what comes before and after the passage. So, Philemon vv. 4-7 is between vv. 1-3 which is the opening and x. 8-22 which is the body. Paul in these verses is highlighting Philemon's good qualities in 4-7 that will motivate Philemon to do what Paul is about to request from him in the rest of the letter.

<u>**SAY:**</u> **NEXT** is word studies. We will be discussing studying the words of Scripture.

Doing a word-study consists of three steps, which are:

1. Choose your words,
2. Determine what the word could mean, and
3. Determine what the word does mean in context.

When studying words there are some common mistakes that an interpreter can make. They are called a fallacy, which means a mistaken belief. There are a couple of them, let's review them.

English-only fallacy	Is when you word study on the English word rather than the original Hebrew and Greek.
Root fallacy	To think that the real meaning of a word is found in its original root. If you switch from English to a biblical language does not mean it will automatically change things.
Time-frame fallacy	When we hold onto a late word meaning and reads it back into the Bible. You can hold onto an early word meaning as fact since it is now obsolete.
Overload fallacy	Words can mean several different things. This fallacy is the idea that it would include several different things every time it is used.
Word-count fallacy	When we insist that a word must have the same meaning every time it occurs.
Word-concept fallacy	When we assume that once we study the word, we should have studied the entire concept.
Selective-evidence fallacy	Is when we cite only the evidence that supports our favored interpretation, or we dismiss evidence that seems to argue against our view.

The purpose of word studies is to help you to try to understand as precisely as possible what the author meant when using a word in a specific context.

Read Romans 12:1-2 and Matthew 28:18-20.

Romans 12:1-2

12 Therefore, I urge you, brothers and sisters, in view of God's mercy, to offer your bodies as a living sacrifice, holy and pleasing to God—this is your true and proper worship. 2 Do not conform to the pattern of this world but be transformed by the renewing of your mind. Then you will be able to test and approve what God's will is—his good, pleasing and perfect will.

Matthew 28:18-20

18 Then Jesus came to them and said, "All authority in heaven and on earth has been given to me. 19 Therefore go and make disciples of all nations, baptizing them in the name of the Father and of the Son and of the Holy Spirit, 20 and teaching them to obey everything I have commanded you. And surely I am with you always, to the very end of the age."

If you picked different words to study that is okay. You should know why you would want to study the words you selected.

SAY: Let's now determine what the word could mean. Most words can mean several different things but can carry one of those meanings in a particular context. When we see all the possible meanings of a word, it is referred to as the range of meaning or the semantic range. When we are looking for the range of meaning for a word from the Bible, you will be looking for the range of meaning for the Greek or Hebrew word, not the English word. The original Hebrew or Greek and the English word that was used to translate it will have a semantic range. So we must determine what the Greek or Hebrew word, not the English Word could mean. To determine that you can use a concordance to locate the original Hebrew or Greek word.

When you determine the word has more than one meaning, then you have to determine the specific context. The context determines the word meaning, which is the second thing you can do to determine the word's range of meaning. If it is OT we look at the Hebrew and if it is the NT we look at the Greek in the concordance.

SAY: LET's look at Philippians 3:12.

If you are having difficulty deciding the most likely meaning of a word in its context, then:

- look for a contrast or comparison to define the word
- subject matter or topic dictates the word meaning
- look to see if the author's usage of the word elsewhere in a context that is similar helps to fit the word
- author's argument suggests a meaning
- historical situation directs the evidence in a certain direction

15. Role of the Holy Spirit

We know the Holy Spirit is the divine author of the Bible. This section was designed for you to discover the meaning of the biblical text and apply that meaning to your life. You learned about the methods, steps, how to analyze words, sentences and paragraphs and the discourses.

The Holy Spirit is a vital part of biblical interpretation. The Holy Spirit worked in the lives of the human authors of Scripture and they wrote what God wanted to communicate to His people. The Holy Spirit of God has breathed the character of Almighty God into the Scriptures. As you read and study the Bible, the Bible has the power and authority to shape our lives. The Scripture are inspired ("God-breathed").

The night before Jesus was crucified, Jesus promised his followers that the Holy Spirit would guide into all truth in John 16:12-14.

12 "I still have many things to say to you, but you cannot bear them now. 13 However, when He, the Spirit of truth, has come, He will guide you into all truth; for He will not speak on His own authority, but whatever He hears He will speak; and He will tell you things to come. 14 He will glorify Me, for He will take of what is Mine and declare it to you."

The Spirit and the Word work together and should not be set against one another. Nothing should be put above the Spirit-inspired Word of God. The Holy Spirit helps believers to understand and apply the meaning that is already there.

SAY: Let's answer the question," Can a person grasp the word of God without the Holy Spirt? There are three answers to that. The first answer is "Yes".

(1) Yes. If an unbeliever applies the interpretive methods, they will be able to comprehend the Bible. If read effectively, people will be able to understand the Bible.

(2) "Yes, but only to a degree. Persons without the Spirit can understand the meaning of a biblical passage, but it is limited because of sin which will dull the ability to listen to spiritual truth, limited by the effects of unbelieving or preunderstanding that a person brings to the text. There will be distortion.

Understanding the meaning of scripture involves the mind, emotions, body and so forth (whole person). An unbeliever does not accept the things of the Spirit of God.

(3) "No". People without the Spirit will not accept the truth of the Bible nor apply it to their lives. 1 Cor. 2:14 tells us no. A person will understand the basics of it, but they will also reject it. A person that does not have the Spirit cannot know the things of God because they have no experience. We need the help of the Holy Spirit to apply the Word of God.

SAY: Here are some examples, I will be talking about what the Spirit will and will not do.

When you are interpreting the Bible, what should you expect the Holy Spirit to do for you or enable you to do? What should you not expect the Holy Spirit to do?

For example, when interpreting the Bible, the Holy Spirit is not going to do all of it for you. When we study the Bible, God expects us to use our minds by thinking clearing and reasoning soundly. We must study the Word diligently and faithfully. We must use tools that are available such as, dictionaries, atlases, concordance, and commentaries. The Holy Spirit will not add to the sixty-six books of the Bible. No new information or meanings will be created by the Holy Spirit. The Holy Spirit will help us to grasp God's Word at a deeper level. The Holy Spirit will not change the Word of God to suit our desires or situations. The Holy Spirit works with the Word to transform the life of the interpreter, which is you. The Spirit will convict us that the Bible is divinely inspired, you will be made to understand the importance of a command, a promise and so much more that is in the Word of God, and works on our hearts to receive the Word of God. As you grow in Christ, the Holy Spirit will transform your character to become the character of God which is described in Rom. 12:1-2. The Holy Spirit will restore you to your senses. Your spiritual maturity will affect your ability to hear the voice of the Holy Spirit. The Holy Spirit will use devotional reading and prayer to encourage your spiritual growth. When you are studying the Word of God and seeking and engaging in a personal intimate time with God, you are now engaging in devotional reading.

In ancient times the reading of the Bible focused on prayerfully listening to God and allow him to transform you. It was called lectio divina (holy or prayerful reading). It is similar to the journey process you learned to interpret the Word of God. Let's discuss those five steps:

Slencio-Settle yourself in one place and quiet yourself before the Lord.

Lectio – read a passage of Scripture slowly and out loud.

Meditatio – Read the passage again, let the words sink into your mind and heart. If a particular word catches your attention, then repeat it a couple of times. Think about what God is saying to you right now and how does it connect with your life now

Oratio – Read the passage a third time by praying the passage. Talk to God about what he seems to be saying to you. Respond from your heart what God is saying.

Contemplatio – Just rest and wait patiently in God's presence. Yield to God. Entrust everything to Him. Ask the Lord to continue to transform you throughout the day and conclude with a prayer of thanksgiving.

As you continue in reading and interpreting the Word of God, do so prayerfully. Remember to use your mind, interpretive methods, and good study tools. As you move forward you will have a dynamic interaction with the Spirit of God to hear what he is saying.

16. Living Out the Learned

The interpretive journey had five steps. Steps 1-4 dealt with the meaning of the text, but step five answers how should we live out the meaning through application. Let's look at Philippians 4:13: "I can do all things through him [Christ] who strengthens me (ESV).

Step 1, is Paul is in prison awaiting trial (1:7, 13-14, 17). He thanks the Philippians for ministering to him. He tells them he is grateful and his ministry is dependent on Christ. In step 2, we look at the biblical situation and our situation. The difference is Paul is an apostle and we are not. He is in prison for his faith and we are not. The similarities are we are members of Christ's body, the church. In step 3, we list the theological principles of the passage. In this passage believers can learn to be content in their variety of circumstance through Christ. In step 4, we consult the biblical map. We didn't see anything in the principle that is refuted by the rest of the Bible.

Step 5 is where you apply it to live out the theological principles. So, the principles for Paul was he was a Christian, experiencing trying circumstances, and he knew Christ would give him strength to endure any circumstance.

Then you look for a situation in your life that parallels with the biblical situation. Once you know the parallel situations, think about specific ways the biblical principle(s) apply to you. As you go through life and encounter real-life situations, going through the interpretive journey will guide on how to apply it your real-life situation you are in. It will also help you to apply it for your children, grandchildren, and great grandchildren. Amen

Assignment A

Deuteronomy 8:6-18. Let's look at this passage and apply the interpretive journey.

₆ "Therefore you shall keep the commandments of the Lord your God, to walk in His ways and to fear Him. ₇ For the Lord your God is bringing you into a good land, a land of brooks of water, of fountains and springs, that flow out of valleys and hills; ₈ a land of wheat and barley, of vines and fig trees and pomegranates, a land of olive oil and honey; ₉ a land in which you will eat bread without scarcity, in which you will lack nothing; a land whose stones are iron and out of whose hills you can dig copper. ₁₀ When you have eaten and are full, then you shall bless the Lord your God for the good land which He has given you.

₁₁ "Beware that you do not forget the Lord your God by not keeping His commandments, His judgments, and His statutes which I command you today, ₁₂ lest—when you have eaten and are full, and have built beautiful houses and dwell in them; ₁₃ and when your herds and your flocks multiply, and your silver and your gold are multiplied, and all that you have is multiplied; ₁₄ when your heart is lifted up, and you forget the Lord your God who brought you out of the land of Egypt, from the house of bondage; ₁₅ who led you through that great and terrible wilderness, in which were fiery serpents and scorpions and thirsty land where there was no water; who brought water for you out of the flinty rock; ₁₆ who fed you in the wilderness with manna, which your fathers did not know, that He might humble you and that He might test you, to do you good in the end— ₁₇ then you say in your heart, 'My power and the might of my hand have gained me this wealth.'

₁₈ "And you shall remember the Lord your God, for it is He who gives you power to get wealth, that He may establish His covenant which He swore to your fathers, as it is this day.

Now we are going to continue this journey of the Old Testament. Here you will apply the genres of the Old Testament that you have learned in Step 3 which is the principalizing bridge becomes more critical. Yes, we are New Testament Christians, but we do not ignore the Old Testament. We will read, interpret and apply it.

The narrative stories comprise nearly half of the Old Testament. Narrative is a literary form that is characterized by sequential time action, involving the plot, setting and characters. God is using these narratives to teach us theology. Narratives challenge us, interest us, rebuke us, puzzle us, and entertain us. They remain in our memory and we think and reflect on it, which God wants for us. They are life lessons.

In reading narratives, we are going to review the book of Joshua 2. The early chapters, explain the Israelites are beginning their conquest of the Promised land. In Chapter 1, God exhorts Joshua to be courageous and to lead the people of Israel across Jordan river to victory in the Promised

Land. In Joshua 2 that conquest slows down because of what happened about Rahab the harlot who hides the spies on the roof. So, as you are reading, you should notice the points of the sentences, paragraphs, and discourses.

In Joshua 3 and 5, Israel prepares for attack on Jericho (Rehab's city). Joshua 6 discusses the capture of Jericho. Joshua 6 vv. 17, 23, 25 are important to notice about Rahab. Joshua 7 introduces Achan who steals money devoted to God. He is the opposite of Rahab. There is a contrast of the two. Read Joshua 2:2-7. List as many contrasts as you can in the table below.

RAHAB	ACHAN
Woman	Man
Canaanite	Hebrew, tribe of Judah
Prostitute(disrespectable)	Respectable
Should have died, but survived and prospered	Should have prospered, but died
Her family and all she owned survived	His family and all he owned perished
Nation perishes	Nation prospers
Hides the spies from the King	Hides the loot from God and Joshua
Fears the God of Israel	Does not fear the God of Israel
Has only heard of God, but believes	Has seen the acts of God, but disobeys
Her house survives, where the city is burned	His tent is buried
Cattle, sheep, and donkeys of Jericho perish	Cattle, sheep, and donkeys of Achan perish
She becomes like an Israelite and lives	He becomes like a Canaanite and dies

A narrative has four elements, which are:

1. Plot- Who? and How? questions
2. Setting- When? and the Where? questions
3. Characters- Who? questions

   - Viewpoint of the Narrator- the author conveys the meaning to the reads through the story. Always ask the Who? What? When? Why? Where? Why? and How?
   - Comparison/Contrast- it develops the plot and moves the story forward.
   - Irony- used to describe situations where the literal or surface meaning of an event or episode is quite different.

ASSIGNMENT

<u>SAY</u>: **I am giving you an assignment to complete.** You will be reading Deuteronomy 17:4-17 which are the rules for the king and 1 Samuel 8:10-18 which are warnings about the king. Then you will read the story of Solomon (1 Kings 1-11).

Hand Out

ASSIGNMENT

Read Deuteronomy 17:4-17 which are the rules for king and 1 Samuel 8:10-18 which are warnings about the king. Then read the story of Solomon (1 Kings 1-11). Discuss the ways in which Solomon violates the rules for the king and how he fulfils the warnings. Contrast his good deeds with the bad deeds. In the narrators mind, is Solomon a good character or a bad character? Is he a hero or a bum?

SAY: Next you will learn interpretation of Old Testament Law. The first five books of the Bible is laws. Do we obey some laws and ignore others? Yes. There are different types of Old Testament laws. There are:

- moral laws – God's intention for human behavior. Lev. 19:18
- civil laws – describes aspects that are in a country's legal system. Deut. 15:1
- ceremonial laws – those that dealt with sacrifices, festivals, and priestly activities. Deut. 6:13

So, the moral laws are universal and timeless. They still apply as law to Christians today. The civil and ceremonial laws apply to ancient Israel, not believers today.

Remember the narrative context runs from Genesis 12 to 2 Kings 25. It is presented as a theological narrative. It describes how God delivered Israel from Egypt to establish his people in the promised land. The law defined the covenant relationship between God and Israel. The law was theological. Let me define theological which means, "relating the study of religion and religious belief". The Old Testament law is firmly embedded into Israel's theological history.

This is also true for the books that contain elements of the Old Testament law. For example, the law in Leviticus are part of a dialogue between God and Moses. The covenant context is introduced by God in Ex. 19:5. The people agree to keep the terms (Ex. 24:3), and Moses sealed it with the blood (Ex. 24:8). God promises to dwell in Israel's midst. Israel disobeys God's covenant and enters the Promised Land (Num. 13-14) and God sends them into the desert for thirty-eight more years and that disobedient generation dies out. God leads them back to Canaan, but before entering God calls them to a covenant renewal. It is now a new, younger generation and the Lord reinstates the Mosaic covenant that he made with their parents. The Mosaic covenant was associated with Israel's conquest and occupation of the land, the blessings are conditional (Deut. 28:1-68; 30:15-18). The Mosaic covenant does not apply to the New Testament believers (Heb. 8-9). The Old Testament law is no longer applicable over us as law. Interpret the law through the New Testament teaching (2 Tim. 3:16).

SAY: So, let's talk about Deut. 8:16-18 and apply the interpretive journey.

In Step 1: What did the text mean to the biblical audience?

A: Israel must continue to obey God's commands.

In Step 2: What are the differences between the biblical audience and us?

A: We are not under the old covenant.

In Step 3: What is the theological principle in this text?

A: God's people should obey God.

In Step 4: How does the theological principle fit with the rest of the Bible?

A: Obedience to God still stands. The New Testament stresses obedience in following Christ. Obey the command to love each other (John 13:34)

In Step 5: How should individual Christians today live out this modified theological principle?

A: All of our real blessings come from our relationship with Christ.

In the Old Testament we have the law, which you learned. Also, there is poetry, prophets, and wisdom.

SAY: Let's learn about the prophets.

We have four major prophets and twelve minor prophets in the Old Testament. Major and minor refer to the length of the books. The prophetic books are short spoken or preached messages proclaimed by the prophet to the nations of Israel or Judah. There are also visions from God, short narrative sections and symbolic acts. The majority of the prophetic books addresses Israel's and Judah's disobedience and the consequences of judgment. Much of the prophet's message is poetry. Hebrew poetry uses figure soft speech extensively. Poetry affects the emotions of the reader or listener. The prophets throughout the books expresses the Lord's deep love toward his people and pain he feels as the people reject him. The prophets describe in detailed description of the coming horrible judgment.

The books are primarily anthologies, which are collections of shorter units, they are oral messages the prophets publicly proclaim to the people of Israel or Judah. Sometimes it can be a vision or oracle. The overall theme of the prophetic books are judgment and deliverance. Since the prophetic books are unique, we must not interpret it out of context. The historical-cultural context in step 1 must be applied.

Remember the narrative context ran from Genesis 12 to 2 Kings 25. The books of 1 and 2 Kings tells us how the nations of the Hebrews, Israel and Judah fall away from the Lord to and go to their neighbors idols. Theologically the prophets proclaim their message from Mosaic covenant context, which is in Deuteronomy.

The prophets stand before the Lord, they accuse and warn the people of the consequences of violating the covenant. They focused on three items:

1. You broke the covenant, you better repent!
2. If you don't repent, then receive judgment!
3. There is hope beyond judgment from future restoration.

Israel violated covenant by idolatry, social injustice, and religious ritualism. Idolatry included syncretism (blending of religions) (Ezek. 8). Idolatry is whatever draws our worship and focus from our relationship with God. Social injustice was how the weaker individuals in society were treated (Jer. 5:28-29). For example, judicial bribery, marketplace dishonesty, or failure to pay just wages. Religious ritualism is they depended on instead of relationship (Micah 6:7-8). Israel lost the concept of relationship with God by ritualism. They used ritualism to replace the relationship rather than enhancing the relationship.

The prophets were in direct conflict with attitudes of their culture. Their messages was the social view of God's people should be directed by the Word of God, not the culture. For politics we should have Christian views, not democrat or republican which is the secular culture.

SAY: So as far as the interpretive journey of the prophets and now, we know that in Step 1 we observe what the text meant to the biblical audience. In Step 2 identify the differences between us and the biblical audience. We are not under the old covenant, nor the curses in Deuteronomy. Today's audience is believer and unbeliever. In Step 3 cross the principalizing bridge and develop one or more of the theological principles. The theological principle in the prophetic books are that God is forgiving and restoring his people in the New Testament. It must be faithful to the text and correspond to the rest of the teaching of the Scripture. In Step 4 consult the biblical map and pass it through the New Testament teaching. Finally, in step 5 the application is to translate into real-life situations of Christians.

The prophets also gave messages about the future. They can shift from one future event to another within the passage, or even the same verse. These are called near view-far view. The prophets also give messages about future hope and restoration, the focus can be on the return of the Jewish exiles to Israel under Ezra and Nehemiah, the first coming of Christ, or the second coming of Christ. There can also be in the prophetic books are biblical prophecies appear to have aspects of conditions attached to the fulfilment (Jer. 18:7-10). The prophets use imagery and figures of speech to describe the future. There is a lot of poetry.

SAY: We are now going to interpret the book of Acts.

The book of Acts was written by Luke and he tells us what Jesus began to do and to teach. Luke tells us how Jesus acted by his Spirit through his church. Some of the miracles in Luke and Acts are similar. Luke presents to us God's salvation. Acts is considered a narrative. Luke explained the purpose of Acts in the first few verses that he addresses to Theophilus. He starts in Acts 1:4 with the Spirit of God. In Acts 1 Jesus promises that the Father will send the Holy Spirit. In Acts 2, which is Pentecost the Spirit descends and indwells the disciples of Jesus. The book of Acts tells us the acts and deeds of the Spirit through the church. God is sovereign which means he is in control. The Holy Spirit works through the church which were the people of God. The community of people worshipped God, they cared for each other, grew spiritually, and also joined in the mission. Prayer is a major theme in the book of Acts. The people of that time prayed in every part of Acts. Prayer was central to the church. The early Christians suffered imprisonment, beatings, rejection, violent storms, persecution and death. The gospel comes first to the Jews but then spreads quickly to the Gentiles. Luke's message in Acts tells us to be a follower of Jesus Christ means to be a faithful witness. The themes of Acts are the work of the Spirit, God's sovereignty, the role of the church, prayer, suffering, gospel for the Jews and Gentiles, and the power of witness.

SAY: How do you think Acts is organized?

A: Chapters 1-12 is the good news is preached to the Jews in and around Jerusalem by Peter. Chapters 13-28 is where it is spread to the Gentiles by Paul.

In my reading of Acts I believe that we as Christians should imitate the experiences and practices of the early church (normative) and also focus on what was valuable and inspiring to the early church (descriptive).

For the theological principles, focus on the standard narrative questions which are Who? What? When? Where? Why? and How? This is a simple plan to understand a story. We can take some parts of Acts as normative and others as descriptive.

Acts was written by Luke and we should be focusing on the intent of the author. Look for what Luke is communicating to you. Look for what the common themes or patterns in his writing. For example, when I was reading Acts 8, I asked the question what does the Samaritan and the eunuch have in common? A Samaritan was considered a half-breed and the eunuch was considered a physical reject. God accepts us no matter who we are, and it is because of what he has done for us through our Lord and Savior Jesus Christ.

The book of Acts does focus on discipleship. It starts with the Holy Spirit in Acts 1 and 2. It continues with the sovereignty of God. Signs and wonders are performed by the power of God. The Holy Spirt works through the church which is the people of God to accomplish his will. The people fellowshipped, worship God, cared for each other and they grew spiritually. A lot of prayer occurred in the book of Acts. The Christians also suffered many tragedies and persecution. The gospel is first received by the Jews but also spreads to the Gentiles. Being a faithful witness is demonstrated also in the book of Acts.

Applying the five questions of Who? (the characters) What? (story line) When? (time) Where? (place) Why? (reason) and How? (means) helps us to also interpret the gospels and the new testament letters.

17 Closing

Reflection in Action by Connection
Answer the questions on the lines provided.

Question 1: Colossians 3:16 tells us "Let the word of Christ dwell in you richly". How does this happen in your life?

A:_____
Answer: Studying the Word of God daily.

Question 2: How will you become a person who knows the truth of God in a deep personal way that will bring honor to God, bless others, and joy to your soul?
A: _____
Answer: By hearing the Word of God being read, listen to the preaching of God's Word, reading the Word of God on your own, discussing God's Word with other believers, studying God's Word, memorizing God's Word, by trusting God's Word, sharing the Word of God with others, and reflecting on God's Word.

Question 3: In what ways has God helped you to gain knowledge of Christ and His truth?
A: _____
Answer: The primary way is the reading of the Word of God. Prayer.

Question 4: Which Scriptures show us how Christ taught his followers?
A: _____
Answer: Mark 1:21; Mark 2:13; Mark 4:2; Mark 13:28; Matthew 11:28

Question 5: Which Scripture tells us that the Bible guides us?
A: _____
Answer: 2 Timothy 3: 16-17

SAY: So, have learned about the greatest book ever written. This completes goal three on the Bible and how to apply the meaning of the Bible through the interpretive journey. Now it is time to learn about prayer and spiritual warfare in Goal Four.

GOAL FOUR

WEAPONS OF SPIRITUAL WARFARE

LESSON PLAN

Date & Time:	Curriculum Area: Weapons of Spiritual Warfare	Goal /Unit Topic: Goal Four

Key enduring understandings, concepts, abilities, and/or values.
Explained in the Introduction

Intended learning outcomes (to know, to do, to create, to value, etc.)
Explained in the Overview

Assessment Strategies: How will you assess attainment of the intended learning outcome? Questions & Answers, Dialect, Interaction

Materials/Preparation/ Area Setup:

Materials: Poster board, Dry Erase Markers

Preparation: Decorations, Poster board

Area Setup: For each disciple, place on the desk a blue pen, highlighter, notebook, goal four Participant Guide

Introduction	Setting the Stage: engaging, motivating, experiencing, connecting with prior knowledge, reflecting, conjecturing, posing problems
Once the Introduction and Overview have been completed, then move on to the Bible book recitals. It will be recited every time that we meet with the disciples.	

Guided learning steps

The learning steps are as follows:

Introduction	
Overview	
1. Spiritual Warfare	2. Blessings and Curses
3. Levels of Spiritual Warfare	4. What Are our Weapons?
5. Spiritual Attack	6. Deliverance
7. Angels	8. Consecration
9. Satan the Adversary	10. Blessings and Curses
	11. Closing

Disclosing: acquiring knowledge/skills, conceptualizing, developing, understanding, integrating

Practicing, Reinforcing: modeling, giving instruction, checking for understanding, guided practice, independent practice, applying, posing and solving problems

Closure

Prayer, Questions & Answers, Comments

Transcending: summing up, responding, creating, performing, committing, evaluating

Modifications:
How will you change the lesson to meet the needs of the individual students?

Personal notes/reminders/homework/assignments

Post-lesson reflections

INTRODUCTION

When a person becomes a Christian, their destined journey and calling of life begins and that is where warfare also begins with Satan. God has given us as soldiers of Christ, powerful weapons of defense against Satan and his accusations against us.

It exists in the unseen, spiritual dimension, where God is all powerful and Satan is in revolt. God instructs Christians to use the armor and weapons of God. Christians have many weapons that they can use against Satan. It is a battle against the spiritual powers in the spiritual realm. The keys to success in spiritual warfare are to rely on God's power, not your own. Put on the whole armor of God, draw upon the power of Scripture which is God's Word. Pray in perseverance and holiness and appeal to God. Stand firm, submit to God and resist the devil. God is the Lord of hosts which protects us. Amen.

Overview

I. Goal Lessons:

Goal four teaches about spiritual warfare, how you will use those weapons and to receive the blessings that God has for you.

II. Goal Objectives

Upon completion of this goal, the disciple will be able to:

    a. explain the weapons of warfare, spiritual attack,
    b. pray, decree, declare, and confess the word of God over their life,
    c. describe Satan and the demonic devices he is establishing on the earth against the people of God,
    d. walk in faith,
    e. fight the plan of the enemy in the spiritual realm, and
    f. understand how heaven operates and how to access it.

III. Bible Books Recital

Genesis to Revelation

1. Spiritual Warfare

Spiritual warfare is real. God revealed it through the prophets in the Bible. To understand this war, we need to see what scriptures says. Understanding the spiritual war requires revelation from God. The Bible tells us there is an invisible realm, which is distinct from our physical realm. The target of this battle is the souls of humanity (1 Pet. 5:8-9), and the battlefield is the mind of humanity, binding them from the truth, that they perish without salvation.

The kingdom of Satan is raging war on the Kingdom of God, for the souls of humanity. Let me explain. In the spiritual realms, when someone comes to Christ and is born again, things happen

The scriptural basis for warfare in prayer is based upon:

1. the BELIEVERS AUTHORITY (Lk. 10:17,19; Jn. 14:13,14)
2. the PRAYER OF BINDING AND LOOSING (Mt. 16:19)
3. Job 22:28- you WILL DECREE a thing and it WILL come to pass!
4. John 14:13, 14 ASKING in the Name of Jesus.
5. Ephesians 6:16 FAITH in Christ, which stops EVERY fiery dart of the enemy!

The new Christian finds themselves in the middle of a war, not understanding the conflict and how to move forward in victory, rather in defeat. Our goal as children of God is to advance the Kingdom of God, take territory from the enemy, and bring souls into the kingdom. Satan understands the born-again Christians are his mortal enemy. His goal is to remove the advantage of victory they have in Christ, by causing the saved to be in bondage and defeated through strongholds. A defeated Christian is one less enemy Satan has to worry about. We need to understand how Satan wages war in our lives, and in the lives around us. Knowing the method of spiritual warfare, allows us to go on the offense, rather responding from a position of defense and weakness.

Satan's work against the Kingdom of God takes place in the invisible realms (Rom. 1:20; Heb. 11:27; Col. 1:16). In Ephesians chapter 6 Paul tells us the spiritual realm is invisible, but it is organized with a structure of rule. The angelic world and the demonic (fallen angels) conflicts are being played out in the physical realms, which involve us. Another example of the invisible world is in the New Testament scripture, Mark 5:13.

2. Levels of Spiritual Warfare

Jesus recognized and declared that there is a satanic kingdom and that it exists. It is a shame that there are Christian churches that do not recognize that a Satanic kingdom exists back then or even now.

There are four levels of spiritual warfare working for Satan, which are:

1. **Principalities**: Evil spiritual princes in Satan's kingdom who are assigned to control large

portions of the world, nations, states of large political or religious segments of the country. They do this by influencing rulers, kings, presidents, government officials, parliaments, congress, judges and all who have legal, political influence or rule over regions of the Earth.

2. **Powers**: Powers are behind witchcraft, occultism, psychic powers, mental powers, dark arts, transcendental meditation, invisible powers, and universal life force. They operate much like how electricity works.

3. **Rulers of Darkness**: They rule regions under the legal authority of principality. They include governors, county managers, mayors, and they have specific areas of a country or city given over to them to rule. This also includes organized crime, incidental and immoral behavior, gambling, prostitution, adultery, influencing people to justify doing wrong.

4. **Spiritual hosts of wickedness in heavenly places**: There is a blanket of wickedness covering the people of Earth to cause wicked events to happen such as floods, hurricanes, earthquakes, tornadoes, tsunami, tidal waves, forest fires, or any wicked event that could cause theft, death, and destruction. It is from this realm that Satan directs his demons and targets not only specific areas but people. It is from this realm Satan assigns demons, as people are given over to evil practices and rebellion against God.

There is another level of warfare spoken about. It is found in our mind. Romans 7:23-25 and 2 Corinthians 10:3-6. Paul writes both to the Romans and to the Corinthians, that there is a war going on in our minds. Thoughts that bring us into captivity; imaginations; arguments, that would cause us to be in disobedience to God.

So, when we declare and speak things in the name of Jesus Christ to the demonic realm whether they are in the air above us or in our minds, or battling them in the members of our body, we should expect the command to be obeyed. Whenever God calls you to do great things, the devil will attack your imaginations.

So where is the warfare that is stated in Ephesians 6 actually located? It must be located here on Earth with the world forces of darkness, and also in the second heaven above us with the prince of the power of the air (Ephesians 2:2). The prince of the power of the air is located in our immediate atmosphere above our heads in the clouds surrounding the Earth above our cities, counties, states, in countries and further beyond with principalities in the stars.

Marzullo writes, "Spiritual warfare is a battle between the people who are loyal to God and a network of evil spirits that are loyal to Satan. It is the warfare between these two kingdoms that is fought in the spiritual realm.

We must fight spiritual warfare because Jesus fought spiritual warfare.

1. Destroy the devil's works (John 14:12).
2. Put off the old man (Ephesians 4:22-24).
3. Escape the devil's snares (2 Timothy 2:26).

4. To open people's eyes (Acts 26:17-18).
5. We are to minister the Gospel to the brokenhearted, the captives, the infirmed, and the oppressed because Jesus did. (Luke 4:18).
6. To maintain our victory (1 Timothy 6:12)."[1]

3. Spiritual Attack

Every Christian as they walk on their journey will face the attacks, accusations, and condemnations of the enemy. We must know WHAT to do, how to react and respond according to Scripture. A believer must learn how to develop prayer strategies against satanic attack, accusation, and condemnation, and much more.

There are Biblical strategies you must know and follow to see the victory which Jesus has already obtained for you, which are:

- Do not pray for victory, because you already have the victory in Christ. You must take possession of victory through your faith.
- Confess to possess. Our words are faith seeds. We speak it and release it in the physical realm; the Holy Spirit takes root in our hearts through our faith of the unseen from the realm of the Spirit.
- Plead the blood of Jesus against the attack of the enemy.
- Bind the demons, binding Satan first and all strongman spirits, first.
- Pray the Holy Spirit.

Decree and destroy Satan and his demonic spirits, in the name of Jesus. Job 22:28 says that WHAT you DECREE WILL come to pass.

4. Angels

There are different angels in the heaven. The Angels are for us, not against us. Amen.

Definition of *Angels*

Enns writes, "There are a number of different words used in Scripture to define angelic beings.

Angel. The Hebrew word malak simply means "messenger"; it may refer to human messenger (1 Kings 19:2) or a divine messenger (Gen. 28:12). The basic meaning of the word is "one who is sent." As a divine messenger an angel is a "heavenly being charged by God with some commission."

Sons of God. Angels are called "Sons of Gods" in that in their unfallen state they are God's sons by His creation (Job 1:6; 38-7).

---

[1] Frank Marzullo Jr, *Spiritual Warfare Now-Fighting for the Sons of Men,* 2013, 190-

Holy Ones. Angels are also referred to as the "host" which can be understood to denote the armies of heaven (Ps.89:6, 8; 1 Sam.17:45).

Existence of Angels

The existence of angels is uniformly presented in Scripture. The thirty-four books of the Bible make reference to angels (seventeen in the Old Testament; seventeen in the New Testament)."[2]

Nature and Attributes of Angels

Enns writes, "*Angels are spirit beings.* Although angels may reveal themselves to mankind in the form of human bodies (Gen. 18:3) they nonetheless are called "spirits' (Heb.1:14), suggesting they do not have corporeal bodies. Hence, they do not function as human beings as in terms of marriage (Mark 12:25), nor are they subject to death (Luke 20:36).

Angels are created beings. Along with the celestial bodies, the Lord created the angels by His Word (Ps.148:2-5).

Angels were created simultaneously and innumerable in number. The number of their creation is "myriads" (Heb.12:22).

Angels are a higher order than man. Mankind, including our incarnate Lord, is "lower than the angels" (Heb.2:7). Angels are not subject to the limitations of man, especially since they are incapable of death (Luke 20:36). Angels have greater wisdom than man (2 Sam. 14:20), yet they are limited in power (Dan. 10:13). Angels are not created in the image of God; therefore, they do not share man's glorious destiny of redemption in Christ. "[3]

Classification of Angels

Enns writes, "*Angels who are governmental rulers.* Ephesians 6:12 refers to "rankings of fallen angels": Rulers are "those who are first or high in rank"; powers are "those invested with authority"; world-forces of this darkness" expresses the power or authority which they exercise over the world"; spiritual forces of wickedness describes the wicked spirits, "expressing their character and nature."

Angels who are highest ranking. Michael is called the archangel in Jude 9 and the great prince in Daniel 12:1. Michael is the only angel designated archangel and may possibly be the only one of this rank. The mission of the archangel is protector of Israel. (He is called "Michael your prince" in Dan. 10:21.) There are chief princes (Dan.10:13), of whom Michael is one, the highest-ranking angels of God. Ruling angels (Eph. 3:10) are also mentioned, but no further details are given.

Angels who are prominent individuals. **(1)** Michael (Dan. 10:13; 12:1; Jude 9). The name Michael

---

[2] Paul Enns, *The Moody Handbook of Theology,* 2014, 301.
[3] Ibid, 302.

means "who is like God?" and identifies the only one classified as an archangel in Scripture. Michael is the defender of Israel who will wage war on behalf of Israel against Satan and his hordes in the tribulation (Rev. 12:1-9). **(2)** Gabriel (Dan. 9:21; Luke 1:26). His name means "man of God" or "God is strong." Gabriel means to be God's messenger of His kingdom program in each of the four times he appears in the Bible record. He reveals and interprets God's purpose and program concerning Messiah and His kingdom to the prophets and the people of Israel. **(3)** Lucifer (Isa. 14:12) means "shining one" or "star of the morning." He may have been the wisest and most beautiful of all Gods created beings and was originally placed in a position of authority over the cherubim surrounding the throne of God.

Angels who are divine attendants. **(1)** Cherubim are "of the highest order or class, created with indescribable powers and beauty… Their main purpose and activity might be summarized this way: they are proclaimers and protectors of God's glorious presence, His sovereignty, and His holiness. They stood guard at the gate of the Garden of Eden, preventing sinful man from entering (Gen. 3:24); were the golden figures covering the mercy seat above the ark in the Holy of Holies (Ex. 25:17-22); and attended the glory of God in Ezekiel's vision (Ezek. 1).

(2) Seraphim, meaning "burning ones," are pictured surrounding the throne of God in Isaiah 6: 2. They are each described as each having six wings in their threefold proclamation, "holy, holy, holy" (Isa. 6:3), it means "to recognize God as extremely perfectly holy. Therefore, they praise and proclaim the perfect holiness of God. The seraphim also express the holiness of God in that they proclaim that man must be cleansed of sin's moral defilement before he can stand before God and serve Him."[4]

Ministry of Angels

Enns writes, "*Ministry to God.* The cherubim have a ministry to God in defending the holiness of God; seraphim have a ministry to God in surrounding the throne of God as they attend to his holiness.

Ministry to Christ. Angels have a significant ministry to Christ from prior to His birth until His second advent. **(1)** angels predicted His birth (Luke 1:26-38); **(2)** Angels protected Him in infancy (Matt. 2:13); **(3)** Angels ministered to Him after the temptation (Matt. 4:11); **(4)** Angels strengthened Him at Gethsemane (Luke 22:43); **(5)** Angels announced His resurrection (Matt. 28:5-7; Mark 16:6-7); **(6)** Angels attended His ascension (Acts 1:10); **(7)** Angels will attend His second coming (Matt. 25:31)

Ministry to believers. Angels are termed "ministering spirits" In Hebrews 1:14. The following responsibilities are carried out in angels' ministry to believers. (1) Physical protection; (2) Physical provision; (3) Encouragement; (4) Direction; (5) Assist in answers to prayers; and (6) Carry believer's home.

<u>Relationship</u> *to unbelievers.* Angels have been and will be involved in meeting our judgment on

[4] Paul Enns, *The Moody Handbook of Theology*, 2014, 302-304.

unbelievers. Angels will also be instrumental in judgment at the end of the age when they cast out unbelievers into the furnace of fire (Matt.13:39-42); angels will sound the trumpet during the tribulation (Rev. 8:2-12; 9:1, 13; 11:15); angels pour out the fowl judgments on the earth (Rev. 16:2-17)."[5]

There Are Different Types of Angels:

Herzog writes, [6]**"Healing angels**: that help to speed up the healing power.

Territorial angels: are the ones that help take your city. They are "the earth or land angels". They are assigned to your territory.

Healing, miracle, and signs and wonders angels: Signs and wonders, healings, and miracles will occur; validating the message of the gospel with a harvest of souls following.

Angels of transportation help you to arrive at your destination miraculously fast.

Angel of time: This angel can take you back and forth through time; sometimes in your sleep, prayers, or other.

Angels of finances: Angels can supernaturally be released to bring finances in time of need or things that are needed on time.

Legions of angels: We have a right to a legion of angels. Once you have access and a right to something, you start to have faith to activate it.

Angels over creation: These are angels assigned to the oceans, mountains, deserts, etc. There are also angels over wind, rain, snow, lighting, and thunder that will come out of the treasuries of heaven. The enemy also tries to manipulate the weather patterns that God put over creation.

Planetary angels: There are angels that have been given spheres of authority over planets and galaxies. They are there to make sure everything in outer space that God created is functioning and rotating normally.

Angels over government: There is a glory that God put over government."[7]

5. Satan the Adversary

Satan was an angel in heaven. Satan is a fallen angel (Is. 14:12-15) and as such is only a created being. He is in no way equal to God, the Creator. While Satan is superior in intellect and strength to mankind, he is inferior to God in every way. Believers have the power of the indwelling resurrected Christ over them and protecting them (1 John 4:4).

The activity of Satan against believers is described throughout the Bible. Satan tempts believers

5   Ibid, 2014, 304-306.
6   David Herzog, *The Courts of Heaven*, 2013, 32-39.

to lie (Acts 5:3); he accuses and slanders them (Rev. 12:10); he entices them toward sexual sin (1 Cor. 7:5); he places obstacles in their path (1 Thess. 2:18); he causes persecution (Rev.2:10); and he causes Christians that are not fully serving God to infiltrate among true Christians to promote confusion and division in the church (Matt. 13:38, 39). The Christian's defence involves being on guard, sober, vigilant (Pet. 5:8), taking a stand against the devil and resisting him (James 4:7; Eph. 6:11-18).

SAY: Let's learn about the demonic spirits that Satan has created here on earth in the natural to destroy God's children. There is a history behind demonic spirits and it all began once Satan was cast out of heaven into the sea with the fallen angels that followed him. I will discuss four of them, but there are more.

Succubus Spirits: A succubus is a demon that takes the form of a woman in order to have intercourse with a man in his dreams. A demon who tempts men sexually at night and who tries to kill infants at birth.

Marine Spirits: Marine spirits are generally referred to as spirits which have operational base in the waters. They are spirits thrown down from heaven (Rev 12:12) and (13:1) and made the oceans, seas, rivers, streams and lakes their abode. The Marine kingdom (WHICH IS SPIRITUAL) is established beneath the Atlantic Ocean and the Headquarters of Marine kingdom of Satan is said to be located beneath India's Sea. The **"Queen of India's sea"** is the head of Marine kingdom, while the **"Queen of the Coast"** is next in command and resides within the Atlantic Ocean. It is said that both are also among the fallen angels and travel in the form of half humanoid and half fish.

Incubus Spirits: An incubus was supposedly a male demon who would lie with sleeping human women in order to have sexual intercourse with them. Incubi were thought to be able to father children, and the half-human offspring of an incubus was called a "cambion. Incubus spirits do have form, but it is not a physical form. However, they can project an image in order for us to see them. They have the ability to choose and project an image that they feel would be pleasing and acceptable to us. They have the ability to convince people that they are deceased lovers, out of body spirits from people that you might have feelings for, and whoever is necessary for them to convince you to let them touch you, lay in bed with you, and/or have sex with you.

Leviathan Spirits: According to Strong's Concordance #3882, Leviathan is depicted as "a serpent or crocodile." The most detailed description of Leviathan can be found in the 41st chapter of the book of Job, in which God asks Job if he can handle a battle with this apparently unbeatable monster. Leviathan is described as exhaling smoke and having scales, breath like hot coals and sharp teeth that are "terrible" round about.

You have to break all soul ties and attachments to them. Do this by using the Sword of the Spirit, and visualize cutting the cords to them, while saying, *"In the name of Jesus Christ, and with the Sword of the Spirit, I cut and severe all soul ties, and attachments to all incubus, marine, leviathan and succubus spirits"*.

As Christians, we are warned against worshiping demons (Leviticus 17:7), and even their names should be forgotten (Zechariah 13:2). Some people study demons thinking that will help them carry on spiritual warfare. All we really need to know about the enemy is this: "Every spirit that does not confess that Jesus Christ has come in the flesh is not of God" (1 John 4:3, NKJV). Our focus should be on learning more about the One who "has delivered us from the power of darkness and conveyed us into the kingdom of the Son of His love, in whom we have redemption through His blood, the forgiveness of sins" (Colossians 1:13-14, NKJV). When we hide God's Word in our hearts, it keeps us from sinning against Him (Psalm 119:11) and gives us the weaponry to fight off any attack of Satan or his demons (Ephesians 6:17).

His Character	Scripture
Cunning	Gen. 3:1
Created with superior wisdom	Is.14:13,16; Ezek. 28:2; 3:12
Resident of Eden	Gen. 3:1 (serpent); Ezek. 28:13
Essentially violent	Ezek. 28:15
Liar and violent	Gen. 3:4; John 8:44
Ambitious to be as God	Is. 14:13,14; Ezek. 28:2, 3, 6; Luke 4:6-8; 2 Thess. 2:3 4
Deceptive in appearance	Gen. 3:1; Ezek. 28:14; 2 Cor. 11:14; Acts 5:3

His Work	Scripture
Urges people to renounce God	Gen. 3:4, 5
Perverts and hinders scripture	Gen. 3:1, 4, 5; Matt. 4:6
Hinders the Gospel	Matt. 13:19; 16:23
He lost his position and is under judgment because of rebellion	Is. 4:12, 15; Ezek. 28:7, 8, 10, 16-18; Matt. 25:41; Rev.19:20, 21, 20:13-15

Names for Satan	
Name	Reference
The accuser of our brethren	Rev. 12:10
The adversary	1 Pet. 5:8
Angel of the bottomless pit	Rev. 9:11
Beelzebub, ruler of the demons	Matt. 12:24
Belial	2 Cor. 6:15
The dragon	Rev. 12:7; 20:2
The enemy	Matt. 13:39
The god of this age	2 Cor. 4:4
Liar	John 8:44
Lucifer	Is. 14:12-21
Murderer	John 8:44

The prince of the power of the air	Eph. 2:2
The ruler of the darkness	Eph. 6:12
Satan	Mark 1:12,13
The tempter	1 Thess. 3:5
The wicked one	Matt. 13:19

Satan, also known as the Accuser, goes to the courts of heaven day and night and accuses us to the Judge, who is God. Jesus is our Advocate or lawyer. The accuser of the brethren accuses God's people day and night," Then I heard a loud noise in heaven, saying, "Now the salvation, and the power, and the kingdom of our God and the authority of His Christ have come, for the accuser of our brethren have been thrown down, he who accuses them before our God day and night" (Rev. 12:10).

Before you go to the courts of heaven and plead your case, you must repent of anything he could use against you. Everything in your life like your marriage, children, ministry, job, business, sickness, lack, etc. can be taken to the courts of heaven.

Satan uses many things to build cases against us which he takes to the courts of heaven, such as:

1. Sin: Psalm 32; Psalm 51
2. Transgressions: Psalm 32; Psalm 51
3. Iniquity: sin of the bloodline, look at your family's sin.
4. Your own personal words you speak over yourselves can be used against you. Words can be used to justify us or condemn us. Matt. 12:37
5. The words that have spiritual authority (ministry gifts, teachers, apostles, pastors, prophets). If they speak against you it can be used in the courts of heaven.
6. Those who have spiritual authority over you. There words can devastate you in the spiritual realm.
7. Motives of the heart can be used.
8. Unforgiveness and not showing mercy to others (James 2:13).
9. Covenants with demons in the spiritual realm.
10. Contracts in the spirit realm. Powers of darkness agreements are made in the spiritual realm with demonic gods. They will try to rule in your family line.
11. Dedications in the spirit realm.
12. Trades or making trades. The satanic realm uses blood to make trades.

6. Blessings and Curses

The Bible has a lot to say about blessings and curses and they are very real. Blessings and curses are usually expressed in words—spoken, written or inwardly uttered. The book of Proverbs describes the power of words: Prov. 12:18; 15:4; 18:21. The book of James speaks about words in

James 3:5-6, 9-10. James explains that words can be either for good or for evil. Physical objects can also be a means of blessing and cursing. For blessing, it was used in Exo. 30:22-33; Lev. 8; 1-12; 1 Sam.16:13. For cursing, it was described in 1 Cor.10:16 that it can be used for blessing or judgment; Exo. 20:4-5.

Curses were to come upon you, pursue you, overtake you, and destroy you.

Curses and blessings are words that can be activated with the supernatural power of God or the devil. Words can affect or impact people's lives and alter their destiny. It can last from one generation to the next and repeat itself for many years.

In Deuteronomy 28 Moses speaks about the blessing and curses to the Israelites. In the new covenant in John 10:27, it is also speaking to the same blessings and curses. In the Old and New Testament, it was telling the people the same thing, which is to recognize the Lord's voice and follow Him in obedience.

In Deuteronomy 28 the blessings were exaltation—being lifted up high, health, fertility, prosperity, victory, and God's favor. The curses were humiliation, inability to reproduce in an area of your life, mental and physical sickness, family breakdowns, poverty, defeat, oppression, failure, and Gods' disfavor.

There are seven indications of a curse:

1. **Mental and emotional breakdown** (Deut. 28:20, 28, 65, 66, 67). People can be cursed by feeling confused, anxious, dread or even terror. The mind is attacked by hostile forces. People can lose control over how they think, how they feel and how they react.

2. **Repeated or chronic illness** (Deut. 28:22, 27, 35, 59, 61). All types of conditions such as, sickness, disease, fever, tumors, inflammations, hereditary sickness, and sores. Sometimes there is no cure. There are also sicknesses that God will allow to keep us humble. We can be blessed with spiritual insight like the Apostle Paul.

3. **Barrenness, repeated miscarriages and related female problems** (Deut. 28: 18). The curse affects the woman's reproductive organs and how it should be working. Women can experience inability to conceive, miscarriages, tumors, cysts, other growths like fibroids, menstruation issues. All affects the reproductive organs.

4. **Marriage breakdown and alienation in families** (Deut. 28:41). Many parents in today's generation are experiencing curses upon their children, such as, rebellion, drug use, sexual promiscuity, alcohol, music of Satan and more.

5. **Continuing financial or material insufficiency** (Deut. 28:17, 29, 47-48). People can experience temporary financial issues. Faith in God will be tested. People will have to be content with what they have until God can trust His people with abundance to be used for His glory.

6. **Being "accident-prone"** (Deut. 28: 29). People who are prone to accidents. Sometimes they make rash, quick moves.

7. **A history of suicides or unnatural deaths** (Deut. 28). The references to unnatural or untimely death in Deuteronomy 28 are too numerous to mention. The curse affects a person but also a larger group which could be the family. It can include suicides, unnatural or untimely deaths. People have a negative faith which can invite evil spirits to take over their lives.

Are any of these indications of curses present in your personal or family life?

_____

In Proverbs 26:2 Solomon makes it clear that there is a reason for every curse: "Like a fluttering sparrow or a darting swallow, an undeserved curse does not come to rest."

Let's discuss the causes of curses:

1. **Idolatry and false gods** (Exo. 20:1-5; Rom. 1: 22-23): There are nations and cultures that have worshipped false gods for many years which has caused the generations that came after them to be exposed to a curse.

2. **Injustice to the weak and helpless** (Deut. 27): Oppression and injustice is condemned especially against the weak and helpless.

3. **Wrong sexual practices** (Deut. 27: 20-23): Any form of unnatural sex brings a curse. Unnatural sexual acts include with family members or animals, also known as bestiality, and any expression of homosexuality (Lev. 18:22).

4. **Anti-Semitism** (Gen. 12:1-3): God calls every man and woman to fulfill an assignment on the earth and in turn Satan will target you to stop that fulfilment from coming to pass. So, whoever curses the Jewish people will be cursed. (Gen.12:1-3; Gen. 27:29; Numbers 4:29)

5. **Legalism and carnality:** Jeremiah 17:5-6 gives an example. The Christian church has received and tasted the grace of God, but they begin to do their own thing and trust in their own efforts. The fleshly way of doing things is put in front of God's divine grace.

6. **Stealing, perjury and robbing God:** The prophet Zechariah had a vision of a scroll that contained curses on one side that cursed thieves, and the other side cursed people who lied and swore falsely (committed perjury) in the name of the Lord. In the household when this curse is applied, all the people are destroyed in the house. Robbing God (Malachi 3:8-9).

SAY: What causes of curses may be present in your own life?

_____

_____

_____

Now let's discuss blessing and curses through authority figures.

Blessings and curses are part of an invisible spiritual realm that affects the lives of all people. God alone has absolute authority. God is the supreme source of authority to those He chooses. God placed His authority in the hands of Jesus. Jesus delegates His authority to others. A person may exercise authority by blessing those under his or her authority or that same person can also curse. In marriage, husband and wife share the authority jointly.

A father, mother, or even a teacher can inflict curses. How we respond to authority figures, including our parents, can bring or perpetuate a curse on us. You are automatically exposed to a curse if you dishonor your parents. The words of religious leaders that are used can have a potential for good or evil according to the authority of their office. Blessings and curses can affect families, tribes, communities or whole nations. They can continue from generation to generation to generation.

Legitimate Curses from Servants of God

Prince notes, "Curses can legitimately proceed from people representing God. For example: Joshua pronounced a curse in Joshua 6:26, David in 2 Samuel 1:21, Elisha in 1 Kings 5:26, Jesus cursed the fig tree in Mark 11:12-13, Jesus in Matthew 23:23, Jesus authorized the disciples to curse in Acts 13:9-12, Paul curses those who bring heretical teachings to the Church in Gal. 1:6-9.

A curse must only be uttered by Christians when it is expressing the sovereign judgment of God. It must not proceed from the mind or will of the speaker, nor express human anger or vindictiveness. Luke 9:51-56"[8].

SAY: Do you know of any examples of such a curse in your experience?

_____

_____

_____

---

[8] Derek Prince, *Blessings and* Curses, 2003, 9-42.

Self-imposed Curses

Prince notes "In Matthew 12:36-37 Jesus gives a solemn warning about the danger of words carelessly spoken: "I tell you that people will have to give account on the day of judgment for every careless word they have spoken. For by your words you will be acquitted, and by your words you will be condemned."

Jesus here focuses on careless words-those spoken idly, without premeditation. Even if we do not really mean them, they can have power. We need to remember God takes our words seriously, even when we ourselves do not."[9]

Christians are in a covenant relationship with the Lord. A covenant is very powerful and once you inter into a covenant relationship on an unscriptural basis, the result will be a curse. There is also the marriage covenant between a husband and wife. There is a business covenant when you enter into a legitimate business agreement, you must honor it. Church members are in covenant with each other to walk in holiness, righteousness, faith, and building the kingdom of God together. A covenant must be honored once you enter into any of them.

SAY: What kinds of statements might open you to a curse? Do you commonly have any of these?

_____

_____

_____

Curses from Servants of Satan

Prince notes, "Satan is a created being, a rebellious angel, who was cast out of God's heaven. He rules over a spiritual kingdom of evil angels, together with lesser evil spirits, who are collectively called demons. His name means "adversary" or "one who opposes: He is the implacable enemy of God. His aim is to control the entire human race, and his primary tactic is deception. Primary targets of Satanic curses and other occult weapons are the servants of God and Jesus Christ. Satanists recognize who their main enemies are and direct their attacks accordingly."[10]

SAY: Have you inadvertently exposed yourself to occult influences?

_____

_____

_____

---

9   Ibid, 43.
10   Derek Prince, *Blessings and* Curses, 2003, 49.

Soulish Prayers or Utterances

Prince explains, "Many Christians would be surprised to learn that they can be harmed by spiritual forces emanating from their fellow believers. James says, "But if you harbor bitter envy and selfish ambition in your hearts, do not boast about it or deny the truth. Such 'wisdom' does not come down from heaven but is earthly, unspiritual, or the devil" (James 3:14-15). In Jude 16-19 the apostle describes a class of persons who are associated with the Church but are nevertheless "Grumblers and faultfinders; they follow their own evil desires" (verse 16). He concludes by saying of them, "These are the people who divide you, who follow mere natural instincts and do not have the Spirit" (verse 19). In Titus 3:2 Paul says that we are to "slander no one." One Greek verb translated "to slander", or "to speak evil" is blasphemy—from which is derived the word blaspheme. The sin of blasphemy includes not only evil words spoken against God, but also evil words spoken against our fellow human beings.

James deals specifically with words that Christians speak about one another: "Brothers, do not slander one another"" (James 4:11). The word translated 'slander' is katalalo, which means simply to "speak against." Many Christians interpret this to mean we are not to say anything false against other believers. What he actually says, however, is that we are not to speak against fellow believers at all—even if what we say about them is true. This includes gossip, which is classed by many Christians as a relatively harmless practice. Yet in Romans 1:29-30, Paul groups it with many serious sins. If we have been guilty of speaking against one another or praying wrongly, we need to repent and seek God's forgiveness."[11]

SAY:

Have you been guilty of speaking against someone or praying wrongly? Who? What? Why? _____

_____

What should you do about it? _____

The response is to repent, pray, and do not commit that sin anymore.

The Divine Exchange

Through the death of Jesus on the cross, God has made full provision for every human need, including release from a curse. The purpose accomplished by Jesus' sacrifice is summed up in Isaiah 53:6.

- His righteousness for our sin
- His life for our death
- His healing for our wounds
- His riches for our poverty

---

11 Derek Prince, *Blessings and* Curses, 2003, 52-53.

- His glory and acceptance for our shame and rejection

The divine exchange could be summed in one grand, all-inclusive word: salvation (Derek Prince, 2003, p. 54-56).

How to Pass from Curse to Blessing

The basic pattern is stated in four simple words:

- *Recognize* your problem and its cause.
- *Repent* of anything that ever opened you to it.
- *Renounce* the curse.
- *Resist* every attempt of Satan to keep you under the curse.

Specific steps

1. *Confess your faith in Christ and in His sacrifice on your behalf*
2. Repent of all your rebellion and sins (Here is where you change your heart and mind attitude and go the way of God instead of the way of self)
3. Claim forgiveness of all sins
4. Forgive all other persons, including anyone who was the cause of the curse
5. Renounce all contact with the occult or with secret societies
6. You are now ready to pray for release from any curse

(Derek Prince, 2003, p. 58-61)

SAY: Are you ready to pray the prayer of release?

7. What are our Weapons?

The weapons of Warfare are as follows:

A	The Gospel	(John 12:46; Ephesians 5:8; 1 Thess. 5:5; 1 Peter 2:9; 1 John 1:6, 7),
B	The Blood of Jesus	Satan's defeat (Rev. 12:11; 1 John 1:6, 7),
C	Faith	which empowers prayer (Heb. 11:1; Ephesians 6:12; Rev. 12:11; James 1:6,7),
D	Your faith confession (the shield of faith)	these are your faith-filled words, spoken aloud from the applied Word of God, over another person, self, or circumstances. (Mark 11:23,24; Proverbs 18:21; Ephesians 6:16; Rev. 12:11),

E	Prayer	(Matthew 7:7; 1 John 3:22; 1 John 5:14; Mark 11:23, 24; Proverbs 23:7; Proverbs 18:21),
F	The Believer's Authority	Believers must understand their position in Christ, that they are joined to His Spirit (1 Cor. 6:17) and are therefore, one with Him (Romans 6). The believer must, therefore, know who he or she is, and the power that has been delegated to them by the Holy Spirit (Luke 10:17; Luke 10:19; Matthew 11:12; John 14:12; Jeremiah 51:20; Matthew 16:19; Matthew 12:29; Job 22:28; 1 Cor. 6:17; Mark 11: 23-24; Proverbs 23:7; Proverbs 18:21; Revelation 12:11),
G	The full armor of God	(Ephesians 6:11-17),
H	The Word of God	(James 4:7; Matthew 4:1-11),
I	Binding and loosing prayer	(Matthew 16:18-19; Matthew 12:29), and
J	Agreeing	Matthew 18:19, **and decreeing** (Job 22:28) in the name of Jesus (Luke 10:17)

SAY: Let's discuss each weapon and how to use them.

A. The Gospel

The gospel is to preach, proclaim good news of Jesus Christ, and what he has done to reconcile sinners to God. Renn explains, "The "gospel" of the kingdom of God, emphasizes the omnipotent rule or control of God over his people, is noted in Matt. 4:23; 24:14; Mark 1:14,12

B. The Blood of Jesus

The blood of Jesus Christ was absolutely necessary to remit sins (Mt. 26:28; Jn. 6:53-56; 19:34; Acts 20:28; Rom. 3:24-25; 5:9; 1 Cor. 10:16; 11:25; Eph. 1:7; 2:13; Col. 1:14, 20; Heb. 9:6-28; 10:19-20, 29; 12:254; 13:12; 20; 1 Pet. 1:2; 18-23; 1 Jn. 1:7; 5:6-8; Rev. 1:5-6; 5:9; 7:14; 12:11. The reconciliation of sinners with God has come about only as a result of Christ's work of atonement through his death on the cross (Rom. 5:11; 11:15; 2 Cor. 5:18,19).

C. Faith

Faith is complete trust and commitment to God (Phil. 3:2-9). We must have "now" faith. Faith depends on Christ. We understand and know it is the sole command of God. But without faith, it is impossible to please him. 1 Cor 12:9 speaks to an extraordinary trust in God under the most difficult or dangerous circumstances. (Matt 17:20; Heb. 11: 1, 3, 6; Gal 3:23, 25, Tim 4: 12, 6:11; 2

---

12 Renn, Stephen, *Expository Dictionary of Bible Words*, 2005, 446.

Pet 1:5; Jude 3). Pray for faith "Increase our faith (Luke 17:5), then confess your weaknesses (Mk 9:24). Ask for more faith, so you can pray for bigger things. Romans 10:17 says, "17 So then faith cometh by hearing, and hearing by the word of God." When God puts a desire in you to do a task for Him, two things will happen. First God will help you do it. Second, you'll grow your faith to trust Him for bigger things in the future. As you look at your life purpose, focus on God and His plan for your life. God will provide if you're focused on Him.

Belief is what truly activates the act and process of faith. The substance or conviction of things hoped for, the assurance of things not seen. It is absolute dependence upon and reliance in the Word of God and of Christ. Faith in God involves right belief about God.

Exercise-Experiencing Faith

Write one sentence statement of your life purpose. Make sure this is what God wants for your life. Next, review your life plan.

1. Look at your changes-make a list of two or three steps of faith that you are facing now and in the distant future.

2. Focus on one step of faith- pray over the list and target one challenge for today. Here's what you can do:

   - Pray and ask God to help you to know what to do,
   - Aim focus on what you want to accomplish with this step of faith,
   - Count the cost, figure out the problems or consequences in taking this step, and
   - Pray again and ask God to help you and to guide each step you take.

As you go from one faith, one project to another, you grow from "faith to faith"- Rom 1:17.

Confessions for your Faith

- My faith is "now faith". When I speak in faith, I believe that I have received it "now". For my faith is the substance of things hoped for, and the evidence of things not yet seen. (Hebrews 11:1).

- I am a person of faith. I walk by faith; I talk by faith; I live by faith, and I therefore have an expectancy to receive that which I confess and pray for by faith. For I walk by faith and not by sight. (2 Corinthians 5:7).

- The righteousness of God is revealed from faith to faith. I am the just, and I live by faith (Romans 1:17).

When my faith is tried in the fire, my faith shall stand, and come through the fire victorious – as pure gold (1 Peter 1:7).

D. Your Faith Confession

Confessions

Confessing the word of God is simply exercising our authority that God has given us to speak, decree, and declare His word through faith. The Greek word for confession is the word "homologue". This word has several definitions, which are, to speak the same thing, to come in agreement with, to unify with, and to declare. This brings one's life situations in line and in accord with God's word.

When we speak the same thing, God has spoken in His Word, causing us to be of one mind and opinion with His Word

      1) confession is "to speak the same thing",
      2) agreement is "to be of the same opinion and mind",
      3) unity is "to come together and become united with one cause or purpose", and
      4) declare is to "proclaim, pronounce, or make a declaration

Do you speak life or death?

We must know that we can speak death and destruction to our lives by speaking negative words and confessions of doubt, fear and unbelief. We are to speak the abundance of God by speaking what God says about our lives.

God created us to be able to speak in the spirit to create, change things and rule as He does in our lives through His Word. There are two forces that are waiting for us to speak to bring actions to our words, and it is the angels and the demons. Psalm 103:20 tells us that angels hearken to the voice of God.

Satan and his demonic spirits understand the authority and power of words we speak. The angels of God move out to bring to pass every positive word of God that we speak. The demons and devils also have been given the authority to move out and bring to pass the negative words that we speak.

Do you rehearse your script?

When we confess God's word, we are confessing the Word of God. As we speak the word of God it becomes our script, which comes from scripture in the Bible. As we continue to speak our script, it is now being rehearsed. As we say it continually, it activates life to every current situation or anything we are going through. God's divine authority and the power of God's word will manifest changes to those situations and everything you are going through.

God is saying that regardless of your circumstances, call (pray and confess) those things which are not the way your desire or need them to be, as though they were the way that you desire or need them to be; because in the spiritual realm, they are already that way (Scott, 2002, Vol III, p. 11). Always pray and confess what God has said in His Word.

Consistency in Confession

We must start our day in prayer, getting into His presence with praise, worship, and thanksgiving. Seek his face, get in His presence, and His anointing comes. Then we petition Him for our daily bread (needs and desires). For the rest of the day, do what Jesus did, which is speaking, decreeing, and declaring His word. For the rest of the day, just confess (speak, decree, and declare His Word).

Before bedtime, pray and cover family, neighbors, brothers and sisters, the unsaved, the earth and yourself during the night from the enemy, and ask for rest, dreams and visions, and to rise again the next day, renewed and restored in the name of Jesus Christ. Our actions must coincide with our confessions.

E. Prayer

Prayer is to communicate with or talk to God. We ask or petition God for something. Ask for things that God has promised to give (John 15:7). You apply the word of God as you pray. Sin in your life will block answers to your prayers. You have to deal with sin before you ask God for anything with true repentance (Psalm 66:18). There are different forms of prayer, such as, prayer of praise, prayer of authority, prayer of thanksgiving, prayer of asking, and prayer of intercession.

Prayer is:

1. **You must have a personal relationship with God.** It must be intimate fellowship with God. John 15:7. You must approach God with a one-on-one, intimate, personal relationship with Him. Going to church once a week, sing songs in church, paying tithes and offerings many believe is a relationship with God. God wants you 7 days a week. Talk with Him. Read the Bible, study and meditate so His words will abide in you.

2. **Your prayer requests must always line up with the will of God in your life.** (1 John 5:14). If God tells you that what you are asking for is not in His perfect will for you and your life, then you must let it go, trust God and move on. To know if it's God's will (a) analyze your prayer request, and (b) ask the Holy Spirit if you should approach God with this prayer request. You will have an inner knowing from Him if you should proceed or not.

3. **The prayers of the righteous he will hear, not the prayers of someone not keeping commandments or living a righteous life.** If it is a no to both of these , you will not have

success in your prayer closet. Sometimes you will have a hard time in getting victory over certain things. Sanctification will be necessary, so we can be saved and born- again. While God molds you, you will see the boundaries God will set up for you. It will be made clear to you through convictions of the Holy Spirit (Prov. 15:29; 1 Peter 3:11; 1 John 3:22; James 5:16) To "repent" means to turn away from those sins (Isa. 59:2; Prove. 28:9). Mark 11:25 speaks to unforgiveness. Ask the Holy Spirit if unforgiveness is a hindrance in your walk and personal prayer life with God. For husbands make sure you "honor your wives", 1 Peter 3:7 and "dwell with them with understanding", or it will hinder your prayers. If there is no love, respect, kindness and proper understanding, you will have a tough time in your prayer closet.

4. **Here is where you will state your case before God in the courts of heaven.** You will "reason together" with Him (Isa. 1:18) and "state your case" before Him and "contend together" with Him (Isa. 43:25). Talk to God and state your case before God, tell Him your reasons and intentions as to what and why you are praying for it.

5. **Now you will ask, seek, and knock.** You will ask God in prayer. You will then seek after Him before HE will answer the prayer. You will then knock which is an earnest desire for whatever it is you are asking of God. Keep knocking until you get some kind of answer from God on your request. The Holy Spirit, who is your helper, will come in to help you. Jacob wrestled with God and he prevailed (Gen. 32:36). The fervent prayer is described in James 5:16-18.
Elijah prayed earnestly and fervently, which is a higher level of intensity to your prayers. You must pray without ceasing (1 Thess. 5:16).

6. **Power of agreement.** Matthew 18:19. If a group of sincere, passionate, and intense believers all approach Him with the exact same prayer request all at the same time, God will move. Amen. There is so much power in united prayer amongst believers. Every Bible-based, Spirit-filled, Christian church should have intercessory prayer teams that are filled with mighty and powerful prayer warriors. The intercessory prayer teams must know to pray powerfully and effectively to God.

7. **Power of intercessory prayer.** A s a believer you must step in to the gap and pray for someone else's prayer needs before God the Father. God is looking for intercessors (Ezek. 22:30; Isa. 59:16; Psalm 106:23). To pray in the gap for someone else would be for example, someone who is not saved, someone who is too sick to pray for themselves anymore, someone whose faith levels are low with the Lord, someone who is weak in the Word, someone who has very little or no relationship with the Lord, someone who has a sudden emergency getting ready to attack them, and praying in agreement with others on an united prayer cause.

Each prayer assignment is for a battle situation for you or someone else. The Lord will guide you as to when to move in and on the situation. You will have to develop connection with the Holy Spirit. The Holy Spirit will prompt you to pray for someone or a situation. You may be kept on assignment for prayer for a short or long length of time, before you will be released from it.

8. **Praying more than one time.** Some believe if you pray for something more than once then you show doubt and unbelief. There are times when you will have to press in and ask more than one time for what you are praying for, which is called "prevailing prayer, prayer warfare, or wrestling with God". It shows maximum intensity and persistence. Luke 11:5-9.

9. **Your heart.** There will be times when you are in prevailing prayer with the Lord and He will not answer your prayer requests on your time. You may become discouraged, frustrated, and impatient. God will test your stamina, patience and perseverance. Saints do not get upset, so not quit, and do not walk asway from the Lord. In Luke 18:1-8, which is a parable, it tells us to always pray and do not lose heart. Continue to come to the Lord and cry out to Him day and night

10. **Jesus Christ and the Holy Spirit.** Rom. 8:26-27 and Heb. 7:25 is telling us about the intercessory ministry of Jesus. Rom. 8:26-27 is telling us about the Holy Spirit. As you pray directly to God the Father, Jesus and the Holy Spirit will also pray directly to God the Father for us as different needs and circumstances arise in our lives. The key word in these verses is intercession, which is prayer offered on behalf of others, to assail with urgent petitions, entreating God for His favor. The Holy Spirit will make intercession for us. We can ask Jesus and the Holy Spirit to intercede for us. We must pray according to the will of God.

    The Holy Spirit will help you with your prayer life (Rom. 8:26). You will earn how to be guided by the Holy Spirit as to what to pray for and what not to pray for, but He can also guide you as to how to word your prayers to God the Father. The Holy Spirit will help you on how to pray, what to pray for, what not to pray for, how to word your prayers to God, what particular Scripture verses to use in your prayers, the timing of exactly when to pray for something, the correct battle strategies to use, how many times to pray to God for the request, whether or not to call upon other believers to pray in agreement with you, whether or not there is anything else that you will need to do on your end before God will grant the prayer request.

11. **Prevailing Prayers.** Isa.64:7 the major verse here is "take hold of you". You put your prevailing prayer by showing Him by both your actions and your words that you mean serious business with Him- and that you are now taking Him at His Word with all of the verses that He has in the Bible.

12. **Thanksgiving prayers.** As you grow on your personal walk with God and He starts to move to answer many of your prayers, you will need to learn to have a thankful and appreciative heart with Him. Your heart must, real, true and authentic. If not, God will see it as manipulation for your own gain and profit. You will see that life should never be taken for granted because you know that you could lose it all in a very short period of time.

    A grateful and thankful heart is gratefulness expressed to another, the aspect of praise that gives thanks to God for what He does for us, natural expression of thanks in response to blessings, protection or love. In the Old Testament they thanked God for protection from their enemies, for keeping the original covenant that was made for Abraham, Isaac, and Jacob and the types of miracles He did for them. In the New Testament Paul tells us to give thanks in all things.

As you grow, you will understand Jesus being the vine and we are the branches. Do not forget who is supporting us, guiding us and protecting us in this life. (Psalm 50:14; 1 Chron. 16:4; Psalm 26:7; Psalm 95;2; Psalm 100:4; Psalm 116:17: Amos 4:5; 1 Thess. 5:18; Phil. 4:6-7; Col. 4:2; Eph.5:19-50; 1 Cor. 1:4); 2 Cor. 9:15; 2 Cor. 2:14; 1 Tim. 1:12; Rom. 6:17; Phil. 1:3; Col. 1:3; 1 Tim. 43; Col. 2:6-7)

Forms of Prayer

There are different forms of prayer.

Prayer of Praise

The Bible gives us insight into the characteristics of our great God and how to express thanks to Him. Many believe this to be the highest form of prayer.

Prayer of Authority

Matthew 18:18 "Assuredly, I say to you, whatever you bind on earth will be bound in heaven, and whatever you loose on earth will be loosed in heaven". It is a loosing prayer as well as a binding prayer. The movement of heaven follows the movement of the earth. Heaven listens to the words on earth and acts on the earth's commands. In Exodus 14:15-16, the rod which God gave to Moses represents authority. The Lord says you pray the prayer of commanding and I will do the work. Command with authority is authoritative prayer. God's overcomers must be faithful in denying themselves, the world, and Satan. They must know how to exercise the authority of Christ. God is to be our source for everything. Authoritative prayer is not to beg, but to command. Isaiah 45:11. Commanding prayer begins at the ascension of Christ. As Christ is far above all rule and authority, so we also are above all rule and authority. A regular prayer is from earth to heaven. Commanding prayer is from heaven to earth. The prayer in Matthew 6 is a petitionary prayer and therefore is upward in direction. The prayer in Ephesians 6 is a commanding prayer and so it is downward. We are heavenly representatives. Spiritual warfare is offensive as well as defensive (Matt. 18:18-19). We are to rule as kings over all things (Mark 11:23).

Prayer of Thanksgiving

Giving thanks to God is important. We are commanded to give thanks to God (Psalm 106:1; 107:1; 118:1; 1 Chron. 16:34; 1 Thess.5:18). Reasons are: (a) He is good – Psalm 118:29, (b) His love endures forever, (c) His mercy is everlasting (Psalm 100:5). We cannot praise and worship God without being thankful. Learn to be thankful for all the gifts He has given us (James 1:17). If we are not grateful, we become arrogant and self-centered. Sacrifice of raise (Heb. 13:15).

Prayer of Asking

Prayer must be practiced to receive an answer. "ask, seek, knock" – Matt. 7:7-11. When you approach the Lord in prayer for something very specific, make sure you ask, seek, and knock.

ASKING: Sometimes you can ask the Lord once or twice for something you are really wanting. The prayer request must be in His perfect will for your life. If you did not or failed to ask in the first place, the Lord will not bring a desire or request. James 4:2. When we pray out of God's will, we are asking "amiss". Amiss means "wrongfully" or "mistakenly". It may not be in your best interest. Do not try to do it on your own without God's help or guidance because pride will now enter in. The result of loss will come after.

SEEKING: If at first you have no success with the Lord in asking Him for something, go into seeking mode with Him to see if that will be what will get Him to answer your prayer. You will have to work, sweat, and seek for whatever it is God is wanting to bring your way.

KNOCKING: Knock means to "to tap on a door". Knock and it will be "opened" to you. Knocking means that you are asking and possibly seeking more than one time for whatever it is that you are asking God for.

Prayer of Intercession

The act of intercession or intercessory prayer to God is on behalf of others needs and situations. Abraham pleaded for the people of Sodom (Gen. 18). Moses petitioned God on behalf of Hebrew people (Exo.15:25). Paul prayed for the believers (Phil. 1:9-11). The church prayed to God while Peter was in prison (Acts 12:5).

To develop an effective prayer life:

- Prayer must be directed to the Father or to the Son. First obey Jesus and bring your requests to Him (John 14:13). If we don't ask, we aren't obedient,
- Before prayer, yield to the Holy Spirit in Jesus name and ask His Spirit of prayer to fall upon you and to lead you with faith-filled words,
- Back your prayers with faith. Faith moves God's heart to action,
- Reject doubt. Choose to believe and stand on your choice,
- Speak your prayers aloud into the air to cancel the devil's power, and
- Pray "through" with persistence until you receive and see the results.

Two of the strongest forms of prayer are praise and tongues. Tongues confound Satan because he cannot understand tongues. Remember when you are praying the prayer of binding and loosing, you bind Satan first, then the ruler spirit assigned to the person, then the demonic spirits below the ruler spirits, and then you lose for i.e. person(s), church, circumstances, finances, whoever or whatever affected, always in the name of Jesus Christ.

The word "bind" means to "tie up". The word "loose" means to "untie". Pray for the needs of others first, before praying for your own needs. Avoid selfish prayers because such prayers are from the "flesh". Pray the solution, not the problem. Pray what the Word of God says about your circumstances and what God promises that He will do on your behalf.

Reasons for unanswered prayer

Tempting or provoking God	Deut. 3:26
Lack of charity or love to others	Prov. 21:13
Lack of humility	2 Chron. 7:14
A hardened heart	Zech. 7:12,13
Forsaking God	2 Chron.15:2
Praying amiss (wrong motives)	James 4:3
Unbelief	Mt. 17:21, 21; Mt. 21:22
Marital strife	1 Pet. 3:7
Parading your prayer life	Mt. 5:6
Sin	Ja. 4:1-5; Is. 59:2; John 9:31
Being discouraged	Lk. 18:1-8
Doubt and double mindedness	Ja. 1:5-8
Anxiety and worry	Phil. 4:6
Hypocrisy	Lk. 18: 9-14
Unforgiveness	Mt. 6:14,15; Mk.11:25, 26
Not tithing	Mal. 3:8-10
Unconfessed sin	Ps. 66:18
Demonic attack	Daniel 10:10
Lack of sincerity	Mt. 6:5
Being unsaved	John 17
Curses	Deut. 28
Willful stubbornness	Jer. 16:12-13

As a believer, prayer should become second nature. It should become a part of all you do. Jesus implored us to pray and never give up (Luke 18:1). Paul also instructed believers to "Keep on praying" (1 Thessalonians 5:17).

In 2 Corinthians 12:2 Paul speaks about the third heaven. Once we understand the 1st, 2nd and 3rd heaven, our prayer life will be different.

1st Heaven: Spiritual realm that sur-rounds the earth.	Powers/authorities are angels of consciousness, intelligence, and are the historians of heaven. Powers work with principalities and war angels. Principalities/rulers given directions by dominions and assigned to bring material blessings to the inhabitants of the earth. They determine where wealth is stored. They determine who is rich and poor (Gen. 22:15-18). Verse 15-16 is the principality and verse 17-18 is speaking about the generations, territory, gates. Gates do not attack, they restrict. Gates refer to territories. It talks about in-come, quality of life, territory. Archangels means chief angels. They have authority in the first heaven as it relates to mankind. These angels constantly ascend and descend. Guardian/ministering angels (Heb.1:14).
2nd Heaven: The Celestial Heaven. Col.1:16; Deut. 4:19; Eph. 6:12	The angels are battling in the 2nd heaven when you are praying. Satan roams from the 1st to 2nd heaven. Angels have to go and contend for what people of God are praying for. This is where spiritual warfare takes place. When you break through the 2nd, you go to the 3rd. Angels assigned to dominions, governing angels, they divide /instruct lower angels' assignments (over entire nation and government) (Dan. 10:1, 13). Virtues angels assigned to ensure the bodies in heaven function in proper order and timing (requires your faith).
3rd Heaven: Rev. 4:1-2	At the throne is the dwelling place of God. The gate to the King-dom is through a relationship with Jesus Christ. There are strategy rooms, meetings, prayer rooms, and upper rooms. Prayers are culti-vated here, and God commands the heavens to respond. Seraphim's serve the throne of God (Isa. 6:1-7). Throne angels are purposed for justice and authority. God sends them to turn injustice to justice (Ezek. 1:18). Cherubim's personally are to protect/guard the throne of God, the glory. They block access into Eden. (Gen. 3:24/Ezek. 1:10). They ensure the enemy does not penetrate your life, your house. They block anything that is not the presence of God.

Remember when we are praying, our prayers must go through three realms of heaven, and simultaneously three realms of demonic angels. God is not the only one who hears our prayers (Eph. 1:20-21; Col.1:15-17; 1 John 3:8).

Mountains	Enemy	Prince	Authority	Missions	Rev. 5:12
Media	Hittites	Apollyon	Evangelists	Airways	Blessing
Government	Girgashite	Lucifer	Apostles	Fill Government	Power
Education	Amorites	Beelzebub	Teachers	Curriculum	Wisdom
Economy	Canaanites	Mammon	Prophets	Wealth Transfer	Riches
Celebration	Hirites	Jezebel	Prophets	Arts	Glory
Religion	Perizzites	Religion	Holy Spirit	Infilling	Honor
Family	Jebusites	Baal	Pastors	Social System	Strength

Courts of Heaven

Let's learn and discuss the courts of heaven. The courts of heaven are in the Old and New Testament. It is a real place where you can go and defend yourself against Satan the accuser during prayer. The whole book of Revelation is about the courtroom operation in heaven. The scriptures that describe the courts of heaven are Daniel 7:9-10; Daniel 7:25; Luke 18; Psalm 82; Jer. 23:8; Psalm 148:2; 1 Kgs. 22:19-22; 2 Chron. 18:18-21; Psalm 103:21; Luke18: 8-15; Daniel 8:10; Psalm 33:6; Neh. 9:6; Isa. 40:26; Isa. 45:12; Zeph. 1:4-5; Isa. 34:4; 2 Kgs. 23:4-5; 2 Kgs. 21:3-5; 2 Chr. 33:3-5; Jer. 19:13; Job 1:6.

Before you access the courts of heaven, you must know the history of your bloodline, such as, parents, relatives and previous family ancestors who had sin, and also gifts and callings. Those gifts and callings get carried from generation to generation to us. The enemy knows all of the weaknesses in your family bloodline.

So, when we are saved, faithful to pray and grow our gifts; we still struggle with sin patterns that was never dealt with when we got saved. Paul was showing that because we have to live in the flesh, there is war between our spirit lives and the flesh life. Jesus sits on the throne in heaven making intercession for us and He alone can deliver us from sin…the Holy Spirit convicts us, we repent turning away from sin (sometimes this is a process but God in His faithfulness does not give up on us but with love and patience, convicts and empowers us to repent). We could also be praying for things outside the will, plan and purpose of God…therefore, we do not get what we ask for. Paul spoke about his struggle in Rom. 7:15; 20-25. Galatians 5:17 explains the fight between sin and the Spirit.

When you partake of the blood of Jesus by faith and it comes into you, it has then power to break off every spiritual pattern in your generational line. Many times you are praying for things with no result and there is a resistance. The resistance is from Satan and he has legal rights when to use what we committed as sin, transgressions, etc. If you still have sin and iniquity in your heart, God does not hear you. If God does not hear you, you cannot have what you have asked for. 1 John speaks of praying according to God's will – confidence comes in when we pray according to God's will and in this confidence, we know God hears us and if we know He hears us then we have what we ask for.

The battlefield is actually a courtroom in heaven. God has allowed us in the spirit to be in that court system. Satan is in the court of heaven telling God what He should not grant you as you make your requests. It can keep you from your destiny and purpose you were made for. Principalities and powers rule regions because they have a legal right to your sin and sins of your forefathers.

SAY: What are you giving Satan as legal rights to accuse you in the courts of heaven before God?

_____

_____

_____

Worship is the atmosphere for the courts of heaven, so be sure to enter it with your worship of our amazing God.

- Begin praying in the Spirit, listening for His directions.
- Confess all personal sins revealed by the Spirit.
- Repent of all personal sins revealed by the Spirit.
- Plead the Blood of Jesus over the sin that is laid upon the altar.
- Confess all generational sin revealed by the Spirit.
- Repent of all revealed generational sin.
- Plead the Blood of Jesus over the generational sin.
- If you are interceding for someone, confess and repent for their personal and generational sin and plead the Blood of Jesus as well.
- Praise God for forgiveness! The legal issues are cleared, and the penalty has been paid.

Now, go ahead and move into your kingly position and begin making decrees about the issue in prayer about. Begin prophesying the future as the Spirit leads you. If there is any binding or losing, rebuking, it is to be done now. Follow the leading of the Holy Spirit!

Prayer Time

Our prayer time with God is very important to our relationship with Him.

Zumpano explains,

"As a believer:

1. Pray regularly. God wants to hear us pray throughout the day (Acts 10:2).
2. Pray without hindrance. Sins and other distractions can negatively affect your prayer life (Luke 22:39-46).
3. Pray expecting to get answers. The Bible gives us guidelines to follow so that our prayers will be answered (1 John 5:14-15).
4. Pray effectively. Prayer can work powerfully in the face of a crisis when God's people come together and call out to him (Acts 12:1-17).

Pray persistently. God honors persistent prayer (Luke 18:1-8).

Let's discuss praying in "tongues and its importance in spiritual warfare. Praying in "tongues" comes from the Holy Spirit through the baptism-in the-Holy Spirit. It must be asked for (Lk. 11:10-13). The believer must EXPECT to receive it, by ASKING and by FAITH, in Jesus' name. There are two types of "tongues. "Gift of tongues" manifests only in the congregation or assembly of the brethren, and usually, when it manifests, the interpretation of what is being said will be placed on the heart of another believer who is present, or the person speaking will interpret. Another type, called praying in-the-Spirit, or "personal tongues", it is for private use and personal prayer. The language of "tongues" is fluent, not repetitive. It is different for every person, and frequently varies in the same person."[13]

Our prayers must be personal. Our confessions can be spoken as death or life (Proverbs 18:21).

SAY: So, let me ask this. If you are praying for something and have not received it yet, but God has released it to us, where do you think it is?

Answer: "It's already in the spiritual realm.", Ephesians1:3. There are many jobs of the angels and one of them is to war and fight on our behalf to get it to us what you prayed for. The angels are always met with demonic opposition. (Daniel 10:12-20).

SAY: So, what do you think you must do to help the angels get your blessings to you?

Answer: You must pray and confess more of God's Word with "faith in God's Word" and "the confession of God's Word". You need faith to activate the Word of God. In the natural we fight with our faith and confession. If you give up, the angels will also give up.

Daily Confessions

Daily confessions must become a lifestyle. If you have a specific area of need in your life, then confess it in the morning, afternoon, lunch break, on your way home, and before you go to bed. Life experiences will bring many confessions and discipline is key. Daily confessions will help your prayer life.

---

13   Ben Zumpano, M.D., *Spiritual Warfare Prayers,* 1999, digital, 33.

Prayer Watches

In the Bible there were specific times when the watchmen watched over the walls of the city. Intercessors are called to the same time of watch in their prayers (Matt. 14:15-23; Psalm 119:62; Job 33:15; 22:27-28; Habakkuk 2:1; Acts 2:1-8; 2 Kings 9:17-18). At different times and seasons in your life you may find that your prayer watch time changes. Each prayer watch has a purpose. The Bible speaks about prayer watches. As you pray, you stand watch over your family, cities, and nations. You are to watch for the enemy's activities and the manifestation of God's plan. The watches are the times of the day or night that God calls us to pray. It covers 24 hours. Let's discuss and learn about the eight prayer watches.

You must pray ad seek the mind of the Lord, which is "Thy kingdom, come. Thy will be done on earth, as it is in heaven." (Matthew 6:10). You must set yourself to watch which is to set yourself to see what God will say to you. (Hab. 2:1) Practicing hearing the voice of God is essential to all the watches.

Watch	Time	Focus and Purpose
1st	6:00pm-9:00pm	**Evening Watch**. The witches go through the cities to take hold of the gates of the day (Psalm 59). Renew every covenant you have with God during this time.
2nd	9:00pm-12:00 Midnight	**Second watch; midnight watch**. Time for divine favor. **(Exo.3:21-22, 11:3-4, 12:35-36; Psalm 5:12; 45:12; Esther 2:9, 15, 17)**. In Acts 23:23 we see Paul enjoying favor from the captain of the soldiers during this same period. Pray for divine protection. (Zech. 1:10; Acts 9:23). Pray for provision to do God's work.

3rd	12:00am (Midnight)-3:00am	**Breaking of day watch** The deep sleep falls upon men according to Acts 20:7-12. According to Matt. 13:25, while men slept the enemy went to sow tares. Satanic activities are heightened. The devil operates at this time because this is the time that men are sleep and there are not so many people praying to oppose him. (Matt. 13:24; 1 Kings 3:20) It is a time for slaying; when the destroying angel goes through the camp, neighborhood, community, city, or nation (Exo. 12:29 cf. 2 Kings 19:35). It is a time to declare Psalm 91:5, 6 for the divine protection for yourself, family, church, city and nation. Its's a time of release from every prison (Isa. 42:22; Jud. 16:3; Acts 16:25; Psa. 18:27-28; 2 Kings 19:35).
4th	3:00am-6:00am	**Morning watch** This is the last watch of the night. Here is the time that the satanic agents who went out to perform their activities are returning back to their bases. This is the time the devil and his cohorts are running back 'home' so that they are not caught. This is the time to release judgment on the wicked, who remain stiff-necked after many warnings and rebukes in line with Prov. 29:1. They will be shaken out by the dayspring in line with Job 38:13. This is a time of divine judgment.
5th	6:00am-9:00am	**Early morning watch** It is a time of declaration and utterances. (Acts 2:15; Psalm 2:7-9) The spiritual significance of sunrise is having Jesus Christ the King of Kings and the Lord of Lords rise over us. Pray for the outpouring of the Holy Spirit to equip you for the day.
6th	9:00am-12 noon	It is a time for harvest, the benefits of the cross of healing, forgiveness, strength, and prosperity. Here is both Christ's sentencing by Pilate and crucifixion, and the descent of the Holy Spirit at Pentecost. Time to put off the old man, crucify the flesh and the behaviors of the devil.

7th	12:00pm-3:00pm	Pray in line with Acts 10:9 and Psalm 91:5, 6, and 14. It is the time to pray to dwell in the secret place of the Most High, abiding under the shadow of the Almighty, and making the Most High your habitation. The midday is the fullness of the day and it is the beginning of the sixth hour. Pray against Destruction that stalks at noon time. (Psalm 91:5) Destruction is released at midday according to Psalm 92:6-7. Pray and cut off all satanic arrows that are released at this time. This is the time Justice shall come to you (Isa. 7:14). This is the time of the secret place of the Most High. In Psalm 91, it says that I will not be afraid of destruction that stalks at noonday nor the arrows that fly by night.
8th	3:00pm-6:00pm	Pray for deliverance during this watch. It is also the time for the miraculous and angelic visitation (Zech. 1:10-11, 18-21). This time also the time of the evening sacrifice. It was at this time that Elijah called forth fire from Heaven to consume the prophets of Baal on Mt. Carmel (1 Kings 18:29, 30, 36-39). Isa; 17:12-14, Matt. 27:45-61; Luke 27:45-47, Mark 15:33-39; Dan. 3:8-30; Gen. 24:63; Rev. 6 and 1 Sam. 17.

F. The Believer's Authority

God has given believers the authority, power and right to rule over the earth. Authority is a general term for "dominion", "rule", or "kingdom". The word authority has many different meanings throughout the Bible.

The original Hebrew word for authority is מֶמְשָׁלָה (Strong's #4475), memshalah (mem-shaw-law'), which means to rule, dominion, or kingdom. There are different meanings for authority. In the Old Testament it has different meanings, such as, first, metaphorically "rule" of the sun or the moon is the created order by which the light of day and night is to be governed (Gen. 1:1; Ps. 136:8,9). Second, it refers to earthly kingdoms with their rulers referred in 1 Kgs.9:19; 2 Chron. 8:6; Dan. 11:5; Jer. 34:1; Jer. 51:28; Isa. 22:21). Lastly, the dominion or kingdom of God as referred in Ps. 103:22; 114:2; 145:13. It is not simply referring to the earthly locations of the divine kingdom (Israel), it is also the nature and quality of God's rule. Micah 4:8 refers to the restored kingdom of Judah.

In the New Testament the Greek word for authority is (Strong's #1849), ἐξουσία, ας, ἡ, exousia, (ex-oo-see'-ah), which means power, authority, right. All the "power" and "authority" is derived from God and may be justly utilized or abused. References to authority in the New Testament are in Luke 19;17; Rom. 9:21. Civil authority is in Luke 23;7; John 19;10; Acts 9:14; 26:10. Submission to a higher authority, for example in Matt. 8:9; Luke 7:8. Heavenly authorities are found in Col. 1:16; Eph. 3:10; 1 Pet. 3:22. God's authority is in Acts 1:7; Jude 25. Authority given to people by God are in Matt. 9:8; Eph. 1:21. Apostolic authority is found in 2 Cor. 10:8; 13:10. Exousia also means "right", 1 Cor. 9:4; 2 Thess. 3:9 which is to derive material support from one's ministry in the gospel. In Rev. 22:14 the saints in heaven are given the "right" to access the tree of life. Authority can also mean "command," "commandment" in the context of Titus 2:15, which denotes the "authority" associated with the pastoral office. In the New Testament Greek (Strong's #2003), **ἐπιταγή, ῆς, ἡ, epitage,** (ep-ee-tag-ay').

The believer's authority is to exercise your authority in Christ Jesus. You are God's ambassadors and you can speak with His authority while you are in prayer (2 Cor.5:20). You use the sword of the Spirit, which is the Word of God (Ephesians 6:17).

G. The Full Armor of God

We begin by putting on the full armor of Father God upon our spouse, each of your children, family members, relatives, friends, acquaintances, all true Christian believers and yourself. Next, put on the helmet of salvation, the breastplate of righteousness, the belt of truth and the shoes of the gospel of peace in which we stand, in your left hand pick up the shield of faith to quench EVERY fiery dart of the enemy, in you right hand pick up the sword of the Spirit which is your Word, which says that no weapon formed against me shall prosper (Ephesians 6:10-17).

In addition, believers have been given the whole armor of God to stand against the wiles of the devil" (Eph. 6:11). Each piece of the armor is to be "put on" to help believers overcome the temptations and attacks of the Evil One.

SAY: Let's learn about each one.

1) Having Girded Your Waist with Truth (v.14): The waist or abdomen was generally thought to be the seat of emotions. To gird this area with truth is to commit your emotions to believe the truth. Often a person knowingly allows herself to believe a lie because of fear of self-pity. Believers must hold a commitment to truth regardless of the repercussions. NT: John 8:32, 36.
OT: Isa. 11:5. Spiritual weapon is truth.

2) Having Put On the Breastplate of Righteousness (Eph. 6:14): The breast is generally thought of as the place of the soul. The heart must be kept pure and righteous because sin gives a foothold to the enemy. Confession and forgiveness on the basis of the blood of Christ cleanses the heart. NT: 1 John 1:9. OT: Isa. 59:17. Spiritual weapon is righteousness.

3) Having Shod Your Feet with the Preparation of the Gospel of Peace (Eph. 6:15): Proper shoes enable the feet to go from place to place. The believer is about her Father's business, which is to spread the gospel of peace and reconciliation. An undaunted sense of this mission keeps the believer headed in the right direction. NT: Matt. 28: 19, 20. OT: Isa.52:7. Spiritual weapon is the gospel of peace.

4) Taking the Shield of Faith (Eph. 6:16): The Wicked One is "the accuser of the brethren" (Rev. 12:10) and will send his fiery darts to install doubt, fear, and guilt. Faith acts as an invisible shield that deflects such false accusation NT: Heb. 6:16. OT: Psalm 35:2; Isa. 21:5. Spiritual weapon is faith.

5) Take the Helmet of Salvation (Eph. 6:17): A helmet protects the head, that is, the brain and thoughts. Assurance of salvation is a mighty defense against doubt and insecurity and the kinds of works bred by them NT: 1 John 5:11-13. OT: Isa. 59:17. Spiritual weapon is salvation.

6) Take the Sword of the Spirit (Eph. 6:17): The Word of God, the only offensive weapon is the armor, was used by the Lord Jesus against Satan (Luke 4:1-13). The living Word is powerful, effective, and instructive NT: Heb. 4:12; 2 Tim. 3:16, 17. OT: Isa. 49:2. Spiritual weapon is the Spirit, Word of God, and prayer.

7) Praying Always (Eph. 6:18): Prayer opens the channels between us and God. In the midst of battle, we as believers must keep in constant communication with our leader for direction and encouragement. Our prayers for one another are important and effectual NT: James 5:16. Spiritual weapon is to pray. (The Women's Study Bible, NKJV, 2006, The Armor of God, p. 1538)

PRAYER: I thank you Father, Lord Jesus, and Holy Spirit for this day.

"Lord Jesus Christ in Your Holy Name I put on the full armor of Father God, this day, upon my spouse, each of my children, immediate family members, relatives, friends, acquaintances, all true Christian believers who I may forget, and lastly myself, covering each and every one of us, and all that we have, and possess, with Your precious blood of protection." Let your blood wash and cleanse sin from our lives. Purify our spirits in the name of Jesus. I release the blood to rule the atmosphere and I command clearance in the air, the earth, the land, and the sea right now in the name of Jesus. Our prayers God will go up to you as a sweet-smelling savor. Jesus release a battalion of angels in this new day. I plead the blood of Jesus and I reinforce the whole armor of God from the crown of my head to the sole of my feet. I put on the helmet of salvation because You are our salvation, the breastplate of righteousness because you are our righteous, Lord, the belt of truth and the shoes of the gospel of peace in which we stand, Lord Jesus, because You are our truth and peace. In my left hand I pick up the shield of faith and I decree by trusting faith that all of Satan's plans are bound, we're loosed, and he is defeated in our lives this day and every day to come. In my right hand I pick up the sword of the Spirit, which is your Word, Lord Jesus Christ and place it in theirs for Your Word says that no weapon formed against me shall prosper. I decree all these things accomplished in Your Name, Lord Jesus Christ, Amen.

NOTES

_____

_____

_____

_____

_____

H. The Word of God

The Bible is the verbally inspired Word of God. The "Word of God," is used of both the Bible and the person of Jesus. The Word of God is inspired: "All scripture is inspired by God and profitable for teaching, for reproof, for correction, for training in righteousness," (2 Tim. 3:16).

I. Binding and Loosing Prayer

With your faith in Jesus Christ, you have his power and authority to bind evil and loose God's plans in any situation. We need to bind evil (Matthew 12:29) because Jesus explained to us that we must first bind the strongman before we can plunder his house. You must use first your inherited authority to bind the evil forces. After that, you loose or call forth God's plan for restoration.

Luke 11:21-22

"21 When a strong man armed keepeth his palace, his goods are in peace: 22 But when a stronger than he shall come upon him, and overcome him, he taketh from him all his armour wherein he trusted, and divideth his spoils."

The goods that are plundered are people, previously held in bondage. The coming of Jesus and the binding of Satan liberates the souls of people who were subject to slavery their whole life.

Binding

To bind is to fasten or tie. Bind is incidental to the picture of a strong man's house being plundered. When you bind something, you are declaring it unlawful or evil based on God's word. As co-heirs in Jesus Christ, you have his authority to execute this judgment on the forces of evil (Psalm 149:5-9). Our faith is what releases the power from heaven that binds or ties up the evil one.
Matthew 16:19; 18;18; Luke 10:19

Loosing

You are calling forth God's plan in the earth. When you loose something on earth, you "permit and declare it as proper and lawful on earth" from scriptures. It must be in accordance with God's word.

Loosing: Mark 11:15; Luke 19:31-33; Acts 27:43

"And I will give unto thee the keys of the kingdom of heaven: and whatsoever thou shalt bind on earth shall be bound in heaven: and whatsoever thou shalt loose on earth shall be loosed in heaven." (Matthew 16:19)

"Verily I say unto you, Whatsoever ye shall bind on earth shall be bound in heaven: and whatsoever ye shall loose on earth shall be loosed in heaven." (Matthew 18:18)

"Behold, I give unto you power to tread on serpents and scorpions, and over all the power of the enemy and nothing shall by any means hurt you." (Luke 10:19)

Example of a Binding Prayer: "Father God, I thank you for sending your Son Jesus to die for me, and resurrecting him to sit at your right hand in Heaven right now. I thank you for bestowing upon Him all power and authority over evil. In the name of Jesus Christ, I speak to any evil spirits, especially spirits of *_____ (fill in the blank), I bind you from attacking me now and throughout this day. Leave me now and go straight to Jesus Christ who will deal with you. I am covered and protected by the blood of Jesus Christ. Amen."

Then we can loose spirits of God into our life or the lives of others, using the name of Jesus:

Example of Loosing Spirits of God Prayer: First, we bind the plans of evil in the situation we are facing in the name of Jesus Christ. Then, we call forth God's will to be done on earth as it is in heaven.

"Father in heaven, I stand in faith on the authority I have as a believer in Jesus Christ, and a co-heir to his kingdom. In the name of Jesus Christ, I bind every evil spirit and every evil plan made in this situation. I cancel the enemy's plans and call forth God's plans for this situation. I break their power and command them to leave me now in the mighty name of Jesus. God's word says that God has plans for good and not evil (Jeremiah 29:11) for us and I claim those plans now. Father, I ask that your will be done in this situation, as it is done in heaven. I give thanks and praise to you.

In Jesus' name I pray, Amen."

"Father, I thank you for sending your Son Jesus to die for me and resurrecting him to sit at your right hand in Heaven right now. I thank you for bestowing upon Him all power and authority over evil. In the name of Jesus Christ, I speak to any evil spirits [especially spirits of _____ fill in the blank] I bind you from attacking me now and throughout this day. Leave me now in the name of Jesus. I am covered and protected by the blood of Jesus. In the name of Jesus Christ, I bind every spirit that is not the spirit. Father, I ask in the name of your precious Son that you would send ministering spirits to me. In the name of Jesus, please loose Your spirits of Adoption, Blessing, Compassion, Consideration, Contrition, Conviction, Counsel, Courage, Deliverance, Devotion, Diligence, Direction, Discernment, Discretion, Edification, Excellence, Fairness, Faith, Faithfulness, Fear of God, Freedom, Forgiveness, Glory, Goodness, Grace, Gratitude, Harmony, Healing, Holiness, Honesty, Humility, Joy, Judgment, Justice, Kindness, Knowledge, Longsuffering, Love, Meekness, Mercy, Might, Newness, Obedience , Patience, Peace, Power, Powerful anointing, Praise, Prayer, Prophecy, Purity, Repentance, Respect, Resurrection, Restoration, Self-control, Sincerity, Sound mind, Supplication, Trust, Truth, Understanding, Unity, Wisdom. Amen.

J. Agreeing

Agree or agreement is "consent given between the parties involved", "be of one mind or like-minded", "come to an agreement", "make a formal pledge". When two or more people are gathered together to pray, and they agree, this is also a powerful spiritual weapon against the enemy. Amen,

Mat 18:19

19 Again I say unto you, That if two of you shall agree on earth as touching anything that they shall ask, it shall be done for them of my Father which is in heaven.

Job 22:28

28 Thou shalt also decree a thing, and it shall be established unto thee: and the light shall shine upon thy ways.

Matt. 5:25; 18:19; 20:13

Mk. 14:56,59; Acts 15:15; 28:25; Rom. 9:16; John 5:8

8. Deliverance

The word proclaims that a believer is sealed for the day of redemption by the Holy Spirit (Eph. 4:30). No demon can break into the sealed area, but they can go into other areas as the "flesh".

Demons can also attach themselves to the soul of man or the heart of man. The heart is the representation of the soul man or the heart of man. The heart is the representation of the soul man (your intellect, will, and emotions in your soul. (Matt. 15:1-20; Mark 17:21-23).

ASK: How do you know if you need deliverance? Most of our problems are of a carnal nature.

Answer: When we do what we do because we want to do what we do and we don't give up what we do, because we just want to do it.

So, what you have to do with flesh is to crucify it. It has to die. Paul tells us how to die to sin in Romans 12:1-2.

The word is telling us to lay our life down as a sacrifice to God and change the way we think to what is good and acceptable to the will of God. So, if you have a problem, and you have crucified the flesh, fasted, prayed and the problem does not go away, then it is of a demonic influence.

There are several ways to know if somebody needs deliverance, which are:

Marzullo explains,

1. "By discerning of spirits: which is when the Holy Spirit discloses to you the source of the problem as you are ministering to others. Some people see the demonic spirits with their eyes or in their mind; others get a word of knowledge or an impression or vision from the Holy Spirit. It works with a word of knowledge, or impressions, or visions. Word of knowledge is knowledge that only God knows and then He reveals it to you, and when that word is declared and spoken, then He reveals it to you, and when that word is declared and spoken, it reveals what was hidden in the dark and brings it into the light.

2. By the symptoms, confusion, irrationality: These indicate the presence of demons by their conversation by their speech, by what they say, i.e. lying, cursing, telling dirty stories, filthy speech, always gossiping, bragging, complaining, criticizing, judging everyone, taking offense easily

3. When the person is having problem in the sexual realm: I.e. Unclean sexual acts, perversion, sexual fantasies. The source of the problem is lust.

4. Addiction Problems: Tobacco, alcohol, drugs, caffeine, coca cola, tea, sugar, sweets. The root of addiction must be dealt with.

5. Infirmities: The evil spirit of infirmity had to be cast out first, and then the laying on of hands for healing in Jesus' name.

6. Involvement in the realm of the occult: For example, channeling, divination, zodiac astrology, horoscope, hypnotism, Spiritism, spiritualism, Chinese astrology, numerology, tarot cards,

Taosim, I Ching, Kabbalah, Zen eastern practices and religions, Buddhism, Hinduism, Vedanta, Brahmanism, Reiki, astral projection, automatic writing, runes, Ouija board, telepathy, readings from psychics, drugs, acupuncture, Mayan philosophy, fairy tales, reincarnation, karma, four leaf clover superstition, spells, fortune cookie superstition, spiritual healers, transcendental meditation, yoga, chakra, third eye, E.S.P., Ramtha cult, channeling the gods of this world, worshiping Roman, Greek, Egyptian gods, psychic powers, black magic, white magic, necromancy, soul travel, crystal powers, para psychology, magic healings, demon worship, Satan worship, Lucifer worship.

7. Your natural eye: When you are ministering or praying for a person and the demons will start making them roll their eyes back in their sockets, so all you see is the white of their eyes, twitching nose or their hands and feet claw-up, means presence of occult or witchcraft spirits."[14]

There are many more. If you have ever been involved in any occult practice, you must ask God to forgive you for it, it is sin and renounce it, then you must also cast out the spirit of it in the name of Jesus and the spirit of the covenant you made with the devil when you walked in agreement with him when you practiced these things.

The word "occult" is derived from the Latin occultus, which means something "hidden" or "concealed," referring to that which is inner, secret, mysterious, and beyond the range of ordinary human knowledge.
(The Woman's Study Bible, NKJV, 2006, The Occult, p. 248)

Deliverance is a gift which helps man and woman live an aggressive and effective Christian life. In Matthew 15:27 Jesus declares that deliverance is the children's bread. In order to receive and keep your deliverance, you must change your mind and be tired of being in sin, sick, and want to be set free. You must submit to God and take a stand against the devil.

SAY: Are there any questions? (Discussion Opportunity)

_____
_____
_____
_____
_____

9. Consecration

Consecration is to devote, separate, dedicate and give wholly over to God. Consecration is the act of dedicating oneself to a specific purpose or intention (Joshua 3:5; Lev. 20:7; 2 Cor. 6:17;

[14] Marzullo Jr., *Spiritual Warfare Now-Fighting for the Sons of Men*, 2013, 30-36.

Rom.12: 1-2). God calls his people to be consecrated to Him. Once you decide to consecrate yourself, God will consecrate you-making you holy. It will prepare you for an unknown future (Joshua 3:4, 8, 14-17) and to stand before God and your enemies (Joshua 7:6-14). It makes you strong ((Heb. 7: 23-28; 10:14). God through the blood of Jesus, intercedes on our behalf (Heb. 7:17-28; Jer. 13: 15-17). It represents your purity (Matt. 5:8; Job 1:1, 5). Consecration is a way of living. You must be prepared to continue pursuing God for the rest of your life.

When you consecrate yourself

- Dedicate your heart to God. You are making a conscious, willing decision to dedicate your soul, mind, heart, and body to God.
- Have a Motive. Christ must be a priority. Remember that your motive is a factor and must be changed when you consecrate yourself to Jesus Christ as Lord and Savior., Repent of your sins and the need for salvation and forgiveness.
- Be baptized.
- Separate yourself from the world and make the spiritual life a priority over the flesh.
- You must draw closer to God through regular prayer.

10. Prayer Session

Each one of you will write want you need deliverance from and we are going to pray. For example, known family bloodline sin, curses, poverty, trials, situations, behaviors, beliefs, addictions, material items, sickness, etc. Even though we will be going into prayer, remember as you walk with God, it will be a lifelong pursuit for you to release things or persons from your life as you go through your life experiences. As you continue in this discipleship plan, the last four sections are vital to you for fulfilling the assignment of the Great Commission given by Jesus Christ. Let's get free, in the name of Jesus!

11. Closing

Reflection in Action by Connection
Answer the questions on the lines provided.

Question 1: What is the believer's authority?
A:_____
Answer: The believer's authority is to exercise your authority in Christ Jesus. The believer is God's ambassador and can speak with His authority while in prayer. You use the sword of the Spirit, which is the Word of God.

Question 2: What are the components of the armor of God?
A: _____

Answer: Gird your waist with truth, put on the breastplate of righteousness, shod your feet with the preparation of the gospel of peace, taking the shield of faith, helmet of salvation, sword of the Spirit, and to pray always.

Question 3: What is binding and loosing?
A:_____
Answer: Binding is when you declare it unlawful, or evil based on God's Word. Faith is key because it releases the power from heaven that binds or ties up the evil one. Loosing is when you loose something on the earth, you "permit and declare it as proper and lawful on the earth".

Question 4: What are two examples of unanswered prayer?
A:_____
Answer: Two examples of unanswered prayer can be lack of sincerity, unbelief.

Question 5: Name the four levels of spiritual warfare working for Satan.
A:_____
Answer: principalities, powers, rulers of darkness, and spiritual host so wickedness in heavenly places.

<u>**SAY**</u>: You have made it this far and you can't and won't turn back.

Amen.

GOAL FIVE

PRAISE & WORSHIP

LESSON PLAN

Date & Time:	Curriculum Area: Praise & Worship	Goal /Unit Topic: Goal Five

Key enduring understandings, concepts, abilities, and/or values.
Explained in the Introduction

Intended learning outcomes (to know, to do, to create, to value, etc.)
Explained in the Overview

Assessment Strategies: How will you assess attainment of the intended learning outcome?
Questions & Answers, Dialect, Interaction, Pre/Post Tests??

Materials/Preparation/ Area Setup:
Materials: Poster board, Dry Erase Markers
Preparation: Decorations, Poster board
Area Setup: For each disciple, place on the desk a blue pen, highlighter, notebook, goal five

Introduction	***Setting the Stage***: engaging, motivating, experiencing, connecting with prior knowledge, reflecting, conjecturing, posing problems
Once the Introduction and Overview have been completed, then move on to the Bible book recitals. It will be recited every time that we meet with the disciples.	
Guided learning steps The learning steps are as follows: 1. Instructions on Praise 2. Forms of Praise 3. Instructions on Worship 4. Expressions of Worship 5. Confessions of Praise & Worship 6. Hebrew Words Relating to Praise & Worship 7. Forms of Worship 8. Closing	***Disclosing***: acquiring knowledge/skills, conceptualizing, developing, understanding, integrating ***Practicing, Reinforcing***: modeling, giving instruction, checking for understanding, guided practice, independent practice, applying, posing and solving problems
Closure Prayer, Questions & Answers, Comments	***Transcending***: summing up, responding, creating, performing, committing, evaluating
Modifications: How will you change the lesson to meet the needs of the individual students?	
Personal notes/reminders/homework/assignments	
Post-lesson reflections	

Goal Five: Praise & Worship

INTRODUCTION

Praise and Worship should be a daily activity in our spiritual walk with Jesus Christ.

ASK: What is praise in the biblical sense?

Christians often speak of "praising God," and the Bible commands all living creatures to praise the Lord (Psalm 150:6). One Hebrew word for "praise" is yadah, meaning "praise, give thanks, or confess." A second word often translated "praise" in the Old Testament is zamar, "sing praise." A third word translated "praise" is halal (the root of hallelujah), meaning "to praise, honor, or commend." All three terms contain the idea of giving thanks and honor to one who is worthy of praise.[1]

Overview

I. Goal Lesson:

Goal five teaches about praise and worship.

II. Goal Objectives:

Upon completion of this lesson, the disciple will be able to:

    a. praise and worship the Lord daily,
    b. explain the act of communion and giving, and
    C. explain the importance of fasting.

III. Bible Books Recital

Genesis to Revelation

1. Instructions on Praise

We praise God by song, music, shabach (to address in a loud tone an attitude of wholehearted praise), lifting up of hands, kneeling down (means to bow low as a sign of reverence and adoration), dance, speaking about God and what he has done in our lives. We say hallelujah, Praise God, Amen and so many more words of praise. The scriptures are full of God's instructions to His people on becoming praisers and worshipers of Him. It is important to spend time reading from His word so that we will know how to praise Him. Psalm 98 gives instructions on praise.

2. Forms of Praise

Who is to praise God? All of God's people, all of creation (Ps. 145: 4, 5; Is. 55:12). Where do you praise God? Praise is fitting wherever you are (Ps. 96:3). How do you praise God? Praise is expressed through words and music (Ps. 33:1-3). When do you praise God? God should be praised at all times (Ps. 34:1). What do you praise God for? God is praised for His greatness (Ps.150:2). Why do you praise God? God is worthy of your praise (Rev. 5:12).

Praise is your best weapon against Satan. When you praise God, you are showing the heavenly hosts, powers, principalities, demons and darkness, and angels of light that your great God is worthy of praise—no matter what your circumstances. Genuine praise must flow from your heart even during times of sorrow, discouragement, trial, and temptation (Ps. 42:5). The praise of His people brings glory to God.

(The Woman's Study Bible, 2006, 774.)

3. Instructions on Worship

Scripture: 1 Tim 2:1-4

Worship activities spring from the heart, such as loving God, praying to God, rejoicing in God, turning to God, seeking God, trusting God, and yielding to God.

Worship "in truth" connects the heart or spirit of worship with the truth about God and his work of redemption as revealed in the person of Jesus Christ and the Scriptures. David understood the importance of worshiping in truth and the necessary linkage between "truth" and the Word of God when he wrote, "Teach me your way, O Lord, and I will walk in your truth; give me an undivided heart, that I may fear [i.e., worship] your name" (Psalm 86:11; Psalm 145:18). Here both the Old and New Covenants agree! The true worship of God is essentially internal, a matter of the heart and spirit rooted in the knowledge of and obedience to the revealed Word of God.

(Retrieved May 21, 2016 from www.biblestudytools.com; Psalm 134:1-3 Worship)

Col. 3:16 instructs worship leaders to teach and admonish through singing psalms, hymns, and spiritual songs. The primary function of a worship leader is to teach and admonish. The songs that we use are simply the method used to accomplish the mission.

4. Expressions of Worship

- Singing (Eph. 5:9)
- Commitment (Rom. 12:1-2)
- Praying (Ps. 5:6)
- Hearing the Word (John 17:17)
- Giving (1 Cor. 6:1-2)
- Baptism (Romans 6:3-4)
- Meditating (Hab. 2:20)
- Lord's Supper (1 Cor. 11: 23-26)

5. Confessions of Praise & Worship

- Jesus is the great Bread of Life unto my soul (John 6:35).
- The name of the Lord is Wonderful, Counselor, the Mighty God, the Everlasting Father, and the Prince of Peace (Isaiah 9:6).
- There is none like the Lord in all the earth. For the Lord is great, and His name is Great and Mighty (Jeremiah 10:6).
- Jesus Christ is the King of all Kings, and He is the Lord of all Lords (1 Timothy 6:1).
- Unto the Lord is the Kingdom, and the power, and the glory, forever and ever (Matthew 6:13).
- Great is the Lord and greatly to be praised. His greatness is unsearchable and will never end (Psalms 145:3).
- Jesus Christ is the Alpha and the Omega. He is the first and the last. He is the beginning and the end. He is the one who is, the one who was, and the one who is soon to come (Revelation 1:8).

6. Hebrew Words Relating to Praise & Worship

The Old Testament was originally written in Hebrew. There are so many Hebrew words that related to praise and worship. Let's go through a couple of them more in detail.

Hebrew Word	Description
Barak	To kneel or bow, to give reverence to God as an act of adoration. To be attuned to him and his presence. Psalm 34:1; Psalm 100:4; Psalm 95:6
Hallal	To praise, to make a show or rave about, to glory in or boast upon, to be clamorously foolish about your adoration of God. Psalm 35:9; Psalm 2:23; Psalm 44:8; Psalm 63:5
Ranan	To creak, to emit a stridulous stand, to shout aloud for joy. Psalm 7:17; Psalm 33:1; Psalm 98:4

Schachah	To depress or prostate in homage or loyalty to God, bow down, fall down flat. Psalm 29:2; Psalm 66:4; Psalm 95:6
Tehillah	To sing hallal, a new song, a hymn of spontaneous praise glorifying God in song. Psalm 34:1; Psalm 40:3; Psalm 149:1
Yadah	To use, hold out the hand, to revere or worship (with extended hands, praise, thankful, thanksgiving). Psalm 33:2; Psalm 61:8; Psalm 18:49
Zamar	To touch the strings or parts of a musical instrument and playing it, make music accompanied by the voice, to celebrate in song and music, give praise, sing forth praises, psalms. Psalm 66:2; Psalm 71:22; Psalm144:9.
Alats	To jump for joy, exult, be joyful, rejoice, triumph. Psalm 5:11; Psalm 9:2; Psalm 68:3
Chuwl	To twist or whirl in a circular spiral manner, to dance. Judges 21:23
Kabod	Splendor, copiousness, glorious, glory, honorable. Psalm 29:1; Psalm 66:2; Psalm 96:8
Kara	To bend he knee, to sink, to prostate, bow down self, bring down low. Psalm 22:9; Psalm 95:6
Macha	To rub or strike the hands together, clap. Psalm 98:8
Nacah	To lift, exalt, extol, hold, up, honorable, magnify, regard, respect, yield. Psalm 28:2; Psalm 63:4; Psalm 13:2
Patsach	To break out (in joyful sound), break forth in joy, make a loud noise. Psalm 98:4; Psalm 98:6; Psalm 100:1
Rinnah	A shrill sound, shout of grief or joy, gladness, proclamation, rejoicing, shouting, triumph, singing. Psalm 107:22; Psalm 118:15; Psalm 126:6
Samach	To brighten up, cheer up, make glad, make merry. Psalm 31:7; Psalm 48:11; Psalm 105:3
Shabach	To address in aloud tone, a loud adoration, a shout, proclaiming with a loud voice (unashamed), to glory, triumph, power, a testimony of praise. Psalm 63:3; Psalm 106:47; Psalm 145:4

7. Forms of Worship

A. Giving –Tithes and Offerings

"Every man according as he purposeth in his heart, so let him give; not grudgingly, or of necessity; for God loveth a cheerful giver (2 Corinthians 9:7).

The grace of giving. "Therefore, as ye abound in everything, in faith, and utterance, and knowledge, and in all diligence, and in your love to us, see that ye abound in this grace also (2 Corinthians 8:7).

Tithes is 1/10th of our wages. Offerings are what we give after we have paid tithes. This offering must come from our 9/10th since 1/10th is already the Lord's.

B. Giving a seed offering

Giving a seed offering is also known as sowing a seed or sowing alms. (Luke 6:38; Matt. 13:13; Luke 8:4-8). Sowing a seed of money into a particular ministry. Alms are sown for the poor, for widows, and orphans. Water your giving of your seed with prayer and scripture. Give from the heart with joy and keep your giving in private in accordance with Matt. 6:1-2.

What happens when you give?

1. You realized your purpose (You were created with the potential to exhibit characteristics of the One whose mark we bear),

- God is pleased (When you give with the right motives, God is pleased. When you act in generosity, God is happy),
- God provides for you (He provides daily bread),
- You gain perspective (A change in perspective can change your life), and
- You partner with God (You are funding a mission with eternal sacrifice).

We must always be willing to give our tithes and offerings and also to others.

Let's discuss some principles of giving.

- As you give to the Lord's work, give with the belief that all we have belongs to God and commit to use all of it as He wants
- It is an act of worship
- It reflects faith in God to provide for your needs.
- Giving should be sacrificial but yet generous. Paul gave an example of that in 2 Corinthians 8:1-5. The poor Christians in Macedonia sacrificed to give generously. They were in poverty but overflowed in a wealth of generosity.
- It reflects spiritual worthiness. If we cannot be entrusted with the unrighteous wealth, how can you be entrusted with the money God entrusts with? If we cannot give to Christ's kingdom, how can we handle spiritual riches?
- If we love God we should be motivated to give to God. Giving should be measured in the heart. Give because of your love for Him.
- Giving must be willingly, thankfully, and cheerfully. In 2 Corinthians 9:7: "Each one must give as he has decided in his heart, not reluctantly or under compulsion, for God loves a cheerful giver." Do you "just give," or do you give to God?
- Give to respond to a real need.
- Giving should be planned and systematic. Give as God prospers and according to a plan.
- As you give generously, you will receive bountiful blessing. Luke 6:38. If you give to God, God will give to you. If you give bountifully, He will give bountifully.

God will bless you in this life if you love and trust Him enough to be generous in giving.

C. Communion

Communion is the act of breaking bread and drinking wine in remembrance of Jesus Christ. The bread represents the body of Jesus Christ and the wine represents the blood he shed on the cross at Calvary. Communion can be done in fellowship with others and as often as you meet.

<u>Scripture:</u> 1 Corinthians 11:23-26; Matthew 26:26-29; Mark 14:22-25; Luke 22:17-20; 1 Corinthians 10:16-17; John 6:47-51; John 6:53-58; John 6:26-27, 35.

D. What is Fasting?

The purpose of fasting is self-humbling. Fasting is abstinence from food for spiritual purposes. It is a scriptural means ordained by God for us to humble ourselves before Him (Matthew 18:4; Matthew 23:12; James 4:10; 1 Peter 5:6; Psalm 35:13; Ezra 8:21-23; Luke 4:1-2). It is to humble the soul (Ezra 8:21), to seek the Lord (2 Chron. 20:3, 4). To chasten the soul (Psalms 69:10), to prepare for spiritual warfare (Matt. 17:21). Fasting was also a part of the life and ministry of Jesus and of the New Testament church. Jesus also taught His disciples to fast. It is an expected discipline of followers of Jesus Christ (Matt. 6:16).

It is our obligation as Christians to fast. Fasting transfers us from the natural to the supernatural. Therefore, the key to successful Christian living is knowing how to release the power of the Holy Spirit in our lives so that we can do the things we could not do in our strength. The carnal nature is in opposition to the Spirit of God. If we yield to the carnal nature, we are opposing the Spirit of God. If we are going to yield to the Holy Spirit, we must deal with the carnal nature. The carnal nature must be brought into subjection to the Holy Spirit. When you fast, you serve notice both on your body and your carnal nature: "You don't control me. I'm not subject to you. You're my servant. You'll obey what the Spirit of God in me declares I have to do."

Faith needs prayer for its development and full growth, and prayer needs fasting for the same reason. Fasting works when combined with prayer and faith. To fast means to abstain from food. Fasting humbles the soul before God (Ps. 35:13); chastens the soul (Ps. 69:10); and crucifies the appetites and denies them so as to give the entire time to prayer (2 Sam. 12:16-23; Mt. 4:1-11). It manifests earnestness before God to the exclusion of all else (1 Cor. 7:5); shows obedience; gives the digestive system a rest (Mt. 6:16-18; 9:15; Lk. 5:33); demonstrates the mastery of man over appetites; aids in victory over temptation; helps to attain power over demons; develops faith; crucifies unbelief; and empowers prayer (Mt. 4:1-11; 17:14-21). Christians should do more fasting until they receive power with God over all powers of the devil.

Promised blessings associated with fasting:

- answered prayer, insight and restoration (Zech. 8:19)
- rewarded by God the Father (Matthew 6:17,18)
- joy, gladness and cheerfulness (Zech. 8:19)
- spiritual power over demons (Mark 9:29)
- effects of fasting (1 Kings 21:28-29; Psalms 109:24; Matthew 15:32; Mark 8:2-3).

There are various types of fasting. The full/normal fast which abstains from all food except water. The partial fast is limitation of the diet, but not abstaining from all food (Daniel 1:2). An absolute fast is avoiding all food and liquid, even water. The Daniel fast is normally for 21 days. When fasting be sure to drink water, 100% apple, cranberry or grape juice (no additives). You may also drink herbal teas (no non-herbal teas or coffee) and sweeten with honey. When you break your fast to eat a meal, pray, stick to healthy foods including lots of vegetables, healthy soups and fruits. Spend time in the word and in prayer as often as you can throughout the day.

If fasting is done without a biblical purpose, it can be miserable, self-entered experience about willpower and endurance. Hunger should be reminding you of your spiritual purpose. When the hunger comes, just pray about your purpose. Here are some biblical purposes for fasting:

- To strengthen your prayer. God is pleased to hear us praying (Neh. 1:4; Dan. 9:3)
- to seek God's guidance
- to express grief (Judges 20:26;1 Sam. 31:13)
- to seek deliverance or protection (2 Chronicles 20:3-4; Esther 4:16; Psalm 109)
- expresses repentance and returning to God. It can signal a commitment to obedience and a new direction (Joel 2:12; Jonah 3:5-8)
- it is an expression of humility before God
- to express concern for the work of God (Nehemiah 1:3-4)
- to minister to the needs of others
- to overcome temptation and to dedicate yourself to God
- to express love and to worship to God

As we fast it should be more important to us than what we are seeking from God during the fast. Before fasting we must have a purpose, a biblical, God-centered purpose.

E. Prayer

Prayer is spiritual communication between man and God. It is a spiritual communion with God in supplication, petition, imprecations, thanksgiving, adoration, confession, and intercession. The Holy Spirit's presence prompts prayer.

Prayer is:

1. Your relationship with God must be personal. You must be intimately fellowshipping with God. You must approach God with a one-on-one, intimate, personal relationship with Him. Read the Bible so His words will abide in you.

2. The will of God. Your prayer request must line up with the will of God in your life (1 John 5:14). You should analyze your prayer request, ask the Holy Spirit if you should approach the Father with the specific prayer request. You will have an "inner feeling" from Him if you should proceed.

3. God hears prayers of the righteous. If you are not keeping His Commandments and living a righteous life in his eyes, God will not hear your prayers. Sanctification is a process that God begins so you can be saved and born again. You will begin to be formed into the image of His Son Jesus Christ. There will be boundaries set by God for your life. The Holy Spirit will give convictions as to how far you can go with God.

4. To state your case with God (Isa. 1:18; 43:25). Learn to talk and dialogue with Him, then state your case before God with your reasons and contentions as to what and why you are praying for.

5. To ask, seek, and knock (Matt. 7:7-11). By asking, the prayer must be in His perfect will for your life. If you pray out of God's will, we are asking "amiss". Amiss means "wrongly" or "mistakenly." By seeking, if at first you have no success, you will have to seek Him for whatever God is wanting to bring your way. By knocking, it means to "tap on a door". Knock and it will be "opened" to you. Knocking means asking and possibly seeking more than one time for whatever is it that you are asking God for.

6. The power of agreement (Matt. 18:19). God moves when a group of sincere, passionate, intense believers approach Him with the same exact prayer request at the same time.

7. The power of intercessory prayer is when you step into the gap and pray for someone's else's prayer need before God the Father. God is looking for intercessors (Ezek. 22:30; Isa. 59:16; Psalm 106:23)

8. To pray for something more than one time. We can pray for something multiple times and it can be doubt or unbelief. There are times that you will have to press in and ask God more than one time for what you are praying for. It is prayer warfare (Luke 11:5-9). It is wrestling with God like Jacob (Gen. 3:26). It is fervent prayer (James 5:16-18). Elijah prayed earnestly and fervently, which is a higher level of intensity to your prayers. Pray without ceasing (1 Thess. 5:16).

9. To not lose heart. Sometimes you go deeper into prayer and you begin to feel discouraged, frustrated, or impatient. God can be testing your patience, stamina, or perseverance. Do not give up, get mad, or walk from the Lord. Luke 18:1-8. God wants to see if you will continue in prayer.

10. The intercessory ministries of Jesus Christ and the Holy Spirit. (Heb. 7:25; Rom. 8:26-27, 34). The Holy Spirit will make intercession for us. The Holy Spirit will guide and lead you as to what to pray for and what not to pray for, but He can also guide to how to Word your prayers to God.

11. Prayers of Thanksgiving.

Praying the Names of God

You are ELELYON: The Most High God.	Gen. 14:18-20
You are ELOHIYM: The God of creation.	Gen. 3:3
You are EL SHADDAI: You the God of the "Much More", and You provide more than enough for me.	Gen. 17:1,2; Gen. 28:3; Gen. 35:11; Gen. 48:3,4; Gen. 49: 24,25; Num. 24: 4,16; Ruth 1:20,21; Isa. 60:15,16; Isa. 66:10-13; Rev. 16:7,14; Rev. 19:15; Rev. 21:22,2
You are JEHOVAH: The Great "I Am".	Gen. 2:4
You are JEHOVAH SHALOM: The Lord My Peace.	Judg. 6:24
You are JEHOVAH NISSI: The Lord, My Banner	Ex. 17:15
You are JEHOVAH JIREH: You are the Lord, my Provider.	Gen. 22:14
You are JEHOVAH RAPHA: The Lord that heals me.	Exo. 15:26; Psalm 30:2; 2 Kgs.20:1,4-5
You are JEHOVAH TSIDKENU: The Lord my righteousness.	Jer. 23:6
You are JEHOVAH M'KADDESH: The Lord my sanctification.	Lev. 20:1-8; Matt. 20:16; John 15:19; Exo. 31:12-31; Lev. 20:7-20; 8; 1 Sam. 2;2
You are JEHOVAH SHAMMAH: You are always there for me.	Ezek. 48:35
You are JEHOVAH SABAOTH: The Lord of hosts.	1 Sam. 1:3
You are JEHOVAH ROHI: The Lord who is my Shepherd, and shall not want or be in lack of any good or needful thing.	Psalm 23
You are ADONAY: The Sovereign God. You bought me with a price.	Ps. 2:4

F Praying the Names of Jesus

The Resurrection & The Life	John 11:25
Advocate	1 John 2:1
Shiloh	Genesis 49:10
Faithful & True Witness	Revelation 3:14
Judge	Acts 10:42
Master	Matthew 8:19
Savior	John 4:42
Rock	1 Corinthians 10:4
Man of Sorrows	Isaiah 53:3
Branch	Isaiah 11:1
Head of the Church	Ephesians 5:23
Shepherd & Bishop of Souls	1 Peter 2:25
High Priest	Hebrews 6:20
Living Water	John 4:10
Rose of Sharon	Song of Solomon 2:1
Image of the Invisible God	Colossians 1:15
Anchor	Hebrews 6:19
Bread of Life	John 6:35
Messiah	Daniel 9:25
Alpha & Omega	Revelation 22:13
Mediator	1 Timothy 2:5
True Vine	John 15:1
The Door	John 10:9
I Am	John 8:58
Teacher	John 3:2
Light of the World	John 8:12
The Beloved	Ephesians 1:6
Good Shepherd	John 10:11
Servant	Matthew 12:18
Carpenter	Mark 6:23
Holy One	Mark 1:24
The Word	John 1:1

Bridegroom	Matthew 9:15
Lamb of God	John 1:29
Chief Cornerstone	Ephesians 2:20
Redeemer	Job 19:25

Author & Finisher of Our Faith	Hebrews 12:2
The Almighty	Revelation 1:8
Everlasting Father	Isaiah 9:6
Wonderful Counselor	Isaiah 9:6
Lamb of God	John 1:29
Lion of the Tribe of Judah	Revelation 5:5
Dayspring	Luke 1:78
The Amen	Revelation 3:14
Immanuel	Matthew 1:23
Son of Man	Matthew 20:28
Prophet	Matthew 21:11
Prince of Peace	Isaiah 9:6
Bright Morning Star	Revelation 2:16
King of the Jews	Mark 15:26
The Way, The Truth, & The Life	John 14:6

We praise and worship Jesus when we pray and say his many names.

G. **Praying the Names of Holy Spirit**

Spirit of God	Matt. 3:16
Spirit of the Lord	Luke 4:18
Spirit of Our God	1 Cor. 6:11
Spirit	Num. 11:25
Spirit of Glory	1 Peter 4:14
Spirit of the Lord God	Isa. 61:1
Spirit of Jesus	Acts 16:7
Spirit of Jesus Christ	Phil. 1:19
Spirit of His Son	Gal. 4:6
Spirit of Counsel & Might	Isa. 11:2
Spirit of the Living God	2 Cor. 3:3
Spirit of Truth	John 14:17
Spirit of Holiness	Rom. 1:4
Spirit of Grace	Heb. 10:29
Spirit of Adoption	Rom. 8:15
Spirit of Faith	2 Cor. 4:13
Comforter	John 14:26

According to Strong's #7307: the noun spirit is related to a verb meaning "to breathe" or "to blow. It can signify breath (Job 9:18,19:17), wind (Gen. 8:1; Ex. 10:13), air (Eccl. 1:14; Is. 26:18), the breath of life (whether animal or human, see Gen. 6:17; 7:15), disposition or mood (Gen.

14:8; Ezek. 21:7; an evil or distressing spirit (1 Sam. 16:14-16, or the Spirit of God (Gen. 1:2; Ps. 51:11. The endowment of God's Holy Spirit is a special gift to believers, which brings spiritual life (Ps. 51:10,11; 143:10, power (Judg. 6:34, wisdom and understanding (Is. 11:12, and divine revelation which leads to a better understanding of God's Word and His perfect ways (Joel 2:28; Is. 61:1,2.

Our daily praise, reading of the word, studying the word, praying, giving in your tithes and offerings, decreeing and declaring of the Word of God are all forms of worship.

8. Closing

Reflection in Action by Connection
Answer the questions on the lines provided.

Question 1: What is prayer? – 3 lines
A; _____

Answer: A personal relationship with God through communication. It is the will of God. Prayer is spiritual communication between man and God.

Question 2: Do you understand the importance of fasting? What is it's importance?- 2 lines
A:
_____

Answer: The importance of fasting is the believer will abstain from food for a spiritual purpose in mind. The importance for the believer is that it will humble the soul, seek the Lord, to chasten the soul, to prepare for spiritual warfare. It is a discipline of the believer's journey.

Question 3: Are you applying the expressions of worship to your life daily? Yes or No. Either answer explain how and why?—3 lines
A: _____

Answer: The expression of worship is also a daily discipline of the believer.

Question 4: Do you believe praise is important for the kingdom, and why?-3 lines
A: _____

Answer: Praise is important for the kingdom because you are showing the heavenly hosts, powers, principalities, demons and darkness, and angels of light that God is worthy of the praise in all circumstances.

Question 5: How often will you make confessions daily for your desired result in your life? What will be your focus? - 3 lines

A: _____

Answer: A minimum of three times a day.

SAY: You have completed goal five on praise and worship. Praise God!

GOAL SIX

KINGDOM AND CHURCH

LESSON PLAN

Date & Time:	Curriculum Area: Kingdom and Church	Goal /Unit Topic: Goal Six
Key enduring understandings, concepts, abilities, and/or values. Explained in the Introduction		
Intended learning outcomes (to know, to do, to create, to value, etc.) Explained in the Overview		
Assessment Strategies: How will you assess attainment of the intended learning outcome? Questions & Answers, Dialect, Interaction, pre/post tests		
Materials/Preparation/ Area Setup: Materials: Poster board, Dry Erase Markers Preparation: Decorations, Poster board Area Setup: For each disciple, place on the desk a blue pen, highlighter, notebook, goal six		

Introduction Once the Introduction and Overview have been completed, then move on to the Bible book recitals. It will be recited every time that we meet with the disciples.	*Setting the Stage*: engaging, motivating, experiencing, connecting with prior knowledge, reflecting, conjecturing, posing problems
Guided learning steps The learning steps are as follows: <table><tr><td>1. Kingdom of God</td><td>15. Salvation</td></tr><tr><td>2. Kingdom of Heaven</td><td>16. Stewardship</td></tr><tr><td>3. Kingdom of God vs Kingdom of Heaven</td><td>17. Church Discipline</td></tr><tr><td>4. Creation</td><td>18. Teaching</td></tr><tr><td>5. The Apostolic Church</td><td>19. Government and Citizenship</td></tr><tr><td>6. Christians and Christianity</td><td>20. Relationships</td></tr><tr><td>7. Five-Fold Ministry</td><td>21. Racial/Class Discrimination</td></tr><tr><td>8. Pastor/Shepherd</td><td>22. Healing</td></tr><tr><td>9. Role of a Disciple Making Pastor</td><td>23. Spiritual Gifts</td></tr><tr><td>10. Role of a Pastor's Spouse (Male or Female)</td><td>24. Grace</td></tr><tr><td>11. Role of a Minister, Reverend, Ordained Reverend, Elder, Deacon</td><td>25. Healthy Body, Healthy Church</td></tr><tr><td>12. Leaders and Leadership</td><td>26. Success</td></tr><tr><td>13. Leadership of Jesus Christ</td><td>27. Warfare Prayer for the Church</td></tr><tr><td>14. Baptism</td><td>28. Closing</td></tr></table>	*Disclosing*: acquiring knowledge/skills, conceptualizing, developing, understanding, integrating *Practicing, Reinforcing*: modeling, giving instruction, checking for understanding, guided practice, independent practice, applying, posing and solving problems
Closure Prayer, Questions & Answers, Comments	*Transcending:* summing up, responding, creating, performing, committing, evaluating
Modifications: How will you change the lesson to meet the needs of the individual students?	
Personal notes/reminders/homework/assignments	
Post-lesson reflections	

INTRODUCTION

The church is both the center and agent for the kingdom of God in the world. The book of Acts gives us the story of God's mission. The story focuses on sending and going into the world, calling peoples of all nations, tongues, and tribes to glorify God through living worshipful lives. The five-fold ministry and the leaders operating in the church are to be the example of the Christian life because the flock and even the unbeliever looks to them for leadership.

Overview

I. Goal Lessons

Goal six explores, explains, and teaches about the Kingdom of God and the Church.

II. Goal Objectives

Upon completion of this lesson, the disciple will be able to explain:

    a. the roles and functions of the five-fold ministry, leadership and the church,

    b. the role of the Pastor's spouse, if applicable, and

    c. the church and its activities.

III. Bible Books Recital

Genesis to Revelation

1. Kingdom of God

What is a kingdom? A kingdom is ruled by a King. The King is the ruler of the kingdom territory. The King expects the people to reflect him and obey the rules that have been put in place. The Kingdom of God is God's government operating on earth from the Kingdom of Heaven. The Kingdom of God is the spiritual reign or authority of God. It is God's rulership and dominion over the heaven and the earth. The Kingdom of Heaven is the administration. The men and women on earth are of His heavenly kingdom. We must walk as ambassadors on the Earth to win souls to fulfill the Great Commission. The Bible is the ambassador's constitution. The earth is in a spiritual battle for a Kingdom, the Kingdom of Heaven, and a Kingdom with its capital, which is Jerusalem.

Here on Earth

God created earth for his people to live on earth as it is in heaven as Kingdom citizens. God created the earth, air, sun, moon, sky, winds, fire, stars, oceans, animals, time, seasons, man and woman. We were to live in His will and His way and to know only love. The key to the Kingdom is love. We were to only know good and never experience evil. The Kingdom of God was to inhabit the earth with the people of God

2. Kingdom of Heaven

God is sovereign over the universe, including the kingdom of heaven. Because the kingdom of heaven is a part of the kingdom of God, some things could be said of both, but there are other things said of the kingdom of God, that could not be spoken of the kingdom of heaven.

(The Gospel according to Matthew, p. 37, Dake Bible, NKJV).

Matthew 13:11

In the present realm of profession, tares and wheat, good and bad, are now mixed together in the same kingdom. At the end of this age the two classes will be separated. The professors will be sent to hell and the possessors of the kingdom will continue in its literal aspect forever (Matthew 13 v 40-43;49-50; 25:31-46; Rev. 20; Zech. 14)

(The Gospel according to Matthew, p. 23, Dake Bible, NKJV).

3. Kingdom of God vs Kingdom of Heaven

SAY: There is a difference between the Kingdom of God and the Kingdom of Heaven.

Kingdom of God	Kingdom of Heaven
God as king (1 Cor. 15:28)	Messiah as King (John 18:3; Rev. 20:6)
In heaven and earth (Ps. 103:19)	From heaven (John 18:36)
In heaven and earth (1 Cor. 15:28)	In earth only (John 18:37; Rev. 5:10)
Scope unlimited (Rev. 4:11; 5:11)	Scope limited (Zech. 14:9)
Moran and spiritual (Rom. 14:17)	Political (Isa. 9:7; Dan. 7:14)
Past, present, & future (Ps. 90:2)	Future (Mt. 6:10; 2 Tim. 4:1)
God over all (Ps. 103:19)	Under Christ (Ps. 2:6; Lk. 1:32-33)
Not given (Ps. 10:16)	Given to Christ (Dan. 7:13-14; Lk. 1:32)
Is now (Ps. 90:2)	Begins at second advent (Zech. 14; 2 Tim. 4:1)
Over all (Ps. 103:19)	Under heaven only (Dan. 7:27; Rev. 11:15)
Angelic-heavenly (Rev. 5:11)	Jewish-earthly (Isa. 9:7; Lk.1:33)
Universal (Rev.5:11)	Local (Rev. 11:15)
Heavenly capital (Heb. 12:22)	Earthly capital (Isa. 2:3; Zech. 1:4)
Eternal in purpose (Eph. 3:11)	Dispensational in purpose (1 Cor. 15:24-28)
Timeless-endless (Ps. 90:2)	Has a beginning (2 Tim. 4:1; Mt. 6:10)
Only born-again ones (John 3:5)	Tares in it now (Mt. 13:38-50)
Without show (Lk. 17:20; Rom. 14:17; 1 Cor. 4:20)	Comes with outward show (Mt. 24:29-31; 25:31-46; 2 Thess. 1:7-10; Jude 14; Zech. 14:1-5; Dan. 7:13-14; Rev. 19:11-21)
Does not, for only resurrected saints inherit all things (Rom. 8:17; 1 Cor. 15:50-58; Rev. 21:7)	"Flesh and blood" inherit it, it is for earthly natural people (Ps. 37:11; Mt. 5:5; 25:34; Dan. 7:18; Ezek. 43:7)

4. Creation

God the Father, God the Son, and God the Holy Spirit are in a relationship of love, purpose, and communication in eternity. The book of the Genesis which is the first book of the Bible tells humanity of God's creation in six days and on the seventh day He rested. We were made in the image of God. (Gen. 1:26,27). Adam and Eve were made for God's purpose and plan. Adam's purpose is described in Gen. 1:27-2:25. Adam was to subdue the earth, to be fruitful and to multiply and to rule over the earth. Man was designed for relationship with God and a soul for worship. God formed Eve from Adam's own body as a helpmeet. They had regular communion with the Father, Son, Holy Spirit.

What went wrong?

Genesis 3:1-24 tells us about the Fall. Eve ate the fruit that the serpent offered, she gave it to Adam and he ate. Their eyes were opened, and they were filled with shame. So now, like God, they know good from evil. Man, who once felt secure under God's protection now fear's God. Disobedience caused a broken communion with God.

So, Adam turns on Eve and blames Eve. In Genesis 3:16-19 it tells us that work and survival come in to replace the paradise that they were once living in. They were now common laborers. Eve suffered pain in childbearing. Adam and Eve had to leave the Garden of Eden. But praise God! God promised that eventually Satan would be destroyed.

When Adam sinned, all mankind sinned (Rom. 5:12-19). Adam was our representative and we are his descendants. So, it is condemnation for all men. All people are sinners from conception. We are dead in trespasses and sins. Our hearts, apart from Christ, are wicked. The only restoration is in the Lord Jesus Christ, who was given by God to overcome sin and its destruction.

All of mankind's original needs for love, communication, and purpose still exist but now are unsatisfied. Romans 1:28-31 describes man's condition. "28 And even as they did not like to retain God in their knowledge, God gave them over to a debased mind, to do those things which are not fitting; 29 being filled with all unrighteousness, [a]sexual immorality, wickedness, [b]covetousness, [c]maliciousness; full of envy, murder, strife, deceit, evil-mindedness; they are whisperers, 30 backbiters, haters of God, violent, proud, boasters, inventors of evil things, disobedient to parents, 31 [d]undiscerning, untrustworthy, unloving, [e]unforgiving, unmerciful;"

God's holiness and justice condemn sin. God cannot overlook sin and it is punished by death. God sent Jesus Christ, His Son, as a substitute for us so we won't be punished eternally. We are saved by faith in the sacrifice Christ made for us on the cross. It is a gift of grace from God our Father to those who believe in the Lord Jesus Christ.

5. The Apostolic Church

SAY: Church, when you hear that word, what comes to your mind?

SAY: Let me hear some thoughts that come to mind.

What is church? People today believe that the church is a building for public Christian worship. Christians today believe that we come together in fellowship, through praise, worship, prayer, song, and dance in one accord, so God can get all of the glory.

The foundation of the church is explained in Ephesians 2:20, "having being built on the foundation of the apostles and prophets, Jesus Christ Himself being the chief cornerstone". The church for the Kingdom of God is not a physical building, it is the people of God worshipping God through Christ in the building. Jesus Christ is the true foundation of the church which are His people. The apostles and prophets have also been made part of the foundation of Christianity. The origin of the church is described in Ephesians 1:3-5; 25-32. The purpose of the church is explained in Mk. 16:15.

After the Day of Pentecost (Acts 2:1-4), the apostolic church was established. Jesus selected after prayer the twelve apostles and gave them a commission (to authorize, appoint, charge, empower, dispatch and entrust with a mission). Jesus directly gave the apostles a commission, but also gave the Great Commandment and the Great commission to the church, which are the people and every generation to come to fulfill.

God's ultimate plan for mankind is found in Romans 8:29, which is, "conformed to the image of His Son". God wants Christlikeness. God wants us to be men and women who demonstrate the character qualities of Jesus Christ. Stedman tells us, "He wants a church filled with men and women who exemplify the extraordinary integrity, temperament, wholeness, compassion, individuality, boldness, earnestness, love, righteousness, forgiveness, selflessness, and faithfulness of Jesus Christ!"[1]. The church therefore needs to be first and foremost an apostolic church if it is to fulfill its assigned mission here on earth as the Kingdom of Heaven.

6. Christians and Christianity

Let's discuss and answer these questions:

Who is a Christian?

A Christian is someone who believes in Christ Jesus. A person professing belief in Jesus Christ with the behavior, activity and speech like Jesus Christ
Every child of God can point to Jesus and before the Father's throne and testify: I'm with

Him.

What make us Christians?

 In Acts 11:26 in Antioch believers who followed Jesus Christ were called Christians. Our faith, our belief, our lifestyle makes us Christians. When God can hear Christ in us and He can love us the way He loves Christ.

What are the marks of true Christianity?

Bearing the fruit of the Spirit daily. Daily faith and action, reading the Word of God, prayer, worship. A true Christian displays his faith by how he or she lives. Christians must not only meditate in certain things, but they are to do certain things. Christianity, Phil. 4:9.

<u>Four Things to Practice and Enjoy</u>:

       1. Things learned—Christian practices.
       2. Things received—Christian blessings.
       3. Things heard—Christian blessings.

---

[1] Stedman, Ray C. *Body Life: The book that Inspired a Return to the Church's Real Meaning and Mission.*, 1995,162

4. Things seen—Christian miracles.

(Dake Annotated Reference Bible, Thomas Nelson, Inc., 1982, p. 373)

How to Live a Christian Life

A Believe in the gospel and the entire Word of God at all times, and walk in the light as you receive it (Jn. 1:7)

B Walk by faith in the newness of life, not by sight or by feelings, for "the just shall live by faith; but if anyone draws back, my soul has no pleasure in him" (Heb. 10:23-39; Rom. 6:1-23; 8:1-13; Gal. 5:16-26).

C Read the Bible daily. Search it. Meditate on it day and night to feed and nurture the spiritual life (Ps. 1:1-3; 119:105; 2 Cor. 10:4-7; Eph. 6:10-18; 1 Pet. 2:2).

D Pray to God daily as your heavenly Father in the name of Jesus Christ, "casting all your care upon Him, for He cares for you" (Jn. 16:23-26; Phil. 4:5-6; 1 Pet. 5:7)

E **Claim all of the benefits** of the promises of God and appropriate by faith all that He has promised (2 Cor. 1:20; 2 Pet. 1:1-4)

F **Keep your mind stayed upon God** (Isa. 26:3) and grow in grace, in all the virtues of grace and God (Phil. 4:8; 1 Pet. 2:4-10; 2 Pet. 1:4-11; Jude 20-24).

G Recognize at all times your own weaknesses as well as God's strength and keeping power (1 Cor. 10:12-31; 1 Pet. 1:5). Faith is the victory that overcomes the world (1 Jn. 5:1-4).

H Confess the Lord Jesus Christ frequently and daily as your personal Savior (Mt. 10:32-33). Be busy at soul-winning and keep occupied in all phases of Christian work possible (Pr. 11:30; Dan. 12:3).

I Avoid temptations and shun evil companions (Ps. 1; Pr. 1:10-16); 1 Tim. 4:6-16). Resist sin and Satan (Jas. 4:7; 1 Pet. 5:8-9), make friends with God's people, and strive to be a blessing to them and all others (Rom. 12:1; 1 Cor. 13; Col. 3:5-10).

J Attend church regularly (Heb. 10:25), cooperating with the pastor in all of his many labors (Mt. 28:19-20; Acts 1:8; 2 Cor. 6:1; 2 Tim. 2:15; 3:15-17).

K Seek God constantly for the full anointing of the Holy Spirit, the fruit and gifts of the Spirit, and yield to and obey the Holy Spirit in all things (Lk. 11:13; 24:49; Jn. 7:37-39; 14:12-17; 15:26; 16:7-13; Acts 1:8; 2:38-39; 5:32; Rom. 12; 1 Cor. 12; Gal. 5:16-26; Eph. 5:18; 6:10-18; 1 Th. 5:19).

(Dake Annotated Reference Bible, Thomas Nelson, Inc., 1982, Cyclopedic Index, p. 584)

10 Daily Duties of Christians

1 Pray (Mt. 6:11; Lk. 11:3)

2 Take up daily cross (Lk. 9:23)
3 Continue in one accord (Acts 2:46)
4 Teach (Mt. 26:55; Lk. 19:47)
5 Win souls (Acts 2:47; 16:5)
6 Preach Jesus (Acts 5:42)
7 Search the Scripture (Acts 17:11)
8 Discuss Scripture (Acts 19:9)
9 Carry responsibility (2 Cor. 11:28)
10 Exhort one another (Heb. 3:13)

(Dake Annotated Reference Bible, Thomas Nelson, Inc., 1982, Cyclopedic Index, p. 585-586).

7. Five-Fold Ministry

The five-fold ministry consists of the Apostle, Prophet, Pastor, Teacher, and Evangelist. It is for edification, exhortation and comfort. Apostles, prophets, pastors, teachers and evangelists are all called and sent by the Lord. They each have a dimension of Christ to impart to the Church. It is presented in the New Testament.

In other words, when the Lord ascended, He divided his mantle into five parts. He gave the apostolic mantle to some (not all). He gave His prophetic mantle to some (not all). He gave His evangelistic mantle to some (not all). He gave His pastoral mantle to some (not all). He gave His teaching mantle to some (not all). Each mantle carries a certain amount of grace.

You are going to learn the importance of the five-fold ministry and its purpose here on Earth as God created it to operate. Each part of the body of Christ has a function, each function is anointed for what they are called to do. The Apostle and the Prophet are the foundational gifts of the church. Ephesians 4:13 is the purpose of the apostolic and prophetic team. Ephesians 4:9 is the commission for the apostolic and prophetic team.

Ephesians 4:11 speaks of the five-fold designations. Let's learn about them.

1). The **Apostle** catches what God has got in his heart for the church. An apostle is concerned about what God wants the church to accomplish. The Apostles thinking is addressing what God wants the church to be. The apostolic gift should always be at the heart of the church. God's point of view from the apostolic point of view, has to do with governance, of actually bringing things into kingdom order and alignment, the governance of God over finances. So, the apostolic ministry is concerned about the kingdom of God advancing in the world, and so when a church has apostolic leadership, it will increasingly have spiritual dimensions, and a movement of the church to engage community, and to advance the gospel into the world. Apostles must have corresponding signs, wonders, and miracles. Every Apostle must prophesy. Apostles are the spiritual commanders of the Church. Remember that Apostle and Apostolic are two different things.

2). The **Prophet** guards over what God says for the earth. A Prophet's job is to call for the destiny or assignment in the lives of God's people, bringing them

from where they are to where they are called to be. To be called means to be awakened to your assignment. The Prophet has a sphere of the fear of the Lord around them. The essence of the prophet is to hear God.

Prophets must be pure and have credibility. Prophets must be set in a house of worship. Prophets are called to be intercessors. The prophetic ministry is to do with connecting people into the realm of the spirit, so a prophet will bring revelation and insight into the spirit world and will activate people to get closer to the Lord. So, in a prophetic ministry, you become very aware of the spirit world, the spiritual realm, but also you become challenged to get your life nearer to God, and to deal with sin issues and so on.

So, a prophet will bring people closer to God, and address issues which have spiritual dimensions around them and raise up other people with this same gift to flow that way. Remember that Prophet and Prophetic are two different things. Also, prophecy is the word coming forth from the mouth of God unto a person.

Let me explain the difference between a prophet and the prophetic. The prophet is to hear God and call forth the destiny or assignment in the lives of God's people. The prophet is a man or woman of God that they speak as oracles of God. Prophets speak on the behalf of God to the people. The Prophetic releases the heavens into the earth.

3). The **Pastor** is concerned about the people and their needs.

We will discuss more in detail the Pastor in the next section of this goal.

4). The **Teacher** is a person who is called to teach and establish people, and they have an anointing, a way of thinking, and a flow of God's presence to enable them to do that. It involves establishing people. We will discuss more in detail about the teacher and teaching in this goal.

5). The **Evangelist** is called to connect with God's people, with unsaved people, and draw or bring them to Christ, and then raise up others with an evangelistic gifting. We will discuss more in detail about the evangelist and evangelism in goal eight.

8. Pastor/Shepherd

The key verse for pastors and church planters in the Bible is Eph. 4:11-13, which tells us that the goal of the leaders (Apostles, Prophets, Evangelists, Pastors, and Teachers) is to equip people for works of service or ministry so that the body of Christ can be built up, so that we will all reach unity and spiritual maturity.

A pastor must be immersed in the word of God, yielded to the Holy Spirit, and in relationship with other people, but also a disciple maker (1 Tim. 3; Titus 1). The pastor must cast the vision, teach discipleship as priority, teach and preach the gospel, equip and empower the saints to go out and disciple others for the kingdom.

As a senior or lead pastor, he/she must set the tone for what spiritual maturity looks like in your congregation. The pastor is also responsible (with the Lord's help) to live in such a way that people can see true discipleship and spiritual maturity in the actions of their lives. As the head goes, the body follows.

The pastor must create a foundation that is of God. There must be no segregation because that is where the enemy comes in. Every church today has some form of segregation and that is crippling the church. There must be more emphasis on the home being whole and not to focus on church programs and focus on the Great Commandment and the Great Commission. The church should be slowly moved into launching new ministries as the body of Christ is growing spiritually.

Some characteristics of a good shepherd include feeding the flock, tending the weak and sick, searching for the lost, guiding with love, gathering and protecting the sheep, and giving one's best to them. On the other hand, a bad shepherd is more concerned about feeding himself, worrying about his own health, giving with a heavy hand, abandoning or scattering his flock, and keeping the best for himself.

9. Role of a Disciple Making Pastor

- **An Authentic Disciple**

A Pastor must learn to walk with God daily.

- **A Discipleship-system builder**

Every Christian is a disciple and is to become a disciple maker. A pastor should be more than that. He must lead the church and create a system in which people are taught how to be disciples. The Pastor and his team are called to lead in the development of a church-wide system that will make disciples who make disciples. A church planter should follow Timothy and Titus and build small churches that serve as the "household of God" and the "pillar and buttress of the truth" (1 Tim. 3:14-16).

- **A Developer of Leaders**

A church planter, Pastor, or leadership team should be able to identify emerging, gifted leaders and help them to grow. Focus should be on one of the primary spiritual gifts we need in the church which is the gift of administration (leadership).

- **A Vision Caster**

A church leader must be able to cast the vision to create a disciple-making culture. The church is a community which develops people who follow Jesus, which then are changed by Jesus, and then decide to join Jesus on his mission. The vision must be stated, then state it again and again and again.

10. Role of the Pastor's Spouse (Male or Female)

Let's discuss first the role of the female spouse. The female spouse should be focused first on God, and then be the pastor's wife. An example of a mother of their children if they have children. The Bible instructs the wife to submit to her husband in all decisions.

Along with supporting her husband, the female spouse must conduct herself with reverence in her behavior. She must lead the other females in the congregation by example. She should act according to God's word and portrays this behavior in order for other females to emulate.

The role of the male spouse is still to be the priest of the home, supportive in ministry, love his wife as Christ loved the church and lead his household.

11. Role of a Minister, Reverend, Ordained Reverend, Elder, Deacon

Minister: A "minister" is to "SERVE" the Lord's flock. Guide them, edify them, and teach them. "Take heed to yourselves, and to all the flock, over which the Holy Spirit hath made you overseers, to FEED THE CHURCH OF GOD, which He hath purchased with His own blood." (Acts 20:28)

Reverend: May only preach at his/her church.

Ordained Reverend-Duties:

- *Preaching:* One of the primary goals of an ordained reverend is to preach weekly sermons to the church congregation. Sermons are usually based on spiritual or biblical texts. The reverend is regarded as the spiritual guide or "shepherd" of the congregation. An ordained reverend may preach to other congregations; a reverend who is not ordained may preach only to his/her church.

- *Counseling:* An ordained reverend often serves as a counselor for the members of the church. He might be called upon to provide premarital and marital counseling, or to counsel members who are battling problems such as depression or substance abuse.

- *Prayer:* The reverend is often asked to pray for members of the church as well as for their friends and their family. Congregants can call him/her to pray even when he/she is not at the church.

- *Community Outreach:* An ordained reverend is expected to reach out to members of the community who are unable to attend the church. This includes visiting the sick and ministering to the homeless.

Elder

According to the New Testament, elders are responsible for the primary leadership and oversight of a church. The function and role of an elder is well summarized by Alexander Strauch in his book *Biblical Eldership*: "Elders lead the church 1 Tim 5:17; Titus 1:7; 1 Peter 5:1–2 , teach and preach the Word 1 Timothy 3:2; 2 Timothy 4:2; Titus 1:9, protect the church from false teachers Acts 20:17, 28–31, exhort and admonish the saints in sound doctrine 1 Timothy 4:13; 2 Timothy 3:13–17; Titus 1:9, visit the sick and pray James 5:14; Acts 6:4, and judge doctrinal issues Acts 15:6.

In biblical terminology, elders shepherd, oversee, lead, and care for the local church". "Elder" and "Pastor" are not two different offices.

Deacon

One who ministers or serves. Phil 1:1; 1 Tim. 3:8-12.

12. Leaders and Leadership

A. Leaders

Christian leaders are servants with the credibility and capabilities to influence people in a particular context to pursue their God-given direction. Leaders need to model for their churches what it means to be humble (James 3:2) and yet remain faithful to the path. God calls us to be holy (1 Peter 1:15-16). Scriptures that address the character of a leader (1 Timothy 3; 1 Titus 1).

Author Putnam explains that there are four relational environments, which are:

- "Intimate discipling relationships (one leader interacting with two or three people),
- Personal discipling relationships (one leader, interacting with 10-12 people),
- Social discipling relationships (one leader interacting with up to 120 people), and
- Public discipling relationships (one leader interacting with large crowds of people)."[2]

Note: There are scriptures on feminine leadership (1 Sam. 25); Women's Ministries (Acts 2; Titus 2).

For a leader to be more authentic:

---

[2] Putnam, 2013, 107-109.

God appointed leaders must be filled with the Holy Ghost and operating in their gifting in the Spirit. Start with honest, humble leaders who are living out in their personal relationships what they want other people to live out in theirs. So begin there in your closest relationships. Model authenticity. Be vulnerable. Share your struggle. Be genuine.

A leader's job is to guide and equip the saints so that the entire church becomes a mature community in which disciple's flourish. It involves releasing the ministry and gifts of all believers. It's about creating a place where everybody learns to be a minister by growing, serving, and making disciples themselves. Leading a group or an entire congregation is spiritual business and if done correctly, it will be opposed by the enemy.

As a leader you want people to follow because they have to (rights), because they want to (relationship), because of what you have done for the organization (results), because of what you have done for them (reproduction), and because of who you are and what you represent (respect).

Characters of a Leader

1. Integrity
2. Self-discipline
3. Selfless
4. Accountable
5. Honest
6. Ethical
7. Visionary
8. Love People

SAY: Leadership is where one person can influence others to follow his or her lead. The goal of a leader is to get all to a common purpose. Let's discuss each level of leadership.

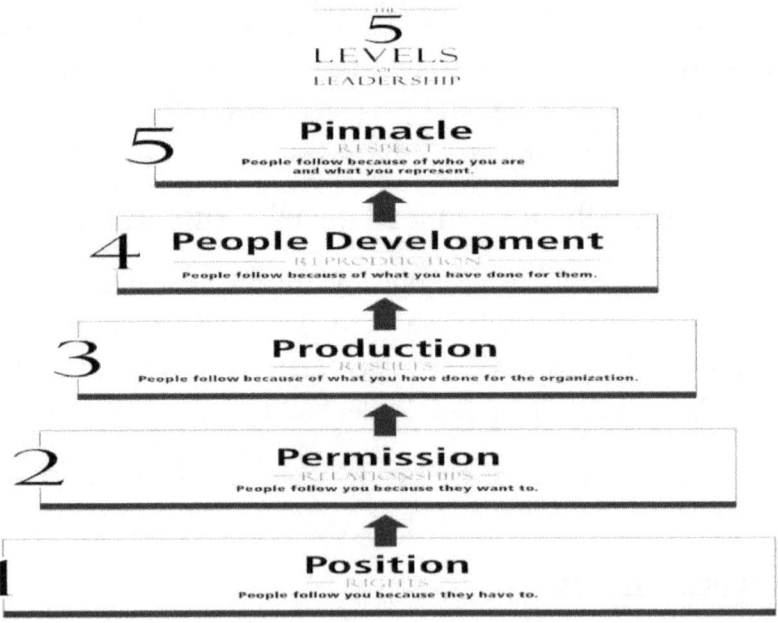

Retrieved from https://alexrister1.files.wordpress.com/2012/01/5-levels-final.jpg.

Level 1: Position

Here is the entry level where you are given a title. The people will only do what they have to do when they are required to do it. Here is where you must ask questions. You must know your job description thoroughly, know the history of the organization, be a team player, and accept responsibility. Your job must be done with consistent excellence, always do more than expected, and always offer creative ideas for change and improvement.

Level 2: Permission

Here is where building relationships begin. There must be a genuine love for people. Have a desire to make those who work with you more successful. Always see through other people's eyes. Remember to love people more than procedures. Have a desire to "win-win" or don't do it. Always include others in your journey and always deal wisely with difficult people.

Level 3: Production

Here is where you begin to see results. You must initiate and accept responsibility for growth. Write, develop and follow a statement of purpose. Include your job description and energy. Ensure people are accountable for results, beginning with yourself. Always communicate the strategy and vision of the organization. Ensure to become a change agent and understand timing. You will always have to make the difficult decisions that will make a difference.

Level 4: People Development

Here is where you have to reproduce. People are your most valuable asset. Always place a priority on developing people. You must be a model for others to follow. Constantly pour your leadership efforts into the top 20 percent of your people. You have to expose key leaders to growth opportunities. You must be able to connect other winners/producers to the common goal. Always surround yourself with an inner core that complements your leadership.

Level 5: Pinnacle

Here is where respect is earned. Your leaders must be loyal and sacrificial. You will have to spend a lot of time making leaders. You will enjoy seeing others grow and develop. You must transcend the organization.

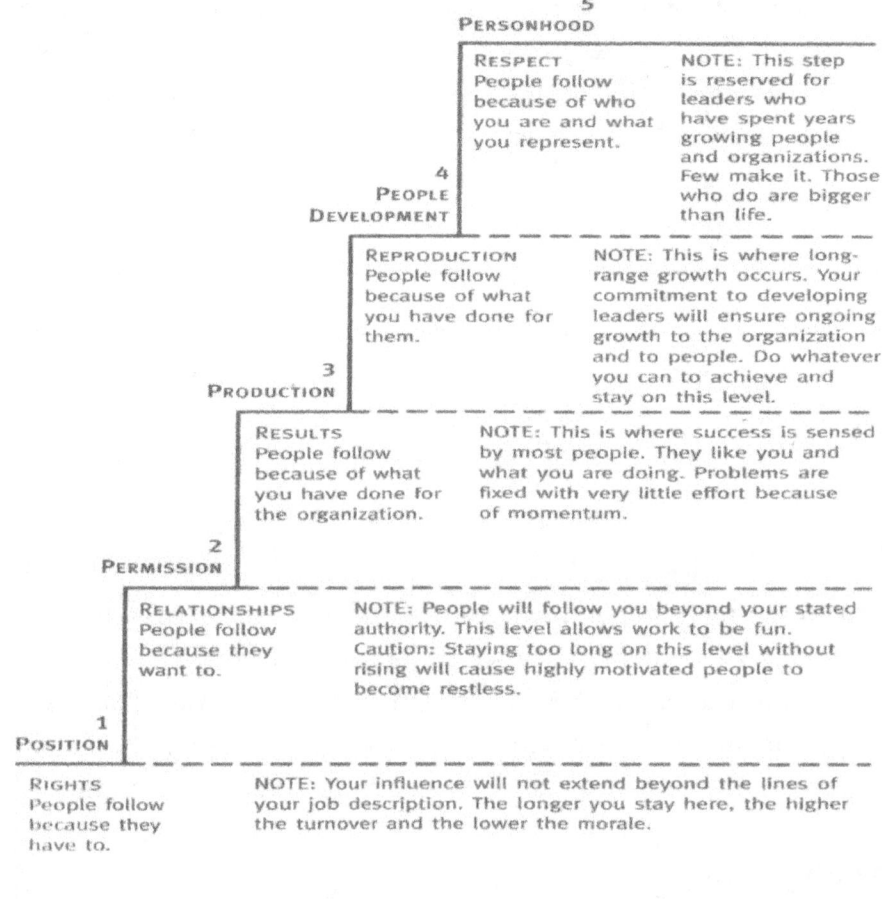

(John Maxwell, 1993, p. 13)

Maxwell, John C., *Developing the Leader Within You.*, Nashville, TN: Thomas Nelson, Inc., 1993, 13.

Level 1: Position

Here is the entry level where you are given a title. The people will only do what they have to do when they are required to do it. Here is where you must ask questions. You must know your job description thoroughly, know the history of the organization, be a team player, and accept responsibility. Your job must be done with consistent excellence, always do more than expected, and always offer creative ideas for change and improvement.

Level 2: Permission

Here is where building relationships begin. There must be a genuine love for people. Have a desire to make those who work with you more successful. Always see through other people's eyes. Remember to love people more than procedures. Have a desire to "win-win" or don't do it. Always include others in your journey and always deal wisely with difficult people.

Level 3: Production

Here is where you begin to see results. You must initiate and accept responsibility for growth. Write, develop and follow a statement of purpose. Include your job description and energy. Ensure people are accountable for results, beginning with yourself. Always communicate the strategy and vision of the organization. Ensure to become a change agent and understand timing. You will always have to make the difficult decisions that will make a difference.

Level 4: People Development

Here is where you have to reproduce. People are your most valuable asset. Always place a priority on developing people. You must be a model for others to follow. Constantly pour your leadership efforts into the top 20 percent of your people. You have to expose key leaders to growth opportunities. You must be able to connect other winners/producers to the common goal. Always surround yourself with an inner core that complements your leadership.

Level 5: Personhood

Here is where respect is earned. Your leaders must be loyal and sacrificial. You will have to spend a lot of time making leaders. You will enjoy seeing others grow and develop. You must transcend the organization.

As a leader you will experience attacks from the enemy to hinder your progress. Let's discuss four spirits that will attach to leaders and attack the church. There are many more.

1. **Jezebel spirit**: Jezebel learned her religious practices from her father and she married King Ahab of Israel. Her father sacrificed children to Baal and she continued that practice in the kingdom of Israel. She brought Asherah worship to Israel. It worshiped carved poles or trees for the goddess of fertility, sex orgies, lust, and sexual immorality. Asherah was the mother of Baal. Jezebel searched for prophets to kill. This spirit seeks to destroy the word of God and the works of God and the people of God. (I Kings 18:19-26). The spirit of Jezebel will lead others to do evil by controlling, manipulation, and domination. She is against the anointed people and the true prophets. When this spirit is identified, get rid of it because it is to destroy the prophets and their ministry. It can operate in the man and woman.

2. **Ahab spirit**: A spirit that attaches to a man who has been given the position of authority. It can be by marriage or by society, the government or church, those who abdicates his authority and allows others to trample, abuse, use, misuse his authority in any way they want to. The spirit of Ahab and the spirit of Jezebel are attracted to each other, so they seek out to attach to each other.

3. **Celebrity spirit**: This spirit is attracted to famous people and those who want to be famous. Some people who stand up on the pulpit in church have a celebrity atmosphere all around them. Some people may go to a church because they are attracted to the celebrity spirit of that

minister and not to the anointing of God. Many Christians are attached to this spirit and don't even realize their allegiance to this spirit. Christians can get entrenched in their church that has no anointing and won't visit or move to one that has the anointing or offend the pastor by leaving. The celebrity spirit tells us human beings that there is some "good reason", spiritually speaking, to tolerate the compromises or inaccuracies in spiritual leadership that flow from those whose motivation is to procure their own fame or dominance. If you tolerate this spirit, you are worshipping an idol and you will follow and worship it. Example of a celebrity spirit is in Acts 8:9-23.

4. **Absalom spirit**: Absalom was one of King David's sons from his many wives. (2 Sam. 13-18) This spirit positions himself to steal the hearts away from the anointed king or in this spiritual realm, the anointed leader. People can be won over by a false representation of authority instead of true authority which is the leader. This spirit leads people to believe that the leader is too busy to listen to them. People will flee from their God given positions. The Absalom spirit shows disloyalty and rebellion to authority and will be dissatisfied. If you are dissatisfied with your leader, approach the leader privately and make an appeal. If he/she will not hear you, leave your leader or church. Do not rebel against him/her and stir up trouble in the congregation. This spirit will push people to take matters into their own hands, get others to do the dirty work, and then continues manipulate to gain recognition. When ready, there will be rebellion because they want to lead and have authority to glorify self.

It pulls down others to reach the top, will criticize everything and contamination moves into the body of Christ.

There are other spirits, such as, Barabbas, Athaliah, Saul, Sanballat, Tobiah and Geshem.

B. Leadership

Matthew 20: 20-21 is the scripture verses where the mother of James and John asks Jesus to place her sons, one on the left and the other on the right in His kingdom. Jesus' response is in verse 22.

Jesus used this occasion to teach two principles of leadership that the church must never forget.

- The sovereign principality principle of spiritual leadership. "To sit at my right or left is not for me to grant. These places belongs to those for whom they have been prepared" (Mark 10:40). God will assign places of spiritual ministry and leadership.

- The suffering principle of spiritual leadership. "Can you drink the cup I drink and be baptized with the baptism I am baptized with? (Mark 10:38).

Leadership is an awesome responsibility demanding spiritual preparation grounded in consistent personal devotion to Jesus Christ and devotional time to study, worship, and praise (Matt. 6:33).

Leaders must also seek godly counsel (Prov. 15:22). They must work willingly and energetically

(Eccl. 9:10). Essential ingredients in leadership include creativity, encouragement of others (Prov. 15:23; 25:11), inspiration (Prov. 16:24; 17:22), expressions of gratitude (Ps. 13; 6; 69:30; Eph. 5:20), and servant's heart (Prov. 3:27; Matt. 23:11). People must consistently be more important than tasks.

Self-sacrifice, gentleness, service without expected reward, patience, kindness, maturing of relationships, mercy—all of these qualities are a part of the Lord's leadership. We see exemplified in the Lord himself those qualities which are necessary in all godly leaders.

(The Woman's Study Bible, 2006, p. 392)

Let's read 1 Timothy 3:2-7 and discuss the insights of leadership from the Apostle Paul. Paul spoke about leadership in many of his letters to the churches.

Sanders explains, "the qualities of leadership Paul spoke about are:

1. **Social qualifications**: With respect to relationships within the church, the leader is to be above reproach. With respect to relationships outside the church, the spiritual leader is to enjoy a good reputation. Outsiders will criticize, nonetheless they respect the high ideals of Christian character. When a Christian leader full of high ideals lives a holy and joyful life in front of unbelievers, they often want to cultivate a similar experience. (p. 40-41).

2. **Moral qualifications**: Moral principles common to the Christian life are under constant, subtle attack, and none more so than sexual faithfulness. The Christian leader must be blameless on this vital and often unpopular point. Faithfulness to one marriage partner is the biblical norm. The spiritual leader must be temperate, not addicted to alcohol, pornography, drugs, food, and other unwise things. A leader cannot allow a secret indulgence that would undermine public witness (p. 41).

3. **Mental qualifications**: A leader must be prudent, a person with sound judgment. As to behavior, the leader must be respectable. A well-ordered life is the fruit of a will-ordered mind. The life the leaders hold reflect the beauty and orderliness of God. Then the leader must be ready and able to teach. The leader feels the joy of the spirit and wants others to know God as well (p. 42).

4. **Personality qualifications**: The Christian leader must be genial and gentle, not a lover of controversy. Then the leader must show hospitality. (p. 42-43)

5. **Domestic qualifications**: The Christian leader who is married must demonstrate the ability to "manage his own family well and see that his children obey him with proper respect" (1 Timothy 3:4). While a leader cares for church and mission, he must not neglect the family, which is his primary and personal responsibility. (p. 44).

6. **Maturity**: A novice or new convert should not be pushed into leadership. Paul warns that a person not ready for leadership, and thrust into the role, "may become conceited and fall

under the same judgment as the devil" (1 Timothy 3:6)." [3]

Sanders explains, "The essential qualities of leadership are:

1. **Discipline**: Before we can conquer the world, we must first conquer the self. A leader is a person who has learned to obey a discipline imposed from without and has then taken on a more rigorous discipline from within.

2. **Vision**: Vision involves foresight as well as insight. A leader must be able to see the end results of the policies and methods he or she advocates. Vision involves optimism and hope.

3. **Wisdom**: It is insight in to the heart of things. Wisdom involvers knowing God and the subtleties of the human heart. More than knowledge, it is the right application of knowledge in moral and spiritual matters, in handling dilemmas, in negotiating complex relationships. Wisdom gives a leader balance and helps to avoid eccentricity and extravagance. If knowledge comes by study, wisdom comes by Holy Spirit filling. Then a leader can apply knowledge correctly. "Full of wisdom" is one of the requirements for even subordinate leaders in the early church (Acts 6:3).

4. **Decision**: When all of the facts are in, swift and clear decision is another mark of a true leader. A visionary may see, but a leader must decide. Once sure of the will of God, a spiritual leader springs into action, without regard to consequences. The spiritual leader will not procrastinate when faced with a decision, nor vacillate after making it. [4]

5. **Courage**: Courage is that quality of mind that enables people to encounter danger or difficulty firmly without fear or discouragement. God calls leaders to be of good courage and not to capitulate to fear. Because fear is a real part of life, God gives us the Holy Spirit, who fills us with power. But we must let that power do its work, and not fear. Leaders strengthen followers in the middle of discouraging setbacks and shattering reverses.[5]

6. **Humility**: Humility is also a hallmark of the spiritual leader. The spiritual leader will choose the hidden path of sacrificial service and approval of the Lord over the flamboyant self-advertising of the world. A leader's humility should grow with the passing of years, like other attitudes and qualities. The spiritual leader of today is the one who gladly worked as an assistant and associate, humbly helping another achieve great things."[6]

7. **Integrity and Sincerity**: These two qualities of leadership were a part of God's law for the Israelites (Deuteronomy 18:13). God wants His people to show a transparent character, open and innocent of guile. Surely the spiritual leader must be sincere in promise, faithful in discharge of duty, upright in finances, loyal in service, and honest in speech.[7]

---

[3] Oswald Sanders, *Spiritual Leadership*, 2007, 42-58.
[4] Oswald Sanders, *Spiritual Leadership*, 2007, 59-60.
[5] Ibid, 60-62.
[6] Ibid, 62-63.
[7] Ibid, 64.

8. **Humor**: Our sense of humor is a gift from God that should be controlled as well as cultivated. Clean, wholesome humor will relax tension and relieve difficult situations. A good test of the appropriateness of a joke is whether the humor controls us, or we control it.[8]

Let's go deeper into the more essential qualities of leadership.

9. **Anger**: Jesus had this quality, and when we use it rightly, we follow Him. In Mark 3:5, Jesus looked "at them with anger". Holy anger has its roots in genuine love. But holy anger is open to abuse. Paul argues for holy anger when he repeats the advice of Psalm 4:4: "In your anger do not sin" (Ephesians 4:26). This anger is not selfish and does not center on the pain you currently feel.[9]

10. **Patience:** Spiritual leaders need a healthy endowment of patience. Patience meets its most difficult test in personal relationships. A leader shows patience by not running too far ahead of his followers and thus discouraging them. While keeping ahead, he stays neat enough for them to keep him in sight and hear his call forward. He is not so strong that he cannot show strengthening sympathy for the weakness of his fellow travelers. The person who is impatient with weakness will be ineffective in his leadership."[10]

11. **Friendship**: You can measure leaders by the number and quality if their friends. Leaders must draw the best out of people, and friendship does that far better than prolonged argument or mere logic. [11]

12. **Tact and Diplomacy**: Concerning relationships, tact is the ability to deal with people sensitively, to avoid giving offense, to have a "feel" for the proper words or responses to a delicate situation. Diplomacy is the ability to manage delicate situations, especially involving people from different cultures, and certainly from differing opinions. A leader should be able to project into the life and heart and mind of another, then setting aside personal preferences, deal with the other in a fashion that fits the other best. These skills can be learned and developed. A leader needs the ability to negotiate differences in a way that recognizes mutual rights and intelligence and yet leads to a harmonious solution. Fundamental to this skill is understanding how people feel, how people react. [12]

13. **Inspirational Power**: The power of inspiring others to service and sacrifice will mark God's leader. Such a leader is like a light for others around.

14. **Executive Ability**: However spiritual a leader may be, he cannot translate vision into action without executive ability. So, God is methodic and orderly. God requires of His managers and stewards that "all things be done decently and in order." Our duty is to reflect the orderliness of God in all we do for Him.

---

8 Ibid, 65-67.
9 J. Oswald Sanders, , *Spiritual Leadership* ,2007, 67-68.
10 Ibid, 68-69.
11 Ibid, 70-71.
12 Ibid, 71.

15. **The Therapy of Listening**: To get at the root of problems, a leader must develop into a skillful listener. But genuine listening seeks to understand another without prejudgment. Leaders who want to show sensitivity should listen often and long and talk short and seldom. True leaders know that time spent listening is well invested.

16. **The Art of Letter Writing**: Any position of leadership involves a considerable amount of correspondence, and letters are self-revealing. Clear language is important in our letters, but more important is the right spirit."[13]

A spiritual leader must be Spirit-led and Spirit-filled. If a leader is selected and is not Spirit-led and Spirit filled, it will lead to unspiritual administration. If a leader has a secular or materialistic outlook, the Holy Spirit will be unable to make spiritual progress. If a leader is not spiritually fit the Holy Spirit will withdraw and leave them to their flesh and to operate in their own standards. The book of Acts demonstrates leadership and how the early church were sensitive to the Spirit. A leader's mission should be the mission of the Holy Spirit.

If a leader is filled with the Holy Spirit, it means you have fully surrendered your life to the will of the Spirit. The leader becomes controlled by the Spirit in your mind, emotions, will, and physical strength. The Holy Spirit will lift the leader to their highest power and the leader is sanctified for a holy purpose. Spirit power is described in John 7:37-39. The leader must remain yielded to Him. Holy Spirit gives natural and spiritual gifts which must be brought into service for the kingdom of God.

The spiritual leader must pray. As a leader prays they will begin to master it. Jesus Christ spent many full nights in prayer (Luke 6:12; Mark 1:35). Spiritual leader must have mental discipline and concentration. The leader must pray in the Spirit. As we pray, true prayer comes from the Spirit's activity in our souls. We must pray in the Spirit because we are to pray in the realm of the Spirit and to pray in the power and energy of the Spirit. The Holy Spirit wants to teach and help us to pray. The leader must come against Satan in spiritual warfare prayers. Prayer must be a daily walk in the leader's life. The leader must have a right relationship with God. The leader must be able to move God.

The leader must use his or her time wisely. Once you lost time, you cannot get it back, it's gone. A leader must know what the priority is for every day. Balance the day wisely. A leader must not put off things that must be taken care of. Set deadlines and get it done.

A leader must be willing to read to learn and to grow. A leader must master the principles of God and His Word. Read the Bible and books to feed the soul. Reading provides spiritual growth, spiritual benefits, preaching and writing style, and receive new information. As you read verify and learn through many resources available, such as a dictionary, verifying history, concordances, and a notepad or journal to keep notes.

As you grow as a leader there may be times where you determine that you need to improve

---

13   Sanders, Oswald J., *Spiritual Leadership*, 2007, 72-75.

on your leadership. We must seek to improve if there is an identified need. A leader must recognize any weaknesses, corrective measures, improving on strengths. Be a leader with intensity and zeal. Sanders explains, "The leader must care for: **1. Administration**—To improve the character of the work. The leader must discover which departments are functioning below standards and remedy the defect. This may involve new job descriptions or establishing new reporting procedures and other lines of communication. **2. Spiritual tone**—to deepen the deity, devotion, and success of the worker. The tone of the church or mission will be a reflection of its leaders. **3. Group morale**—To remove stones of stumbling. Friction among a team should be minimized. When problems are neglected, morale drops and performance decreases. **4. Personal relationships**—To oil the wheels where they stick. Warm relationships among team members are vital. **5. Problem solving**—To amend what is defective. One of the chief duties of leaders is to solve tough problems within the organization. The leader must face the problem realistically and follow through until the solution is reached. **6. Creative planning**—To supplement what is lacking. Criticizing plans is easier than creating them. The leader must see the goal clearly, plan imaginatively, and employ tactics that lead to success. One more matter for improving leadership potential: resist the idea of "leadership from the rear." True leadership is always out front—never from the rear or the sidelines."[14]

What is the cost of being a leader? Sanders answers, "The toll of true leadership is heavy, and the most effective the leadership, the greater the cost."[15] There are some items that will cost you as a leader, for example:

1. **Self-sacrifice**: It is done daily. The scriptures say, "Whoever wants to be first must slave of all. For even the Son of Man did not come to be served, but to serve, and to give his life as a ransom for many" (Mark 10:44-45). You will have to give up personal preferences many times. Paul described his self-sacrifice in 2 Corinthians 4:8-11.

2. **Loneliness**: A leader will always have to be ahead of his followers and there may be times of loneliness. It is not easy when you have to make decisions for your followers and know that it will affect their lives.

3. **Fatigue**: As a leader the work will wear you down. 2 Corinthians 4:16 says, "Therefore do not lose heart. Though outwardly we are wasting away, yet inwardly we are being renewed day by day". Jesus grew weary many times and had to rest. Sometimes a leader has to rise early and work late. Fatigue is a great price of leadership.

4. **Criticism**: Every day a leader will experience criticism and that is where humility is truly tested. Paul experienced criticism of man but knew that the Lord is the true judge.

5. **Rejection**: A leader will be rejected for Christ's sake. Remember that as a leader you are accepted by God.

---

14 Sanders, Oswald J., , *Spiritual Leadership,* 2007, 109-113.
15 Sanders, Oswald J., *Spiritual Leadership*, 2007, 115.

6. **Pressure and Perplexity**: As you grow in Christ it will feel like the pressure gets heavier and heavier.

7. **Cost to others**: Sometimes those who are close to leader pay a hefty price.

SAY: Which do you consider is the most difficult to bear? Write your answer in the space provided.

_____

_____

Why?_____

_____

_____

_____

SAY: We are moving forward now to learn and discuss the responsibilities of leadership.

- **Service**: A leader provides a service whether they are in a secular environment or a church. A leader is concerned about others, not with self. Others must be led to the Lord.

- **Applied Discipline**: Self-discipline a leader must master. You will have to discipline others and show love too. It is a loving discipline. Paul explains discipline in Galatians 6:1, "Brothers, if someone is caught in a sin, you who are spiritual should restore him gently. But watch yourself, or you may also be tempted".

- **Guidance**: A leader must know where they are going before leading others. Leading and guiding others is not an easy task.

- **Initiative**: A leader must initiate movement and visionary plans. A leader must be in front, giving guidance and direction to those who are following. If people are providing caution, a leader should listen but not make it delay or interrupt the vision. Take responsibility and remember God is in control.

Next, as leader you will be tested, temptations will come your way, and trials and tribulations along your journey.

- **Compromise**: As a leader, compromises may be required, it may result in a backward step. Keep moving forward until you succeed.

- **Ambition**: It can be a test.

- **The Impossible Situation**: Deal with obstacles or tasks that seem impossible, and it will grow your competence, teamwork in the team, and faith.

- **Failure**: As a leader you will be met with failure, but don't give up. God is in charge.
- **Jealousy**: There are jealous people out there that love to come against leaders. It is a weapon that Satan uses a lot amongst people. Remember you are protected by God, and he will defend his chosen leaders.

SAY: You are a leader, and you are overwhelmed and have decided that you need to start delegated tasks to balance everything out. Remember when you delegate responsibility to others, you have to lower the reigns for that person to grow into leadership with confidence. Support them in success and failure. Give tasks to those that can do it better for their growth.

SAY: You are a leader and you have determined that you have to replace a leader. What do you think you should do? Handle it differently than the world by making sure God is in it and His spiritual principles. Look for others that can emerge and develop. Seek the Lord in prayer about candidates. God prepares people He has chosen for leadership.

SAY: You have selected a new leader and now you have to train him or her to now lead. What's your next move or strategy? Time will have to be devoted to this task. Training up the younger people is always a great idea because they can handle burdens, embark on new initiatives and making final decisions. There must be trust and respect between leader and trainee. Ensure to apply the pattern of how Jesus Christ trained his disciples. Careful thought must be put into the training along with patience and love. It will take time, patience, instruction, prayer, personal guidance and love. God will assist you through the process.

SAY: As a leader, in the realms of the spirit there are many great dangers. Satan will prey upon any weaknesses you have. Let's learn and discuss them.

- **Pride**: As a leader rises in position, pride can increase. Proverbs16:5.
- **Egotism**: Ego is when one thinks and speaks about themselves directing everything to themselves rather than to God and the people of God.
- **Jealousy**: One who is envious of rivals.
- **Popularity**: Being popular comes with a price. A leader must direct their affections towards Jesus. A leader must not let success get to his head.
- **Infallibility**: A leader must be strong and decisive and stand for what he or she believes. Don't think you cannot make mistakes, no man is perfect.
- **Indispensability**: A leader must remember not to hang onto leadership. He or she must train up the younger and pass on the authority.
- **Elation and Depression**: A leader will experience frustration and joy. Many people will disappoint you, you will be criticized, judged. Learn how to deal with these issues and especially depression. Whether there is success of failure, God must still get all of the glory.

- **Prophet or leader**: If you have to prophesy as what the Lord says, say it. Be a leader always.
- **Disqualification**: Paul explains his struggle with being disqualified in 1 Corinthians 9:27. He was speaking to failure of the body and that he knew he had to be self-disciplined so not to lose the prize.

Before someone is given a leadership role, they must know how to answer these questions:

Why should I lead a group?

Answer: To develop other people to being discipled.

What is a small or large group leader?

Answer: Someone who leads a small group of 8 to 12 regular people. They should remain open with an expectation of new people who can join. It can be closed once the 12 people have been reached. Someone who leads a large group of 12 or more. It can go all the way to 200 people. Meetings should be weekly.

How do I lead small or large group discussions?

Answer: With love, confidence, prayer, being friendly, worship, edification, relational evangelism, truth, and discipleship. Meetings should be weekly.

How do I handle a challenging person or persons?

Answer: The size of the group has a significant impact on both leadership style and effectiveness. There will be times you may have people who are: the one who doesn't want to be there; don't care; won't shut up; won't speak up; the joker, the know-it-all, or doesn't want to know. There's no single response that will work all the time. Have a transparent conversation with them explaining why what they are learning is beneficial to them and their spiritual growth to fulfill their assignment for God.

13. Leadership of Jesus Christ

Malphurs explains, the core distinctive of Christian leadership include:
- "A Christian leader is a Christian. (Rom. 3:23; 6:23; Eph. 2:8-9; 2 Cor. 5:21; John 3:1-21)
- A Christian leader is a committed Christ-follower. (Rom. 6:13)
- A Christian leader's source of truth is divine revelation. There is a twofold- special revelation (Titus 2:11; John 8:32; 2 Tim. 2:15) and general revelation (Matt. 5:45).

- A Christian leader emphasizes Godly character. 1 Tim. 4:7)
- A Christian leader understands the importance of motives. (1 Thess. 2:2-9)
- A Christian leader serves through the power of the Holy Spirit. (John 14:15-17)
- A Christian leader practices godly servant leadership. (John 13:1-17)
- A Christian leader may have the gift of leadership (Rom. 12:9)."[16]

Putnam explains, "Jesus not only expected His followers to practice spiritual disciplines. He modeled them for us. Did Jesus ever…

- Pray?
- Spend time alone with the Father?
- Fast?
- Revere and adore the Father?
- Share the good news?
- Quote the Word of God from memory?

If you read the Gospels, you will find that Jesus did these things all the time. We, as sinful humans need to incorporate these disciplines into our lives."[17]

14. Baptism

Webb-Mitchell notes, "Baptism is a sacred rite that signifies purification, initiation, or identification of an individual with a leader, group, or teaching. In other words, in baptism, we die to ourselves and are initiated into this holy gathering as we are raised up and received into the active life of Christ's body. To Paul the only means of deliverance from the body of death is the body of Christ. Being baptized into Christ (Rom 6:3) means we both die to self and are raised from the dead with Christ (Rom 6:4)."[18]

The Different Types of Baptism in the Scriptures

Jewish baptism: a ceremonial cleansing prescribed for both people and articles (Ex.19:10-14; Lev. 8:6; Heb. 9:10).

John's baptism: a preparatory action which Jews expressed their belief in the imminent coming of the Messiah and their desire to turn away from sin and live righteous lives.

Jesus' baptism: an act of ceremonial righteousness. Instead through baptism, Christ was consecrating Himself to His ministry.

Spirit baptism: the supernatural power of the Holy Spirit by which believers are joined to the

---

16   Malphurs, A., *Being Leaders: The Nature of Authentic Christian Leadership,* 2003, 14-22.
17   Putnam, J., *Discipleshift,* 2013, 118-119.
18   Brett P. Webb-Mitchell, *Christly Gestures,* 2003, 52-53.

body of Christ (Rom. 6:3, 4; 1 Cor 12:13; Gal 3:26, 27; Eph. 4:5; Col. 2:9-12).

Christian baptism: a ceremonial act instituted by Christ (Matt. 28:19) and practiced by the Apostles (Acts 2:38) that depicts a believer's union and identification with Christ in his death, burial, and resurrection.

Baptism by fire: a possible reference either to the judgment at the Second Coming or to the coming of the Spirit at Pentecost (Matt. 3:9-12; Luke 3:16, 17).

(The Nelson Study Bible, 1982, p. 1639).

15. Salvation

In salvation, we experience justification, sanctification, and glorification. Salvation is deliverance from the penalty of power and sin (Eph. 2:8).

Those who repent and trust in Jesus will experience its blessings of:

- **Justification** which is the divine act of declaring sinners to be righteous on account of their faith in Jesus. Closely related to justification is regeneration, in which the Spirit of God indwells a repentant sinner and imparts eternal life to his or her spiritually dead soul (**Eph. 2:1-5**).

Sanctification is the work of the Holy Spirit in the life of the believer, resulting in increasing personal holiness (2 Thess. 2:13).

- **Sanctification** which is the process in which God develops the new life of the believer and gradually brings it to perfection. The act of making a thing pure and holy. For ye know what commandments we gave you by the Lord Jesus. For this is the will of God, even your **SANCTIFICATION**, that ye should abstain from fornication: That every one of you should know how to possess his vessel in **SANCTIFICATION** and honor. (1 Thessalonians 1:1; Mark 4:2-4)

Retrieved July 18, 2016 (http://www.biblestudytools.com/dictionaries/king-james-dictionary/sanctification.html)

- **Glorification** which is the ultimate salvation of the whole person. This comes when we are face to face with our Savior in His coming kingdom. Final act of salvation in which the believer is transformed into the likeness of Christ (Rom. 8:30).

Glorification involves first of all the believer's sanctification or moral perfection (2 Thess. 2:13-14; Heb. 2:10-11), in which the believer will be made glorious, holy, and blameless (Eph. 5:27). The process of sanctification is at work in us now (2 Cor. 3:18) but moves from one degree of glory to another until it reaches final glory.

Second, the body participates in glorification (Rom. 8:23; 1 Col. 15:43; Phil. 3:21), which is the believer's deliverance and liberty (Rom. 8:21). As a result, the glorified body is immortal (Rom. 2:7), imperishable, powerful, and spiritual (1 Cor. 15:43-44). Moreover, creation itself participates in this aspect of glorification (Rom. 8:21).

In the third place, glorification brings participation in the kingdom of God (1 Thess. 2:12), even to the point of our reigning with Christ (2 Tim. 2:10-12). Finally, glorification is in some sense a partaking of God's own glory (Rom. 5:2; 1 Thess. 2:12; 2 Thess. 2:14; 1 Peter 5:10).

(Retrieved July 18,2016 (http://www.biblestudytools.com/dictionaries/bakers-evangelical-dictionary/glorification.html)

16. Stewardship

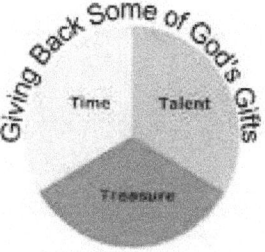

God owns everything, including everything you possess, because He created everything. "All the earth is mine," the Lord said in Exodus 19:5. In Job 41:11, He declared it again, "Whatever is under the whole heaven is mine."

We are managers or stewards of the things God gives to us. God wants us to enjoy the things He has permitted us to have.

As stewards of those things we must remember that they all belong to Him and should be used for the Kingdom. We own nothing that belongs eternally to God. He owns the things we possess, the money in the bank and in our wallets. Haggai 2:8 says, "The silver is mine, and the gold is mine, declares the Lord of hosts."

According to Strong's #3622, the word Stewardship means "household management". A steward is someone who is entrusted with the things of God (1 Cor 9:17).

Principles of Stewardship

1. **Stewardship Principle (His Lordship)**: Recognition that God owns all that we possess.

2. **Voluntary Principle (Our Free Will)**: We are challenged to seek God's will to determine personal giving commitment.

3. **Sacrificial Principle (Pastoral Offering)**: Sacrificial giving, setting apart our financial resources for God.

4. **Commitment Principle (To Purpose in Your Heart)**: A genuine commitment as a result of prayer, sacrifice, and faith.

5. **Witness Principle (That Others May See)**: There are no silent witnesses and no secret disciples.

6. **Teamwork Principle (Unity)**: In stewardship teams we learn principles of stewardship, personal encouragement, develop supportive relationships, and share talents and abilities with others.

7. **Accountability Principle (Standing before God)**: We must all be faithful stewards of all He has placed in our care.

8. **Reward Principle (Universal Justice)**: God's laws are true and applicable to all of us both in this life and in the world to come.

(Retrieved on October 1, 2015 from Stewardship Ministries, 2009)

17. Church Discipline

The pastor, leaders and ministerial team will experience discipline issues in the body of Christ. In 2 Thess. 3:14, Paul instructs the Thessalonians to discipline one of their church members. What does church discipline involve? When should it be employed? What does the Scripture say about it!

The Definition	Church discipline is ultimately the denying of fellowship to a believer in Christ who is continually involved in open sin.
The Occasion	Church discipline involves Christians engaged in overt sin (Matt. 18:15-17; 1 Cor. 5:9-13), especially sexual immorality; those creating division within the body of Christ (Rom. 16:17; Titus 3:10), and those in open obedience of God's appointed leadership in the church (2 Thess. 3: 6, 7, 14; Heb. 13:17).
The Reason	A church must exercise discipline because the church must remain pure (1 Cor.5:8).
The Goal	The goal of church discipline is to cause the sinning person to repent (James 5:19, 20); to "gain back "or restore an erring brother (Matt. 18:15; Gal. 6:1); to make the sinful person feel ashamed enough to change (2 Thess. 3:14).

The Steps	There are several distinct steps to church discipline. First, meet one-on-one with the person. Second, if necessary meet with the person and another church member. Third, if there is no change in behavior, announce the matter to the congregation so that the whole church can corporately encourage the person to repent. Finally, if all else fails put the sinning person out of the assembly (Matt. 15:15-17).
The Attitude	The tone of church discipline should be firm gentleness and love (Gal. 6:1). The people exercising church discipline should put away any spite, hatred, or malice so that they can facilitate true restoration.
The Commands	Matt. 18:15-17; Rom. 16:17; 1 Cor. 5:1-13; Gal. 6:1; 2 Thess. 3:6,7,14,15; Titus 3:10; 11; Heb. 13:17; James 5:19, 20.

Paul is instructing the Thessalonians to withdraw, or withhold fellowship, from a disobedient person. At the time if anyone disobeyed Paul's instructions, their pagan neighbors would think the Thessalonian Christians approved of this person's actions (2 Thess. 3:6, 7, 14).

(The Nelson Study Bible, 1982, p. 2036)

18. Teaching

GOD-CENTERED strategic planning is a disciplined, intentional effort to develop and follow a method to accomplish God's objective for His church in order to meet the enemy under conditions that give us the advantage.

Yount notes, "A series of questions will help us determine what is to be accomplished and how to get there.

- Why does this church exist?
- What are we to be as "church"? (Who and what are we?)
- What is our church profile? (age, family demographics, work patterns, and the like)
- What are the spiritual needs of the people we are reaching? (seeking, new Christians, growing believers, leaders)
- How are we doing? (attendance, baptisms, leadership, outreach)
- Where does God want us to go from here? (What does God want this local body of believers to do in this community and in our world?)
- How will we get there?

Answers to these questions, while generally similar, will be different for each congregation. While all churches have the same universal mission—God's mission—each church plays a unique role with its own specific methods in accomplishing it.

Each program within the teaching ministry of the church should have goals and objectives. The questions that must be answered at this point are:

- How does each program help us accomplish the overall goal of the teaching ministry?
- Are the goals and objectives set for each program and ministry a true reflection of that program or ministry?
- How does each program or ministry fit into the context of our church?
- Is there anything that we are trying to accomplish through the teaching ministry that has nothing in place to help us get there?

When you answer these questions, you may find that some of the goals or objectives or actions will need to be changed, adjusted, or even eliminated. It is important to keep coming back to the question, what are we trying to accomplish and how are we getting there?

Evaluation is only as good as the information on which it is based. Information and data should be current, accurate, and reliable. You will want to evaluate several areas, areas that are objective and easily measured.

Administration

- Is our record-keeping system effective, accurate, and adequate?
- Are we capturing the information that we need?
- Where does each program fit into the overall organizational structure of the church?

Leadership

- How many teachers do we have for each unit? How does this compare with the teacher-student ratio guidelines?
- How many people do we have in leadership positions other than teachers?
- What kind of regular training do we provide for our teachers and leaders?
- How many teachers and leaders attend training opportunities?
- What is the attendance record of the teachers and leaders for program meetings?
- How many teacher or leader vacancies do I have today?

Space and Equipment

- Is the space for each unit adequate?
- Are there classes/departments/groups that have outgrown their current space or are in too large a space?
- What equipment needs to be replaced or repaired?
- Does the classroom environment promote learning?
- Is there a need for additional spaces for groups to meet?

Programming

- What programs are designed to reach people for Christ or to introduce them to the church?
- What programs are designed for discipleship?
- What programs are designed to develop leaders?
- What percentage of your church membership is actively involved in the Foundational Bible Study of your church?
- How many outreach contacts are made by your church members?
- How are members educated in doctrine, church polity, missions, or how to share their faith?

One way of getting a feel for how things are going is to observe classes while they are in session. When you observe a small group, ask yourself questions like these:

- What is the general feel of the group?
- Does everyone seem to be engaged?
- Does the teacher appear prepared?
- Is the space conducive to learning?

Another way to get a feel for what is happening is to solicit feedback from the participants. One final area to consider is teacher evaluation." [19]

19. Government and Citizenship

Contrary to the thinking of most people, government is not limited to state and federal rule and secular jurisdiction. Government—which is management, policy-making, and administration—exists on many levels and in virtually all areas of life.

First and foremost, God's people are called to obey God as Judge, Lawgiver, and King (Is. 33:22). Second, people are called to govern themselves—to rule their spirits (Prov. 25:28). This stands in sharp contrast to the self-judgment spirit of the present age. The family is the primary arena for governance within a God-fearing society.

Husbands are to be the spiritual leaders of their wives and children (Eph. 5:23, 6:1), and parents are to govern their children (Eph. 6:1-4). Schools govern children and employers govern workers (Col. 3:22). Society provides numerous examples of "cultural government", including friendships and associations (Prov. 13:20; 1 Cor. 15:33). Finally, civil government exists to enforce good conduct among its citizenry (Rom. 13:1-7). God, the King of Kings (Rev. 19:16), commissioned government in its multiple forms to promote order and godliness. Our duty as citizens is to obey and pray for all of our leaders (1 Tim. 2:1, 2).

(The Woman's Study Bible, 1982, p. 1461)

The Bible is the Constitution for Christians to obey and live Godly according to His Word.

[19] Yount, W.R., *The Teaching Ministry of the Church,* 2008, Chapter 23, mywsb.com

20. Relationships

Winter & Hawthorne lists, "Ten Ways to Build Multi-Ethnic Bridges between Churches"[20]

1. **Welcome.** We must welcome people of other cultures who want to join our church, and if they so desire, we must help them create niches where they can worship in familiar ways.

2. **Teach.** We must teach, over and over, the contrasting biblical truths of unity and creativity.

3. **Pray.** We must pray with each other regularly across ethnic boundaries.

4. **Evangelize.** We must work together in culturally-relevant local evangelism.

5. **Nurture.** We must work together with ethnic churches in our community to nurture the youth, while encouraging the youth to maintain pride in their heritage.

6. **Repent.** We must repent of hegemonic dominance of neglect on one side and of resentment or dependency on the other.

7. **Link.** We must designate a member to be a "culture broker" who links our congregation with specific churches of other heritage in our community, and who holds the church members accountable for maintaining faithful relationships of depth and substance.

8. **Invest.** We must invest time and money sacrificially and risk ourselves emotionally in strong partnership and exchange patterns.

9. **Build leaders.** We must work together in culturally-relevant leadership training and publishing of useful materials.

10. **Learn.** We must be ready to learn from each other, believing that the word of the Lord may come to us through people very different from ourselves.

21. Racial/Class Discrimination

Discrimination is defined on www.dictionary.com, "as treatment or consideration of, or making a distinction in favor of or against, a person or thing based on the group, class, or category to which that person or thing belongs rather than on individual merit".

Many times, you have gone out somewhere and noticed that someone that is richer, dressed better or smelled very nice was being treated better than you were. Maybe you were ignored while another person was treated with courtesy. Did you ever see this occur or feel a way about it? Remember Christ's command, "love your neighbor as yourself". James 2:1 says, "2 My brethren, do not hold the faith of our Lord Jesus Christ, the Lord of glory, with partiality."

Jesus did not specify any social status or race, he just said neighbor.   He meant anyone you

---

20   Winter & Hawthorne, Miriam Adeney, *Perspectives on the World Christian Movement*, 2009, 419.

interact with regularly. It can be at home, work, church, grocery store, shopping mall, gas station, everywhere. Jesus commanded to treat each of them properly, not show favouritism. If you do this, you are doing right. If not, you sin. When you treat others equally, you show mercy, if not, you are a merciless person. James 2:8-9 says, "8 If you really fulfill the royal law according to the Scripture, "You shall love your neighbor as yourself," you do well; 9 but if you show partiality, you commit sin, and are convicted by the law as transgressors."

Remember to show mercy on others. If you do not show mercy, then God will not show mercy to you when he judges you. James 2:13 says, "13 For judgment is without mercy to the one who has shown no mercy. Mercy triumphs over judgment." Be kind to everyone and treat everyone equally. The rich may be impresses that you are kind to everyone regardless of class. Some may feel insulted that you put them on the same level as a poor person. In either situation, remember that you are following the word of God and refusing to commit a sin which has consequences. There are eternal blessings that await you for obeying the commandments of God. Will you obey the word of God today?

Are you discriminating against a brother or sister? If yes? Why?

Let me explain, you can discriminate against someone because of their skin color, beliefs, financial status, appearance, gifting, and so much more.

The social view of the unbelievers has crept into the church, which are the people. So, there is racial and class discrimination amongst the people.

Racial discrimination involves light skin vs. light skin, dark skin vs. light skin, dark skin vs. dark skin, light skin vs. dark skin. Class discrimination involves rich vs. poor, educated vs. uneducated, and married vs. single.

ASK: **Do you think there can be any other form of discrimination in the church?**

_____

_____

Why? _____

_____

_____

22. Healing

Healing means the restoration of health (Ps. 41:3). Healing makes the person whole or well whether physically, mentally, or spiritually. Sickness is cured by the supernatural intervention of God with or without the use of earthly means. In the healing ministry of Christ faith was a dominant factor. Faith on the part of the person or on behalf of someone is a prerequisite for healing. Healing can be delayed because of a lack of faith.

Some believe that when you seek any type of medical attempt that it is a lack of faith in God's healing power. The Bible does not support this position in belief. In the OT and NT the medical means was utilized (2 Kings 20:2-11; Luke 10:34; 1 Tim, 5:23). In 2 Chronicles 16:12, Asa went to a physician who was a pagan magician.

In Matthew 9:12 Christ shows it is normal to consult physicians. When Jesus commissioned the twelve disciples and sent them out, it continued his healing ministry. The book of Acts and the epistles shows us evidence of the continuance of divine healing. In Janes 5:14-16, he is telling us the healing of the sick through the prayer of faith is a permanent provision and promise of the righteous man.

Scriptures: 1 Cor. 12:9, 28, 30. Gifts of healing by the same spirit. The gifts of healing involve the ability of a person to cure other persons of all forms of sicknesses. It resembles "working of miracles" (powers). Gifts of healing were prominent in the church after Pentecost (Acts 5:15-16; James 5:14-15). "Gifts" indicates the great variety of both the sicknesses healed and the means used in the healings. The person who exercises the gift, and person who was healed had one essential in common, their faith in God. God may heal a person directly. There is a difference between the gift of healing and healing itself.

Jesus said He would send the Holy Spirit, the Comforter to lead, teach, guide, and convict the world of sin. Yes, the Holy Spirit does heal but this is not necessarily why He was sent, or He came into the world. (Acts 1:1-8; 2:33; 1 Cor. 12' Heb. 2:3-4). Gifts of healings are a permanent gift of the Spirit in the church but must be properly exercised only by people of the Spirit and of humility and faith.

Confessions Concerning your Healing:

- The Lord has not given me a spirit of fear or doubt (concerning my healing), but He has given me a spirit of power, and of love, and a sound and confident mind that I shall receive my healing (2 Tim. 1:7),
- The Lord shall remove all sickness and disease from my body (Deuteronomy 7:15), and
- As I serve the Lord, He shall bless me, and He shall take sickness away from me (Exodus 23:25).

23. Spiritual Gifts

Paul gives instruction on spiritual gifts in Romans 12:6-8; 1 Corinthians 12:4-11; 28-30; and Ephesians 4:7-12. Spiritual gifts are gifts of God enabling Christians to perform his or her service. The word charisma ("spiritual gift"), except for 1 Peter 4:10, is used only by Paul. Charisma signifies redemption or salvation as the gift of God's grace (Rom. 5:15; 6:23) and a gift that enables the Christian to perform his service in the church (1 Cor. 7:7), as well as perform a particular ministry in the church.

In 1 Corinthians 12, there is the gifts of the Spirit. You learned about the gifts of the Spirit in goal two.

24. Grace

What is God's grace?

Grace is God's unmerited favor. Grace is undeserved blessing freely bestowed on humans by God. It is kindness from God that we don't deserve. There is nothing we have done, nor can ever do to earn this favor. It is a gift from God.

The word grace in the original language is charis, which the adjective, charismatic, is derived. Webster's New World College Dictionary provides this theological definition of grace: "The unmerited love and favor of God toward human beings; divine influence acting in a person to make the person pure, morally strong; the condition of a person brought to God's favor through this influence; a special virtue, gift, or help given to a person by God."

Grace is undeserved acceptance and love from God (Eph. 2:8). Grace teaches men to deny ungodliness and worldly lusts and to live soberly, righteously, and godly here and now (Titus 2:11-12). If men do not obey its teaching, grace can go no further. Paul tells in the epistles that "Grace was given to each of us according to the measure of Christ's (Ephesians 4:7). We as authentic follower of Christ, have been gifted with a "grace" of the Spirit. God has given us grace for a service capacity for Christians. This grace is given to all true Christians.

<u>Examples of Grace in the Bible</u>

John 1:16-17 For *from his fullness we have all received, grace upon grace. For the law was given through Moses; grace and truth came through Jesus Christ.* (ESV)

Romans 3:23-24... *for all have sinned and fall short of the glory of God, and are justified by his grace as a gift, through the redemption that is in Christ Jesus ...* (ESV)

Romans 6:14 For *sin will have no dominion over you, since you are not under law but under grace.* (ESV)

Ephesians 2:8 For *by grace you have been saved through faith. And this is not your own doing; it is the gift of God ...* (ESV)

Titus 2:11 *For the grace of God has appeared, bringing salvation for all people ...* (ESV)

(Gal. 2:21; Deut. 21:12,13; Rom. 1:7; 1 Thess. 1:1)

25. Healthy Body, Healthy Church

The pastor must get the leadership team to join in prayer as he or she slowly works to build alignment and relationship starting from the top with God. The plans must be built together and sought together to understand the vision. Pastors must ask, how do these principles apply to your church and skill sets? Do it as a team. Use the word to discover these effective visionary principles and allow them to name those principles. Cast the vision, with your actions and then with your words. Tell the church why, reinforce what the benefit will be, and then do it one piece at a time.

All the parts need to be working "according to the proper working of each individual part".

- Pastor is feeding the flock,
- Each person's spiritual gift must be discovered and grown, and
- Every Christian has at least one "manifestation of the Spirit" (spiritual gifting).

As a result of poor choices, a church can become unhealthy. When we receive the precious gift of salvation, we are baptized by the Holy Spirit into the universal church, which is the body of Christ (1 Cor 12:13; Eph 4:5). An evaluation must be done to ensure that the church is healthy.

Healthy, for example:

- People are operating in their gifting
- Blessings are manifesting

Tripp & Tripp notes, "God designed people to live in a community – both physical and spiritual. The family is essential to the growth and development of each of its members. Our families are a precious representation of the family of God, with worship, training, leadership, submission, roles, schedule, laws, accountability, humility, unity, diversity, common goals, love, thanksgiving, praise, nurture, protection, consideration, forgiveness, servanthood, bearing one another's burdens, acceptance, encouragement, communion, companionship, admonition, rebuke, restoration, repentance, reconciliation, prayer and fellowship, to name just a few. These qualities are essential to a healthy, happy family."[21]

26. Success

Renfro notes, "How can the success of a church truly be measured?

Often it is measured by size and budget rather than faithfulness. In evaluating the success of a church, it is necessary to ask questions such as these: Does this structure reflect the ideal structure of New Testament churches? Does the church's leadership meet the qualifications that are spelled out in the Bible? Is the preaching faithful to the text of scripture? Are men leading their families?

---

21   Tripp T. & Tripp M., *Instructing a Child's* Heart, 2008, 134.

Are parent's discipling their children? Are children obeying the fifth commandment? Are those ministries of intergenerational discipleship that reflect the sound teaching principles of Titus 2:1-8 present?

Are wives helping and submitting to their husbands? Are husbands loving their wives as Christ loves the church? Do we practice hospitality toward one another and the world? Are we engaged in biblical evangelism?

A church is successful only to the degree that it lines up with scripture in these areas. To the degree that we lead God's church biblically, we will experience his blessing, not necessarily in buildings and money but in churches that closely resemble what Jesus and the apostles expected churches to look like."[22]

27. Warfare Prayer for the Church

Father, I cover our church, its pastors, people's, ministries, facilities, all that we are, have, and possess, including our families and children, our jobs, incomes, finances, possessions, health, safety, warfare, travels by car-boat-plane, our bodies and all of our body parts systems, organs, structures and functions all with the precious Blood of Christ Jesus, all permanently, immediately, completely, and continually, by trusting and expectant faith, in Christ Jesus Name. I BIND the princes of the north, south, east, and west; the princes over (Continent), (Country), (State), or (Province), (Country), (Community), all territorial spirits everywhere, and all principalities, powers, rulers of the darkness, wicked spirits in high places, and all spirits not of the Holy Spirit. I bind the demonic and devilish ruler spirit over our church and all ruler spirits assigned to all church members, our loved ones, children, me, and all spirits above, around, and below them; I bind and break all of their assignments; I bind all "watcher" spirits, "Scanner" spirits, "eavesdropper" spirits. All spirits of divination, witchcraft Jezebel, Python, Ahab, guile, antichrist, fault-finding, death, slander, scandal, rumor defamation, ill-will, detraction, accusations, false-accusations, persecution, litigation, assassination, character assassination, opposition, hindrance, interference, obstruction, ruin, destruction, theft, murder, discontent, confusion, all warring spirits, the spirits of Cain, Balaam, and Korah, all familiar spirits assigned to all members of all families, and me, all spirits of confusion, lies, deception, division, discord, argument, discontent, seduction, lust, perversion, spiritual or temporal adultery or fornication, pride, presumption, arrogance, unbelief, doubt, fear, all nature spirits, all spirits of indigenous peoples and, the religious spirit, the spirit of unforgiveness, bitterness, anger, resentment, hate, spite, malice, and all of their kindred spirits, I bind all spirits not of the Holy Spirit.

I bind all of their physical-psychic-spiritual attacks, assignments, all operations, all of their seedlings, works, plans, activities, blueprints, plots, plans, designs, traps, wiles, snares, assignments, all curses, hexes, vexes, bewitchments, enchantments, cantrips, ligatures, and judgments of witches and warlocks, all acts of evil, sorcery, witchcraft, magic, candle magic, potion magic, white magic,

---

22 Renfro, P. *Perspectives on Family Ministry: 3 Views*, 2009, p. 77

black magic, voodoo, all blood pacts, blood sacrifices, and blood covenants of witchcraft; all national and continental witchcraft workings and curses; all demonic thoughts, threats, mental locutions, statements and ideations, all self-inflicted curses through negative confession; all curses spoke over the church , its pastors, elders, or peoples, any of our family members or children, or me; any such curses spoken over, formed against, directed at any of our pastors, or our, marriages, families, possessions, health, safety, welfare, jobs, income, our physical bodies or lives, all that they or we are , have, or possess. I take all of these things into captivity to Christ, and by faith, call them all cancelled, made null and void, never manifested, never come to pass, cursed and destroyed at their roots and rendered of no effect, judged, spoiled, never seeded, cast down as vain thoughts and imaginations, and broken off of our pastors, church peoples, families, ministries, and each and every one of us…ALL immediately, completely, permanently, and continually; I cut and sever all ties, binds, cords, and soul ties with corporate or personal sin, repenting, Father, for our people and myself, and renouncing our sin…all by waiting and expectant faith, in Christ Jesus' name and for your glory, Father. Having bound all of these spirits and all spirits not of the Holy Spirit, Father, I now break their communications and supply lines and bind up and off all reinforcements. I speak and decree upon them spiritual: confusion, dumbness deafness, blindness, incapacitation, paralysis; I throw all of their plan into continual confusion and disarray, and decree all of these things accomplished immediately, completely, permanently, and continually ALL in JESUS NAME!

28. *Closing*

Reflection in Action by Connection

Answer the questions on the lines provided.

Question 1: What makes God's people Christians?

A: _____

_____

Answer: The belief that Jesus Christ died on the Cross at Calvary for their sins, and He rose again on the third day, and He will return for the true believers. It is the faith, belief, and the lifestyle.

Question 2: - What is the five-fold designations?

A: _____

_____

Answer: The Apostle, Prophet, Teacher, Evangelist, and the Pastor.

Question 3: What are the eight characteristics of a leader?

A: _____

_____

_____

Answer: The characteristics are integrity, self-discipline, selfless, accountable, honest, ethical, visionary, and to love people.

Question 4: What are ways that you a person can be discriminating against someone inside and outside of the church?

A:_____
_____
_____

Answer: It can be skin color, beliefs, someone's culture, financial status, appearance, gifting, lack of education ad so much more.

Question 5: What is God's grace?

A:_____
_____
_____

Answer: Grace is God's unmerited favor. It is kindness from God that we don't deserve. It is a gift from God.

SAY: God created the Kingdom and the church to operate here on earth as it is in heaven, Amen. Let's move on to goal seven and the mission.

GOAL SEVEN

MISSION & MISSIONS

LESSON PLAN

Date & Time:	**Curriculum Area**: Mission & Missions	**Goal /Unit Topic**: Goal Seven

Key enduring understandings, concepts, abilities, and/or values.
Explained in the Introduction
Intended learning outcomes (to know, to do, to create, to value, etc.)
Explained in the Overview
Assessment Strategies: How will you assess attainment of the intended learning outcome? Questions & Answers, Dialect, Interaction, Pre/Post Tests
Materials/Preparation/ Area Setup:
Materials: Poster board, Dry Erase Markers
Preparation: Decorations, Poster board
Area Setup: For each disciple, place on the desk a blue pen, highlighter, notebook, goal seven

Introduction	*Setting the Stage*: engaging, motivating, experiencing, connecting with prior knowledge, reflecting, conjecturing, posing problems
Once the Introduction and Overview have been completed, then move on to the Bible book recitals. It will be recited every time that we meet with the disciples.	
Guided learning steps	*Disclosing*: acquiring knowledge/skills, conceptualizing, developing, understanding, integrating
The learning steps are as follows: 1. Missio Dei 2. Mission 3. Missions 4. Brainstorm Activity 5. Closing	*Practicing, Reinforcing*: modeling, giving instruction, checking for understanding, guided practice, independent practice, applying, posing and solving problems
Closure	*Transcending*: summing up, responding, creating, performing, committing, evaluating
Prayer, Questions & Answers, Comments	
Modifications:	
How will you change the lesson to meet the needs of the individual students?	
Personal notes/reminders/homework/assignments	
Post-lesson reflections	

INTRODUCTION

Today we will learn and discuss mission and missions for the church and its people. Earley & Wheeler explains, "The early church did five things to align with God's mission, which were:

1. **The Early Church Ministered Through** *Constant Presence* **(Acts 2:46-47)**
   The early church did not hide or run from the community they were called to serve. They engaged the culture. The early church was out in the community on a daily basis, thus creating a constant presence for the purpose of spreading the gospel. As a result, God added to the Church "daily." Our neighborhoods and workplaces become mission fields in which we share Christ in both words and action.

2. **The Early Church Depended on a** *Consuming Power* **(Acts 1:8; 4:8)**

3. **The Early Church Shared a** *Consistent Message* **(Acts 2, 3, 4:12)**. The early apostles never compromised the gospel.

4. **The Early Church Possessed a** *Convicting Boldness* **(Acts 4:31)**. The boldness of the early church was the fruit of a lifestyle of prayer and dependence on the Holy Spirit. Believers had to maintain a posture of prayer to main their spiritual power in life.

5. **The Early Church Consistently Displayed a** *Contagious Courage* **(Acts 4:18-20)**.

The earliest Christians fully realized that life is disposable and can be taken away at any moment. They were not driven by the fear of death."[1]

Overview

I. Goal Lesson:
Goal seven teaches about mission and missions of God.

II. Goal Objectives:
Upon completion of this lesson, the disciple will be able to:

a. explain the mission of God and the kinds of missions, and
   b. develop mission strategies.

III. Bible Books Recital

Genesis to Revelation

1. Missio Dei

Moreau et al notes, "Latin for "the sending of God". God's mission is everything God himself does in establishing his kingdom on earth and everything the church is sent to do on Earth."

```
Missio Dei: All That God does to build the Kingdom



Mission: What the Church Does for God in the World



Missions: Evangelism, Discipleship, and Church Planting
```

2. Mission

Our mission as the people of God is <u>Make Disciples!</u> of the entire world. Jesus commanded us to <u>Go!</u> We should be rubbing elbows and shoulders with those who don't know Christ. We must lead by example.

Moreau explains, "Your heart for people who do not know Christ must be easy to see and emulate. When a person makes a decision to follow Christ, he or she should be baptized in water. <u>Baptize!</u> Take a stand and identify with the death, burial and resurrection of Christ. <u>Teach!</u> New disciples to observe the teachings of Christ. We teach people to love God by connecting them to His word and teaching them to connect. We teach people to love one another by connecting them to each other in groups and encouraging them to use their spiritual gifts to serve each other. We teach people to love their neighbors by connecting them to Christ and to each other and teaching the community to love and serve their community through their gifts.

It is everything that the church does that points toward the kingdom of God. Mission is not limited to evangelistic and church-planting tasks. It includes addressing systematic injustice, enabling social or political liberation, and engaging in dialogue with people of other living faiths.

Mission and spiritual warfare are intertwined. Christians having been declared a new creation (2 Cor. 5:17), are God's children (Rom. 8:15; Eph. 1:4-5), are given Christ's authority (Col. 2:10), and are called to engage in the kingdom conflict (Eph. 6:12) in the power of the Holy Spirit (2 Cor. 10:3-5). They do this by submitting to God and resisting Satan (James 4: 4-9; 1 Pet. 5:5-9)."[2]

Our foundation for the mission is the Bible. The Bible alone has the authority to guide the church through the complex questions that face each new generation.

Mission is to be at the heart of what Christians are and what the church is to be and do. Missions are not the ultimate goal of the church. Worship is because it abides forever.

Moreau notes, "We are saying that the core of our responsibility of reflecting God's glory through worship is (1) to engage in evangelism and church planting, as well as (2) discipling those who enter the kingdom and enabling local churches to thrive and grow, (3) while glorifying God by living lives that act as salt and light in a hurting world is indeed a form of worshipping God, but if it does not include the invitation to the lost to turn to Christ, then it is not truly engaged mission."[3]

SAY: So, what happened? Let's discuss further. Some pressed on and some did not.

3. Missions

Missions is the specific task of making disciples of all nations. Missionaries have the authority to preach the Christian faith (and sometimes to administer baptism, communion), and provide humanitarian work to improve economic development, literacy, education, health care, and orphanages.

4. Brainstorm Activity

This assignment is to consider the people group's history and cultural background, to assess the history of missions work among them, to analyze current mission's strategies at work among them, and to develop a plan for reaching them with the Gospel. Get in a group and plan a mission plan for an unreached people group.

Scenario: We are breaking out into four groups to create a mission plan and incorporate yourself into the community. Each group will be given literature and a specific article to read and determine how you as a group can make a difference in their lives through the love of Jesus Christ. Remember as you read to focus on the specifics such as people who are separated by color, standard of living, prestige, literacy, mode of travel, place of residence and many other factors.

Topics:

1. Proclaiming Jesus Among the Wolves
2. Forgiveness to a people who have had great loss
   Use the tools provided to elaborate on your mission plan.

5. Closing

Reflection in Action by Connection
Answer the questions on the lines provided.

Question 1: What does Missio Dei for God?
A:_____
Answer: It is all that God does to build the kingdom.

Question 2: -What is the mission for the believer?
A:_____
Answer: The mission for the people of God is to make disciples of the entire world.

Question 3: What is missions?
A:_____
Answer: Missions is to make disciples of all nations.

Question 4: How can you make disciples in your community? Write down some ideas of how you can make that happen.
A:_____
Answer: One person at a time or even a small group.

Question 5: How did the brainstorm activity impact you and the importance of the mission and missions?
A:_____
Answer: Gave insight for planning and strategy for the mission.

SAY: You now understand mission and its missions for the kingdom of God. Next is evangelism. Let's get you ready to evangelize!

GOAL EIGHT

EVANGELISM

LESSON PLAN

Date & Time:	Curriculum Area: Evangelism	Goal /Unit Topic: Goal Eight
Key enduring understandings, concepts, abilities, and/or values. Explained in the Introduction		
Intended learning outcomes (to know, to do, to create, to value, etc.) Explained in the Overview		
Assessment Strategies: How will you assess attainment of the intended learning outcome? Questions & Answers, Dialect, Interaction, Pre/Post Tests		
Materials/Preparation/ Area Setup: Materials: Poster board, Dry Erase Markers Preparation: Decorations, Poster board Area Setup: For each disciple, place on the desk a blue pen, highlighter, notebook, goal eight		

Introduction	*Setting the Stage*: engaging, motivating, experiencing, connecting with prior knowledge, reflecting, conjecturing, posing problems
Once the Introduction and Overview have been completed, then move on to the Bible book recitals. It will be recited every time that we meet with the disciples.	

Guided learning steps	*Disclosing*: acquiring knowledge/skills, conceptualizing, developing, understanding, integrating
The learning steps are as follows:	*Practicing, Reinforcing*: modeling, giving instruction, checking for understanding, guided practice, independent practice, applying, posing and solving problems

1. Evangelism	6. Questions Lost People Will Ask
2. Preparing for Evangelism	7. Share Jesus Questions (Witnessing to Others)
3. Evangelist	8. Methods to Evangelize
4. Holiness	9. Lead them to Christ
5. Christianity, Cults & Religions	10. Follow Up
	11. Assignment
	12. Closing

Closure	*Transcending*: summing up, responding, creating performing, committing, evaluating
Prayer, Questions & Answers, Comments	

Modifications:	
How will you change the lesson to meet the needs of the individual students?	
Personal notes/reminders/homework/assignments	
Post-lesson reflections	

INTRODUCTION

What is evangelism? Evangelism is the announcement, proclamation, and/or preaching of the gospel (1 Corinthians 15:1-4), the good news of and about Jesus Christ. Therefore, the gospel is a communicated message–communicated in verbal (Luke 7:22; Romans 10:14-17) and/or written (Luke 1:1-4) form. The English word, "evangelism," comes from the Greek word "euaggelion". Most literally translated in the noun form, euaggelion means: "gospel" or "good news."

Overview

I. Goal Lesson:

Goal eight teaches evangelism. As a result, the disciple will be able to perform the Great Commission and the Great Commandment.

II. Goal Objectives:

Upon completion of this goal, the disciple will be able to:

    a. explain what is evangelism,
    b. explain different kinds of religions,
    c. explain how to evangelize, and
    d. evangelize a lost soul.

III. Bible Books Recital

Genesis to Revelation

1. Evangelism

Evangelism is:

- going and telling the good news of Jesus Christ.
- living as a missionary, not a mission field.

Evangelism is the spreading of the Christian gospel by public preaching or personal witness. Scriptures for witnessing (Matt. 28:19, 20; Acts 1:8; 6:7; 1 Thess. 1:8; 4:9,10; Rev. 11:3). Evangelism, the communication of the gospel message, includes a warning, an explanation, and a call.

Evangelism includes warning people about sin and the consequences of sin (John 16:8; Acts 24:25; Revelation 20:11-15). It includes an explanation of God's remedy for sin—the gospel (Acts 8:29-35; Romans 3:21-26; 2 Corinthians 5:21).

And it includes the clear call to repent (to turn from sin and to turn toward God) and believe the gospel by faith (Mark 1:15; Luke 13:1-5; Acts 17:29-31; Romans 1:17; Romans 10:9-13).

We play various roles in personal evangelism. Biblically we are called to testify (John 1:7-8, 33; 3:11, 28; 15:27; 18:37; Acts 4:33; 10:42-43; 2 Tim. 1:8; 1 John 1:2; 4:14), to witness (Acts 22:15; 26:16), to be ambassadors (2 Cor. 5:20), to proclaim (Matt. 10:27; Luke 4:18; Acts 17:23; 20:27; 1 Cor. 11:26; Col. 1:28; 4:3-4; 1 John 1:2-3; Rev. 14:6), and to persuade (Acts 18:4; 26:28; 2 Cor. 5:11).

(Mc Raney, 2003, Chapter 2, p. 62, digital)

Nothing is any more effective in drawing someone to Jesus Christ than the sharing of personal testimony (John 4:39; 11:32). Believers should always be ready to share. A personal testimony catches the attention of those listening and holds the interest of the unbeliever (John 4:28-30). (The Woman's Study Bible, NKJV, 2006, p. 1635)

2. Preparing for Evangelism

Every Christian is called to be an ambassador for Christ. To be a soul winner you must be saved, develop a desire to lead others to Christ, learn to be led by the Holy Spirit, be trained, and utilize helpful resources.

McRaney explains,

1. An Obedient and Tender Heart

It all begins with a willing spirit. Part of being ready involves making space in our hearts for lost people.

2. Filled with the Holy Spirit

As we are directed by the Holy Spirit, we are in the only position where we are able to follow God's leadership. Believers need continually to demonstrate submission to God's leading.

3. Praying for the Lost and for Clear Communication

Evangelism at its core is a spiritual battle. This battle requires that we enter into it with spiritual weapons. Knowing and using the Word in an appropriate manner is a strong weapon in the spiritual battle. Prayer is another way to become involved in the spiritual battle.

4. Grasp the Gospel Essentials

Before we can share a witness, we need to understand the message and person of Christ. Without a clear understanding of the message, it will be almost impossible for us to encode a message that the lost person can receive."[1]

As the world becomes more anti-Christian and looks more unlike Christ, it is imperative that Christ followers possess different values and behaviors from those without Christ. There is no room for cultural Christianity. In order to be credible, we must demonstrate that the Christian lifestyle works.

3. Evangelist

Anthony explains, "An evangelist equips and encourages believers to share the Good News. (Eph 4:11). To testify is to bear witness. Work of an evangelist- 2 Tim. 4:5. The evangelist lives a life that is at risk of being scrutinized by the world. The posture of the evangelist should be of humility if he or she is to enjoy maximal credibility in the proclamation of the gospel. (Anthony, 2001 p 55). Honesty does a great deal to prepare one for reaching a lost and needy world. Evangelists are not to win arguments but to communicate as clearly and as effectively as possible, the love, forgiveness, and grace of God to all they meet."[2]

4. Holiness

Furthermore, holiness serves as an evangelistic purpose. It is a "holy nation "and "special people" who are able to "proclaim the praises of Him who called you out of the darkness into His marvelous light" (1 Peter 2:9). It is our "honorable" conduct and "good works" that cause evildoers to glory God (1 Peter 2:12). (The Nelson Study Bible, p. 2120)

5. Christianity, Cults & Religions

Christianity is based on what the Bible says. Other religions teach their own doctrines and beliefs that they have created. There are many false gospels today. Galatians 1:8-9 explains how to recognize false gospels. Let's discuss Biblical Christianity and the other religions that man and woman have created their own beliefs to deter the human race from the Bible. Rose Publishing explains,

"1. **Biblical Christianity**: Jesus Christ. Founded about AD 30-33 in the Judean province of Palestine (Israel today), under the Roman empire. Followers of Jesus Christ became known as Christians. The Bible is the key writing which was originally written in Hebrew and Aramaic (OT), and Greek (NT). The Bible tells men and women Who is God? Who is Jesus? Who is the Holy Spirit? How to be saved, What happens after Death, and many facts, beliefs and practices, and more.

2. **Jehovah's Witness (Watchtower & Bible Tract Society)**: Charles Taze Russell (1852-1916), later Joseph T. Rutherford (1869-1942). Began in 1879 in Pennsylvania. These writings are the Watchtower publications, including the Bible (New World Translation only), Reasoning from the Scriptures, what does the Bible Really Teach? Watchtower and Awake! magazines. They believe in a one-person God, called Jehovah. No Trinity. Jesus is the first thing Jehovah created.

3. **Mormonism (Later-day Saints)**: Joseph Smith, Jr. (1805-1844) organized what is now the Church of Jesus Christ of Latter-Day Saints (LDS) in 1830 near Rochester, New York. There are the Book of Mormon, Doctrine and Covenants, Pearl of Great Price, plus the Bible (King James Version only or Smith's Inspired Version), which is seen as less reliable. Authoritative teachings of Mormon prophets and other LDS "general authorities." Ensign and Liahna magazines.

They believe that God the Father was once a man, but "Progressed" to godhood. He has a physical body, as does his wife (Heavenly Mother). No Trinity. Father, Son, and Holy Ghost are three separate gods. Worthy members may one day become "exalted" to godhood themselves.

4. **Scientology**: Founded by L. Ron Hubbard (1911-1986) in 1954 in California. There writings are Dianetics: The Modern Science of Mental Health and others by Hubbard. The Way to Happiness. Their belief about God is that they do not define God or Supreme Being but rejects biblical description of God. Everyone is a "thetan," an immortal spirit with unlimited powers over its own universe, but not all are aware of this. Jesus is rarely mentioned in Scientology. Jesus did not die for sins. The Holy Spirit is not part of this belief. For salvation there is no sin or need to repent. It is freedom from reincarnation. Hell is a myth, and heaven is a "false dream".

5. **Islam**: Founded in Mecca, Arabia by Muhammad (AD 570-632), considered the greatest man who ever lived and the last of more than 124,000 messengers sent by Allah (God). Main types: Sunni ("people of the tradition", Shi'a (party of Ali), Sufi (mystics). Their writings are the Holy Qur'an (Koran), revealed to Muhammed by the angel Gabriel. The Qur'an affirms the biblical Torah, Psalms, and Gospels, but Jews and Christians have corrupted the original texts. Their God is Allah and Allah is One and absolutely unique. He cannot be known. The greatest sin in Islam is shirk, or associating anything with Allah. Many Muslims think Christians believe in three gods

and are therefore guilty of shirk. The belief about Jesus is Jesus was not God or the son of God. His virgin birth is likened to Adam's creation. He was sinless, a worker of miracles, and one of the most respected prophets sent by Allah. He was not crucified or resurrected."[3]

Groothius explains, "Islam insists that there is but one God, whose name is Allah. Allah, a personal God, is the creator, lawgiver and judge of the universe. Allah is the one and only God. The utter transcendence and oneness of God is repeatedly and militantly affirmed by Islam. Islam thus insists that God has no son or cohort."[4]

6. Judaism: Abraham of the Bible, about 2000 BC, and Moses in the Middle East. There are three main branches of Judaism-Orthodox, Conservative, and Reform—each with its own belief. There writings are the Tanakh (OT), and especially the Torah (first five books of the Bible). The Talmud (explanation of the Ganakh). Teachings of each branch. Writings of sages, such as Maimonides. They believe God is spirit. To Orthodox Jews, God is personal, all-powerful, eternal, and compassionate. To other Jews, God is impersonal, unknowable, and defined in a number of ways. No Trinity. Jesus is seen either as an extremist false messiah or a good martyred Jewish rabbi (teacher). Many Jews do not consider Jesus at all. Jews (except Messianic Jews and Hebrew Christian) do not believe he was the Messiah, Son of God, or that he rose from the dead. Orthodox Jews believe the Messiah will restore the Jewish kingdom and eventually rule the earth.

7. Buddhism: Guatama Siddhartha, (563-483 BC), also known as Buddha. Founded in modern day Nepal and India as are formation of Hinduism. Main types: Theravada, Mahayana, Vajrayana. Their writings are the Mahavasta "Great Story," a collection covering the Buddha's life story, the Jutaka Tales (550 stories of the former lives of the Buddha), the Tripitaka ("Three Baskets"), and the Tantras (as recorded in Tibetan Buddhism). Jesus Christ is not part of the historic Buddhist worldview. The Holy Spirit is not part of their belief. Buddhists do believe in spirits, and some practice deity yoga and invite spirit possession. "[5]

Groothius explains, "Buddha taught that spiritual deliverance was found by letting go of desire – the quest to satisfy the non-existent soul and by detaching oneself from impermanent things. Buddhism has many branches with different teachings."[6]

Distribute the pamphlet to the disciples.

6. Questions Lost People Will Ask

Many times, while you are evangelizing, people will ask some questions. Always be prepared to give an answer to everyone who ask you to give the reason for the hope that you have. (1 Peter 3:15) What do you think are the best answers to these questions? Answer but you must provide scripture as a part of your

---

3		Rose Publishing, "Christianity Cults & Religions", Pamphlet, 2010.
4		Groothuis, D., "Christian Apologetics", ,2011, 601.
5		Rose Publishing, "Christianity Cults & Religions", Pamphlet, 2010.
6		Groothuis, D., "Christian Apologetics", , 2011,574,572.

Respond in the lines provided.

1. Which God, or how many gods? _____

   Answer: Read Deut. 6:4, "Hear: O Israel: The Lord our God, the Lord is one!" The Bible makes it clear that there is only one God. The Bible also tells us that all other supposed Gods are idols-figments of man's own imagination gone awry (Mark 12:29; 1 Cor. 8:4; 1 Tim. 2:5). Throughout history mankind has made many false gods. God the Father and Jesus Christ the Son are one mind and purpose (John 4:34; 5:30).

2. Is there a God? _____
   Note: this question can also be Does God exist?

3. How can Jesus be the only way to God?_____

   Answer: Jesus is God. He stated he is truth in John 14:6, "I am the way, the truth, and the life. No one can come to the Father except through me.

4. Was Jesus the Son of God? _____

   Answer: Yes, Jesus was the Son of God. Peter immediately preached the Jesus had been resurrected from the dead and that He was indeed the Christ and Lord and equated Him with God (Acts 2:27,34-35). Jesus of Nazareth was God in the flesh.

5. How can Christianity be true if Christians live like everyone else?_____

   Answer: Christianity is not a religion, but a relationship with God. It has no denomination or church building. It is a relationship between a person and Jesus Christ. Christianity is not based on His teachings, but on Jesus Christ himself.

6. What does Jesus have to do with my life? _____

7. Who was/is Jesus? _____

   Answer: Jesus was the very Son of God. Jesus said of Himself, : I am the good shepherd" (John 10:11). Jesus claimed to be the judge of all men and nations (John 5:22,27). Jesus said," I am the light of the word" (John 8:12). Jesus spoke of Himself as the coming bridegroom (Matthew 25:1).

8. What is God like? _____
   Answer: God is not unapproachable. God is great. God reveals Himself through His Word. God is Creator. God is our Father. God loves us.

9. How can I find meaning and purpose in life? _
   _____

   Answer: Read and reflect upon Genesis 1: 26 where God gave His creation dominion. So, man was made in God's image to rule over His creation. The best self-help book ever published, is the Bible. Take the time to study the Bible because it addresses the ageless issues we will encounter and the questions that will arise during your journey with God here on earth. It records for us God's people vital and profound lessons from real people. The Bible shows the cause and effect of the choices made and the actions taken in life. The Bible tells us how to make life work. To find meaning and purpose in life you must find the will of God for your life, define the will of God in your life, define the call of God upon your life, and steward the call of God upon your life.

10. What happens to me when I die? _____

    Answer: Ecclesiastes 12:7 says tells us what happens when a person dies. It says, "Then shall the dust return to the earth as it was; and the spirit shall return to God who gave it." In other words, when a person dies, his or her spirit goes back to God, the body returns to dust and the soul of that person no longer exist.

11. How can I trust that what Christians are saying is true?——————————————

    Answer: Christianity is based on the birth, death, and resurrection of Jesus Christ. Jesus claimed to be God (Exo. 3:14; John 10:30-33). Jesus rose from the dead! (Mark 15:39) . The Bible presents reliable information concerning Jesus Christ.

12. Aren't all religions basically the same?_____

    Answer: Christianity teaches a unique view of salvation. All religions are not the same. Other religions claim they have one true God but have conflicting views of what He is like and the what He requires of the people following the religion.

7. Share Jesus Questions (Witnessing to Others)

There are five questions to apply when you are sharing the gospel, which are:

1. Do you have any kind of spiritual belief?
2. What's your understanding of who Jesus Christ is? or to you, who is Jesus Christ?
3. Do you think there is a heaven or hell?
4. If you were to die, where would you go? If heaven, why?
5. If what you were believing were not true, would you want to know?

After you go through these questions and get an answer of yes at question five, then open a new Bible and share scriptures. Ask the person or persons, "May I share some scriptures with you." If the answer is yes, then open the Bible. If the answer is no, do nothing. But remember you have not failed. You have been obedient to share the gospel, and the results belong to God.

The power of God's Word penetrates and changes hearts toward his son. There are two basic principles at work when you share scripture.

The first comes from Rom 10:17 and Luke 10:26. In this scripture Jesus is asking the man, "What does this say to you?" There will be objections to the Bible such as, people stating, "Too many errors" or "Too many translations." Your response to many errors should be, "Would you show me one? and the response will be, "Well, I can't. Your response should be, "I can't either, turn to Romans 3:23. Your response to too many translations should be, "Yes you are absolutely right that there are many translations of scripture, but they all say the same thing, turn to Romans 3:23."

Here is the opportunity to share scriptures. Always walk with a new pocket-sized Bible. You will give them the Bible and now ask them to read the scriptures aloud. It represents your commitment of God moving in your life.

Fay explains,

There are seven scriptures that you want them to read, such as:

1. **Rom 3:23: "For all have sinned"**. After it is read aloud, ask, "What does this say to you?" The response you are looking for is "Everyone has sinned."

2. **Rom 6:23: "For the wages of sin is death"**. Ask "What does this say to you?" The response you are looking for is "The result of sin is death, but God gives life through his Son."

3. **John 3:3: "Must be born again"**. Ask, "What does this say to you?" The response you are looking for is "Why did Jesus come to die?"

4. **John 14:6: "I am the way"**. Ask, "What does this say to you?" The response you are looking for is "There is no other way to be with God except through Jesus"

5. **Rom 10:9-11: "If you confess"**. Ask, "What does this say to you?" The response you are looking for is "If I believe God raised Jesus from the dead, I can be saved."

6. **2 Corinthians 5:15. "No longer live for themselves."** Ask, "What does this say to you?" The response you are looking for is "We should live for Christ."

7. **Rev 3:20: ""Here I am standing at your door"**. Ask, 'What does this say to you?" The response you are looking for is "If I ask Jesus to come into my life, he will."

If the person reading the scriptures doesn't understand, Say, "Read it again."[7]

8. Methods to Evangelize

A. Romans Road to Salvation

Here verses are used from the book of Romans. It explains why we need salvation, how God provided salvation, how we can receive salvation, and what are the results of salvation.

1. Romans 3:23
"For all have sinned, and come short of the glory of God (KJV)

2. Romans 6:23
"For the wages of sin is death; but the gift of God is eternal life through Jesus Christ our Lord" (KJV). The punishment that we have earned for our sins is death. Not just physical death but eternal death!"

3. Romans 5:8
"But God demonstrates His own love toward us, in that while we were still sinners, Christ died for us."

4. Romans 10:9,13
"If you confess with your mouth Jesus as Lord and believe in your heart that God raised Him from the dead, you will be saved." (NASB)

"For everyone who calls on the name of the Lord will be saved." (HCSB)

5. Romans 5:1; 8:1; 8:38–39
"Therefore, since we have been justified through faith, we have peace with God through our Lord Jesus Christ." (NIV)

"Therefore, there is now no condemnation for those who are in Christ Jesus." (NIV)

"For I am convinced that neither death nor life, neither angels nor demons, neither the present nor the future, nor any powers, neither height nor depth, nor anything else in all creation, will be able to separate us from the love of God that is in Christ Jesus our Lord." (NIV)

B. Romans Seven Steps to God

1. There is a God, and we are responsible to Him. (Rom. 1:20; 14:12)
2. We have failed to fulfill our responsibility and have sinned. (Rom. 3:10,19,23)
3. It separates us from God. (Rom. 6:23)
4. Jesus never sinned. (Rom. 5:19)
5. Jesus died to pay for our sins. (Rom. 6:23)
6. He rose from the dead to prove He could offer us abundant and eternal life. (Rom 6:23)
7. We need to believe in Jesus in order to be saved. (Rom. 10:9, 13). Ask the person to place themselves on one of the seven steps. If they say that they are at number 7, offer them an opportunity to believe the gospel and be saved.

C. The ABCs of Salvation

When someone is clearly ready to give their lives to Christ, the ABCs are a simple way to help them understand what is necessary in order for them to cross the line of faith.

1. *Admit my need. (Luke 18:9–14)*
2. *Believe completely on Christ. (John 3:16)*
3. *Call upon Him to take control of my life and save me. (Rom. 10:13)*
4. *Do everything He asks. (Matt. 7:21)*

D. The Way of the Master

The Way of the Master uses the Ten Commandments and a series of probing questions as a basis to establish "lostness" and to present Christ. The method these authors advocate for explaining the good news of salvation uses four steppingstones. The stones are represented by four letters: WDJD, which stand for "What Did Jesus Do?"

<u>W (WHAT)</u>: Would you consider yourself to be a good person?

<u>D (DID)</u>: Do you think you have kept the Ten Commandments?

Exodus 20:3–17 reads:

3 "You shall have no other gods before Me.

4 "You shall not make for yourself a carved image—any likeness of anything that is in heaven above, or that is in the earth beneath, or that is in the water under the earth;

5 you shall not bow down to them nor serve them. For I, the LORD your God, am a jealous God, visiting the iniquity of the fathers upon the children to the third and fourth generations of those who hate Me,

6 but showing mercy to thousands, to those who love Me and keep My commandments.

7 "You shall not take the name of the LORD your God in vain, for the LORD will not hold him guiltless who takes His name in vain.

8 "Remember the Sabbath day, to keep it holy.

9 Six days you shall labor and do all your work,

10 but the seventh day is the Sabbath of the LORD your God. In it you shall do no work: you, nor your son, nor your daughter, nor your male servant, nor your female servant, nor your cattle, nor your stranger who is within your gates.

11 For in six days the LORD made the heavens and the earth, the sea, and all that is in them, and rested the seventh day. Therefore the LORD blessed the Sabbath day and hallowed it.

12 "Honor your father and your mother, that your days may be long upon the land which the

LORD your God is giving you.

13 "You shall not murder.

14 "You shall not commit adultery.

15 "You shall not steal.

16 "You shall not bear false witness against your neighbor.

17 "You shall not covet your neighbor's house; you shall not covet your neighbor's wife, nor his male servant, nor his female servant, nor his ox, nor his donkey, nor anything that is your neighbor's."

I normally deal first with lying, stealing, and lust because people can more easily acknowledge them as evident sins. It seems that this is what Jesus does in Luke 18:20.

J (JESUS): On the day of judgment, if God judges you by the Ten Commandments, will you be innocent or guilty?

D (DO): Destiny—Will you go to heaven or hell?

God's Special Plan—A simple and well-prepared presentation of the Gospel for children (www.kidzplace.org).

E. More Good Approaches to Sharing One's Faith:

Along with the evangelistic events, there are several good approaches to sharing one's faith. Some of these are:

Share Jesus Without Fear—A simple approach that uses a series of probing questions combined with the Bible that takes the fear out of sharing (www.sharejesuswithoutfear.com).

FAITH—An easy approach that uses the acrostic FAITH to remember the gospel presentation. It seeks to tie everything back through the Sunday school (www.lifeway.com).

Got Life—An easy outline that uses the acrostic LIFE. It has a strong apologetics application within the overall presentation (www.gotlife.org)

Evangecube—Great visual approach to sharing one's faith. Uses a small cube that is rotated to reveal a snapshot of the Gospel presentation. (www.simplysharejesus.com)

9. Lead them to Christ

After you applied the evangelism methods and they ask you to help them make a personal decision to follow Jesus or they want to rededicate their life to Jesus Christ. Remember, the Holy Spirit is working 24-hours a day, seven days a week preparing people to hear the Gospel. Our job is to be faithful in our witness and testimony and God will lead us to them, and they to us.

For a personal decision have them pray the Prayer for Salvation.

The Prayer for Salvation says, "Dear Heavenly father, I come to you in the Name of Jesus Christ. You said in your Word that if I confess with my mouth that Jesus Christ is my Lord and I believe in my heart that God raised Him from the dad, I will be saved. I believe in my heart that Jesus Christ is the Son of God. I believe that he was raised from the dead for my justification. I do believe with my heart, and now I confess with my mouth Jesus as my Lord. Therefore, I am saved!

Now Lord Jesus, I give you control of my life. Make me the person you want me to be. Thank you for forgiving me for all my sins. Thank you for my salvation! Thank you, Lord Jesus! Amen. Romans 10:9

As soon as you he/she finishes the sinner's prayer, ask them "Did you mean that prayer? Did you ask Jesus into your heart? Show him/her that in Romans 10:13 it says that if you ask Him to save you, He is in your heart. Tell them Hebrews 13:5 says, "I will never leave you nor forsake you." Show them in the Bible the assurance of salvation in John 1:12; John 3:16; and John 10:28-29.

For rededication to Jesus Christ, have them pray the Prayer for Rededication.

The Prayer for Rededication says, "Dear Heavenly Father, I thank You that as I come to you, you will in no way cast me out. I thank you, that You did not send Jesus into the world to condemn the world. But, so that the world could be saved through Him. I am your child because I believe that You raised Jesus from the dead and that He is my Lord. I confess my sin to you now. I thank you that you are faithful to forgive me and to cleanse me from all unrighteousness. I am forgiven. I am washed and cleansed by the blood of Jesus. I thank you that I now have right standing with the Father. In Jesus name. Amen!

10. Follow Up

McRaney explains, "What new Christians need more than a paper to fill out for follow-up is a person to walk with them on their new spiritual journey. No two converts have exactly the same questions or needs. A live person, not a recorded message, is what new converts need most. The best person to do follow-up is the one who led the person to Christ.

Connection is the key to follow-up. If new believers are not connected with other Christians and discipled, they typically will fall into patterns that leave them confused about what to do next. Many will simply do nothing. They will not grow in their relationship with Christ, nor will they encourage others to follow Christ."[8]

---

[8] McRaney, W., *Art of Personal Evangelism*, Chapter 9, 2003, 219, digital.

So now they made a decision and you led them to Christ, what should you do next? Tell them:

1. Read your Bible every day. Ask this person if they have a Bible. If they don't then give them one. Tell them to start reading the Gospel of John, then 1st John, and then the entire New Testament, and then the entire Old Testament.

2. Teach them to pray to God daily and take all of their problems and needs to God. Let them know it is a privilege to pray.

3. Tell him/her to go to attend church where the Bible is preached. Tell them Hebrews 10:25 says, "Do not forsake the assembling of yourselves together." Romans 10:17 says, "Faith comes by hearing, and hearing by the Word of God." Tell them to Bible study services to learn.

4. Tell him/her that he should share their faith in Jesus Christ with others. Matthew 4:19 says, "Follow me and I'll make you fishers of men."

5. Teach the new Christian to make his salvation public by baptism which is in Romans 6:4-6. Baptism pictures the death, burial, and resurrection of Jesus.

6. Stay away from sin.

Leave them with a church, invite them to church and exchange contact information.

Immediate Follow-Up: The people in front of you have just received Christ. What should you do? There is no one answer, but you should do some of the following:

- Celebrate their commitment with them.
- Assure them that they made the best of decisions.
- Encourage and help them communicate with someone who they know would be supportive of their new commitment—sharing their testimony.
- Explain their need and the privilege of talking with God throughout the day (prayer).
- Schedule the next follow-up visit with them.
- Call or write them a note within the first week.
- Provide them with an overall picture of what they might expect.
- Do not bombard them with information.

You are now in your next several contacts with the new convert. You will want to cover some of the following topics.

- Baptism—finding ways to celebrate with new believers. Celebrate baptisms by throwing a party, inviting their friends, clapping, or videotaping the baptism
- Sharing their faith on a consistent basis
- Basics of reading and understanding Scripture (modern translation)

- Church involvement—assisting them in making a connection
- Discipleship matters—spiritual disciplines and basics on how to walk with Jesus daily and for a lifetime
- Carefully addressing assurance of salvation, as the Holy Spirit confirms that a person is in Christ
- Dealing with ongoing problems and sin in their lives
- Helping them find identity in Christ"[9]

McRaney explains, "**Heart: Attitudes and Feelings to Motivate the Witness**

Evangelistic training affects not only the head and the hands but also the heart. Evangelistic activities flow out of a vital, passionate relationship with Christ and a deep concern and passion for lost people. Below are a few tips for developing the heart component of personal evangelism.

- Read and tell the great biblical stories of God's great love for His people.
- Share testimonies of the saving and changing power of God.
- Provide as many different experiences in evangelistic activities as possible.
- Make a big deal of baptism services—invitations to lost relatives and friends, storytelling—and create a celebrative atmosphere.
- Interview lost people.
- Take note of the significant needs in the lives of lost friends.
- Have a quiet time with the evening news and newspaper on your mind about the condition of the world.
- Develop a list of lost people with whom you will begin to cultivate a friendship.
- Pray for lost people by name; prayer walk around your house."[10]

11. Assignment

Based on what you have learned, you will now defend Christianity.

Scenario #1:

You have met someone, and you begin a conversation with the person. Eventually you make the person know you are a Christian. The person asks what Christianity is and you explain. The person asks you to explain the problem of evil. The person also asks, "how I will be able to face and handle the attack of the enemy while I walk with Jesus Christ?"

Scenario #2:

Now we are going to go and evangelize some lost souls for the kingdom of God.

---

9   McRaney, W., *Art of Personal Evangelism*, Chapter 9, 2003, 220.
10   McRaney, W., *Art of Personal Evangelism*, Chapter 9, 2003, 220.

12. Closing

Reflection in Action by Connection

Answer the questions on the lines provided.

Question 1: Have you ever attempted to have a spiritual conversation with an unbeliever about Jesus Christ, and if so, what happened?

A:_____

Question 2: Do you have a reluctancy to talk to others about Jesus Christ? What are your reasons?

A:_____

Answer: Reasons can be fear, lack of training, not enough contact with unbelievers.

Question 3: When you read 1 Peter 3:13-18, what is the challenge that Peter is addressing in this epistle?

A:_____
Answer: Peter is speaking to the believers who were persecuted at that time for their Christian beliefs. Peter is explaining what it means to suffer for doing good. The believer must set apart Christ as Lord in his heart and follow in his footsteps, then the believer can be delivered from the fear of their persecutors, being confident that through suffering they will share his victory.
Read the Scripture and explain its overall meaning.

Question 4: What is evangelism?
A:_____
Answer: Evangelism is the spreading of the Christian gospel by public speaking or personal witness. It communicates the gospel message, with a warning, explanation, and a call.

Question 5: Which method of evangelism do you believe you can apply to evangelize others?
lines

A:_____
Note: Use the one that you are comfortable with. Every situation can give a different result. Don't give up, keep witnessing the gospel of Jesus Christ.

SAY: We are now moving into the last goal. Amen.

GOAL NINE

DISCIPLESHIP: DISCIPLES TO DISCIPLE OTHERS

LESSON PLAN

Date & Time:	Curriculum Area: Discipleship-Disciples to Disciple Others	Goal /Unit Topic: Goal Nine

Key enduring understandings, concepts, abilities, and/or values.
Explained in the Introduction

Intended learning outcomes (to know, to do, to create, to value, etc.)
Explained in the Overview

Assessment Strategies: How will you assess attainment of the intended learning outcome?
Questions & Answers, Dialect, Interaction, post/pre-Test

Materials/Preparation/ Area Setup:
Materials: Poster board, Dry Erase Markers
Preparation: Decorations, Poster board
Area Setup: For each disciple, place on the desk a blue pen, highlighter, notebook, goal nine

Introduction	Setting the Stage: engaging, motivating, experiencing, connecting with prior knowledge, reflecting, conjecturing, posing problems
Once the Introduction and Overview have been completed, then move on to the Bible book recitals. It will be recited every time that we meet with the disciples.	

Guided learning steps The learning steps are as follows:	Disclosing: acquiring knowledge/skills, conceptualizing, developing, understanding, integrating
1. Discipleship	Practicing, Reinforcing: modeling, giving instruction, checking for understanding, guided practice, independent practice, applying, posing and solving problems
2. Disciple(s)	
3. Making Disciples	
4. Five Stage Discussion and Examples	
5. Family Discipleship	
6. Local Congregation	
7. A Child's Heart	
8. Spiritual Disciplines	
9. Small Groups	
10. Closing	
Questions & Answers	
Prayer	
Evaluation	

Closure	Transcending: summing up, responding, creating, performing, committing, evaluating
Prayer, Questions & Answers, Comments	

Modifications:
How will you change the lesson to meet the needs of the individual disciples?

Personal notes/reminders/homework/assignments

Post-lesson reflections

INTRODUCTION

Jesus commanded us to live out the Great Commission (Matt. 28:19-20) and the Great Commandment (Matt. 22:36-40). The early church preached throughout the New Testament in small groups in homes. They used the small group ministry concept to the community of unbelievers. Acts 2:4-47 and Eph 4:11-16 are examples of the early church and the work they did. Let's go to Col 1:28 and examine whether or not you are seeking to represent "everyman" complete (teleois) in Christ. The focus is on the individual. If we are growing and developing disciples, Jesus has promised to "be" with us.

Overview

I. Goal Lesson:

Goal nine teaches discipleship. As a result, the disciple (you) will be able to perform the Great Commission and the Great Commandment to disciple others.

II. Goal Objectives:

Upon completion of this lesson, the disciple (you) will be able to:

    a. explain discipleship, disciples and the stages they have to experience,
    b. explain family discipleship, and
    c. explain the concept of small groups.

III. Bible Books Recital

Genesis to Revelation

1. Discipleship

Discipleship is a relational decision made by a disciple of Jesus Christ by fulfilling and responding to the Great Commission. We need to be disciples who are going out by evangelizing and witnessing to make disciples of Jesus for the Kingdom of God here on earth.

SAY: So, you have made it through all eight goals with God's grace. Now you will begin discipleship, prepare and fulfill your God given assignment with your spiritual giftings and disciple others for the Kingdom of God.

There are three stages of discipleship

1. **Declaration** (Investigation leading to repentance and faith in Jesus. Here is the call to investigate the person and work of Jesus to arrive at a goal which is the place of committed belief. Question to ask: Will you believe in Jesus?

2. **Development** (Immersion, Abandonment and apprenticeship into ministry). Question to ask: Will you follow Jesus?

3. **Deployment** (International Global commissioning). Here is where you are declared fit to reproduce the process in the lives of others.

Question to ask: Will you go for Jesus?

God's plan for spiritual formation of disciples is justification (Conversion, regeneration), sanctification (Discipleship being equipped), and final glorification (does not change).

2. Disciple(s)

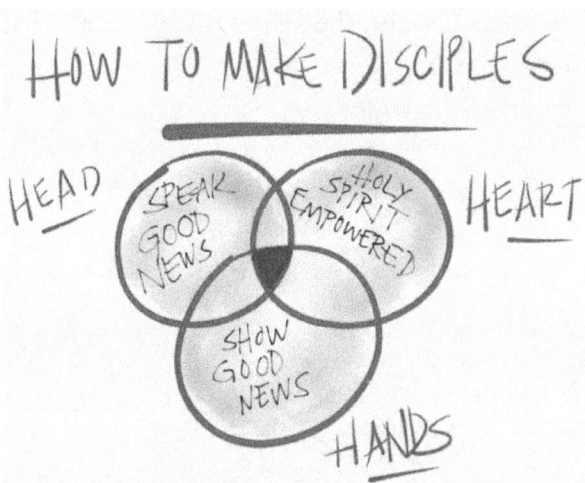

Retrieved from: http://2.bp.blogspot.com/-RMGbdULG5I8/UVX5m4AhKXI/AAAAAAAAEEw/9z-nzal3uqU/s1600/how+to+make+disciples+_+gcmcollective.jpg

The word disciple literally means, "to become a learner or pupil". A disciple of Jesus is a worshiper, a servant, and a witness. Each person in this room is a disciple and those outside of this room, ministry or wherever you are, is a potential disciple for the kingdom of God.

A disciple grows in the four spheres of life:

1. By relationship to God through the head, the heart, and the hands.
2. By relationship with the church which is God's family.
3. By relationship in the home life.
4. By relationship to the world.

The benefit of the four spheres is that being a Christian means that all of these areas need to come under Christ's control. Remember "you cannot be committed to the person of Christ, without being committed to the mission of Christ".

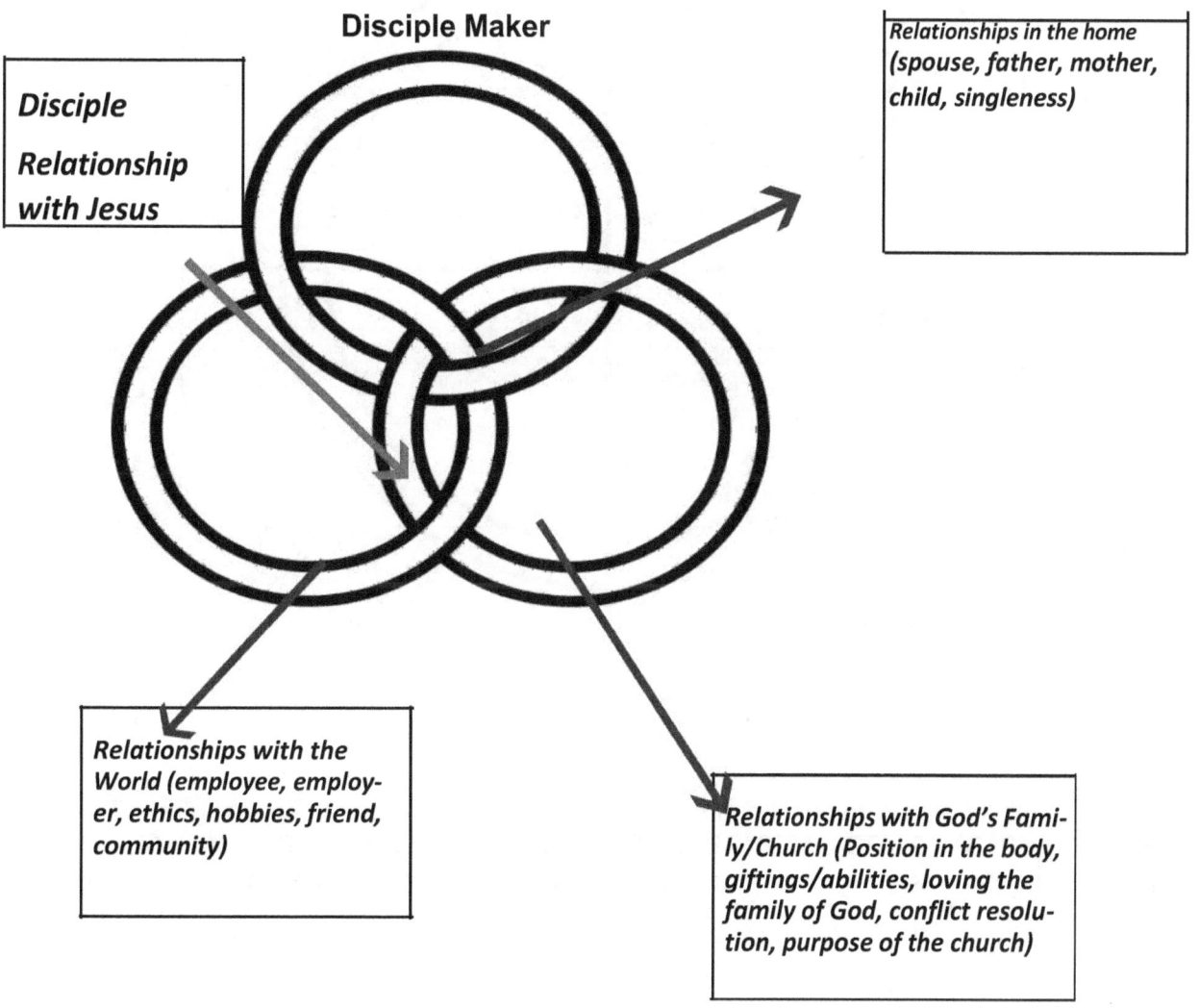

3. Making Disciples

The new disciples will have to go through God's process for their life assignment. Each person will have that encounter with the Holy Spirit which will sustain them as they become disciple makers. Each disciple will move through the five stages of discipleship, and we will discuss those in deeper conversations.

4. Five Stages

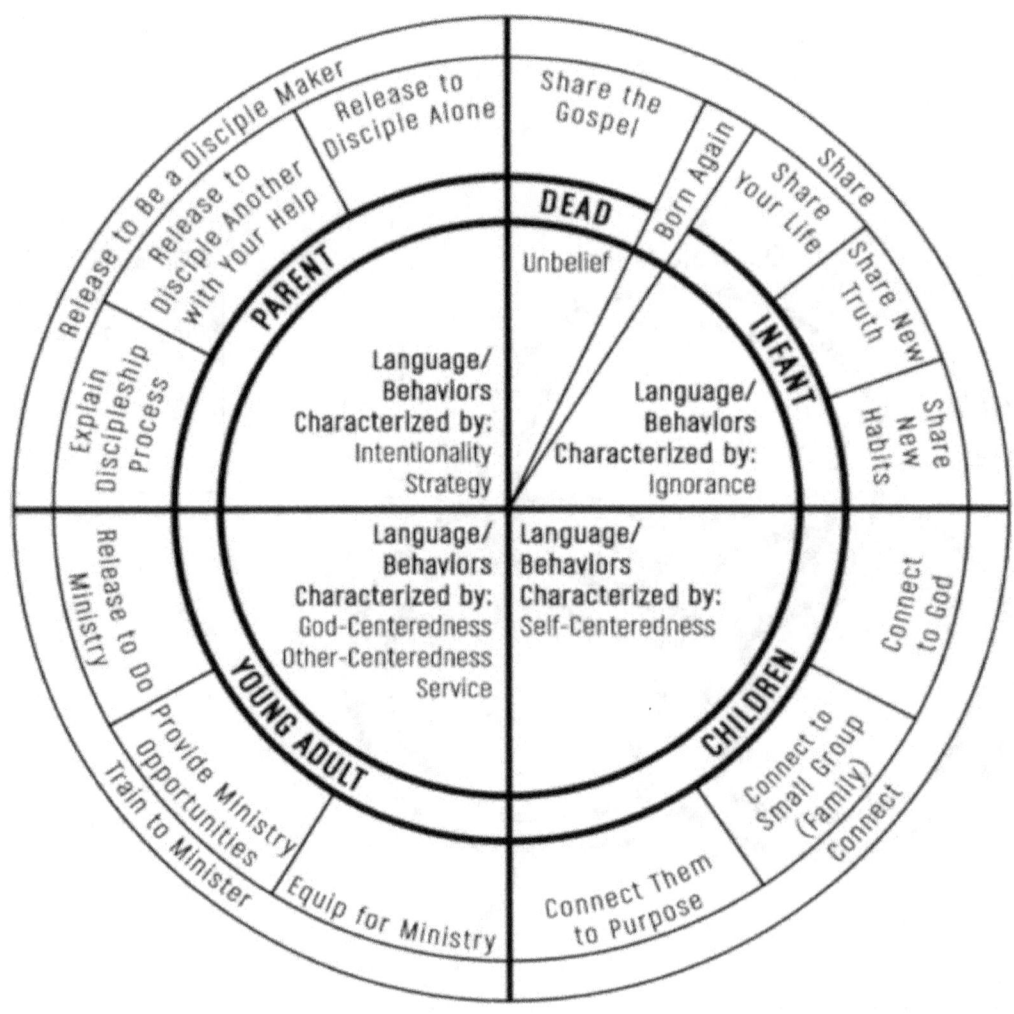

Retrieved from: https://www.bing.com/images/search?view=detailV2&ccid=R767ZW5g&id=FD-120F0BACD6C369A3091264FD4050861DB62060&thid=OIP.R767ZW5gPK2LBcTskAhIoAE-sEa&q=five+stages+of+discipleship+pictures&simid=608009346135164314&selectedIndex=0&ajaxhist=0

Goal Nine: Discipleship: Disciples to Disciple Others

We are going to have discussions and go through each level with examples.

Let's begin at Level 1, here is the spiritually dead and immature person coming to Jesus Christ and knows nothing about the gospel. It can also be a backslider who has repented and will have to go through a new process due to disobedience.

Putnam describes, "**Level 1 Spiritually Dead**. We begin at the top of the circle in the twelve to one o'clock position. Ephesians 2:15 describes those who are dead in their transgressions and sins. So, let's discuss the spiritually dead person. Now we will learn how we approach and help them with the love of Jesus Christ."[1]

They may reject God, they may be seeking God, they may call themselves Christians, but there is no fruit in their lives. They may claim to know Jesus, but they do not have the Holy Spirit living in them. As you interact with those who are spiritually dead to God, you may encounter some who exhibit unbelief or open rebellion. We should not be surprised when spiritually dead people act different ways. They are acting according to their dead human nature, and they cannot change until they have been made alive in Christ.

<u>SAY:</u> Are there any questions? Please write down your questions.

Putnam describes, "**Level 2: Infant**. This is found in the two or three o'clock position. 1 Peter 2:2-3 describes the infant. So, let's discuss the infant.

Spiritual infants tend to lack knowledge about what Jesus taught. They are not unintelligent; they are simply uninformed and in need of truth. But they may have also gotten mixed up with the philosophy of the world, combining it with scripture in a hybrid that works for them at least at this point they think it is working for them. Their lives are generally all about them and what they think works to fulfill their personal needs. People at this stage are spiritually alive; they have made a decision to follow Jesus, but that's about as far as they have gotten!"[2]

Spiritual infants will ask a lot of questions. The key concept is that infants don't know much. They need some to care for and feed them so they can grow and thrive. They need the personal attention of a spiritual parent. They need protection and guidance during this vulnerable stage of discipleship. At this stage, they need the truth of the Christian faith taught and modified for them. They need to develop new habits that form new partners for living as a follower of Christ.

Putnam describes, "**Level 3: Child**, this is found at the three to six o'clock position. Paul describes himself as a spiritual father. 1 Thessalonians 2:10-12.

So, let's discuss the child.

People in this stage are continuing to grow in their relationship with God, and they are beginning to grow in their relationships with other Christians as well. They are beginning to apply God's <u>word in their lives</u> and are walking with other growing disciples in their spiritual journey. Though

---

[1] Putman et al., *DiscipleShift*, 2013, 81.
[2] Ibid, 63.

they are growing, much of their spiritual life revolves around them--meeting their needs, their desires, and their interests. A spiritual child can be a relatively new Christian, or it can be a person who has been a Christian for many years. It's not the amount of time that passes that makes the difference between mature and immature; it's what has happened or not happened in a relational discipleship process during that time. How has he or she allowed the Holy Spirit to bring change and develop to manifest the likeness of Christ?"

Romans 14 teaches us how a child can be. A child can be overconfident, prideful, and full of himself, but they also can be insecure, timid, shy, and full of self-loathing or defeat.

So, what are the needs of spiritual children? Their primary need is a strong relational connection to a mature believer so they can make the transition to a more God and kingdom-focused life. They need someone who will help them learn how to make the developmental transition from dependency to learning how to spiritually feed themselves. They need teaching about who they are in Christ, how to have close friendships with other believers, and what to expect (and not expect) from Christians. They need to learn to trust God in obedience, doing what the word says rather than what their feelings tell them to do. As they grow, their lives will become more and more about God. They will learn to do the right things for the right reasons. And they will learn what it means to have a servant heart, rather than one that is self-centered."[3]

SAY: Are there any questions? Please write down your questions?

Putnam describes, "**Level 4 Young Adult**. This is found at the six to nine o'clock position. 1 John 2: 13-14 describes people who are spiritually young adults. So, let's discuss the young adult.

Spiritual young adults are making a shift from being self-centered to being God-and-other-centered. They are beginning to reorient their lives around God's word and His people and mission. They are starting to understand that God has called them to give to the body of Christ, rather than simply take. They are involved in ministering to others, putting the needs of others first, and being doers of the word-not just people who hear it and accumulate head knowledge. Spiritual young adults are beginning to see that God has created them for a purpose, and their priorities have started to change. They look for places to serve and may join the worship band, serve in the children's ministry or occasionally speak or teach in front of larger groups of people. As they grow more secure in Christ, they tend to be less judgmental and find it easier to overlook others' faults. They are excited about their involvement in the church, and even when they are not, they are learning to be faithful. They have begun maturing in their faith and are learning to focus on fitting their skills and passions to God's kingdom purposes.

What are the needs of these spiritually young adults? First, they need a place where they can learn how to serve. They need a spiritual mentor who will coach and debrief them on their ministry experiences. They need deep, ongoing relationships with people who offer encouragement and accountability. They often need help to establish boundaries. They need guidance in responding to the expectations of people they serve. They need help with identifying their gifts and recurring

[3] Putnam et al., *DiscipleShift*, 2013, 65-67.

skills training. When they get hurt, they need to process the pain so they don't become disillusioned and cynical."[4]

SAY: Are there any questions? Please write down your questions?

Putnam describes, "**Level 5 Parent-Mature**

This is found at the nine to twelve o'clock position. 2 Timothy 2:1-2 describes people who are strong in the grace that is in Christ Jesus.

So, let's discuss the parent or mature one.

A parent must be spiritually mature. In other words, spiritual mature parents make disciples. If the spiritual capable people are not parenting someone, then they are just young adults themselves.

A spiritual parent has a solid understanding of God's word, abiding relationship with God, and a desire to be involved in raising up other disciples. Spiritual parents live out God's word in their daily lives. They are kingdom-centered and God-dependent.

Parents typically know how to determine where a person is in his or her spiritual journey, know where the person needs to go, and know how to get them there. As mature believers, parents understand that you never outgrow your need for a spiritual family, and they are humbled to be involved in the church despite its many imperfections.

What are the needs of spiritual parents? Most important, they need to have close peer relationships with other spiritual parents who are involved in making disciples for encouragement. Peer accountability and ongoing training help spiritual parents hone their skills. They also need assistance in learning how to delegate responsibility so that they can take time to rest and avoid getting burned out. They need to be encouraged and freed to make disciples in the church. They need permission to develop people to maturity. If you define disciple and celebrate disciples making disciples, you create a culture of discipleship."[5]

SAY: Are there any questions? Please write down your questions?

Now I would like each person to tell us which level they believe they are currently walking in and why? Remember no level is more important than another level. All levels are important.

Level: _____

Why? _____

---

    4   Putman et al., *DiscipleShift*, 2013, 67-69.
    5   Putman et al., *DiscipleShift*, 2013, 69-71.

5. Family Discipleship

The family includes married couples, singles, widows, children, youth, elderly which is the entire body of Christ. Once the church receives a new convert, the focus must be to save others living in his or her family household. Here is where the entire family can experience new converts training together.

There will be opposition at the home when that new convert first goes home and he or she may not return to church. The parents will be able to be an example of a disciple training others by training their children. It is the parent's responsibility to disciple by teaching the word, training, disciplining and modeling the behavior and lifestyle according to the word of God. The church is to reinforce what is taught in the home according to the word of God. The responsibility must not be left on the church. We are stewards of our home and those who dwell with us. Once that is done then we can disciple others to fulfill the Great Commission.

For the married couples with children, parents are primarily responsible to disciple their own children. For the married couple without children, they are to disciple each other.

Renfro explains, "Children raised with strong family discipleship are able not only to relate to their peers but also relate to other age groups. They stand against peer pressure and proclaim the truth of Christ because they are not dependent on approval from their peers. Christians must equip their children, grounding them in the truth, and then launch them to be missionaries in the culture.

We reach the parents first and the children naturally follow, allowing us to disciple entire families."[6]

The major scriptures dealing with family are Deut. 6, Eph. 6, and Colossians 3.

Family discipleship should include:

1. A biblical foundation for family integration through the church's proclamation and teaching.
2. Be certain that the church's leadership models family discipleship.
3. Equip the heads of households to become spiritual leaders in their homes.
4. Provide plans for family worship to train a child if yet not learned to sit with their parents in worship service.
5. Encourage heads of households to evaluate their families' priorities and to reevaluate their family's calendars, eliminate items that hinder family time.
6. When times of worship, begin having children and adults worship together.
7. Do not implement age-segregated events.
8. Small groups transition to age-integrated groups.

---

[6] Renfro, P., *Perspectives on Family Ministry: 3 Views*, 2009, 94.

9. Ministries transition to age-integrated groups.

10. Mission efforts transition toward age-integration.

Families must learn and understand the tools of the Bible. Family discipleship should address topics, such as, nontraditional family structures, orphaned children, single moms and dads, divorced and blended families, teenagers with spiritually absent parents, household with two working parents, and so on.

God has commissioned the local church to reach all people, in all family contexts, in every nation, with the gospel of Jesus (Matt. 28:18-20; Acts 1:8). The evangelistic responsibility of the church extends beyond the door of Christian homes.

Renfro explains, "**Family discipleship should include:**

We can apply Deuteronomy 6:7 as a ministry plan for a child's life. The Deuteronomy 6:7 ministry plan hopes that our students and children will:

1	Love God as a way of life (worship). Roman 12:1-2
2	Love others as a way of life (service). Mark 10:45
3	Love the church and understand their roles in the body of Christ (community). Eph 4:4-7
4	Love the Bible and can handle it properly as the authority and foundation for life (Scripture). 2 Tim. 3:5-17
5	Love to tell others about Christ (the gospel) and share their stories (testimony). Rom. 10:14-15
6	Love to grow closer to God through personal spiritual disciplines such as prayer and Bible study (discipleship). 1 Tim. 4:7-12."[7]

These six biblical characteristics truly teach what it means to love God.

For the home, God holds men accountable throughout the Bible for the discipleship that takes place under their roofs (Deut. 6; Psalm 78; Eph. 6:4). Any man with the Holy Spirit and the Word of God can be equipped and expected to carry out his God given duty.

Question: What do you do with the parents who have not caught the vision for discipling their children?

Answer: 2 Tim. 4:1-2. Pastors must call fathers and mothers to obey God's Word. If they are stubborn, reproof and rebuke may be necessary, but with love.

Today, culture sees parenting as an adult care provider. Parenting is to shepherd your child on God's behalf. Training and shepherding are going on whenever you are with your children. Deut. 6-7. If you're going to shepherd your children, you must understand what makes your children

[7] Renfro, P., *Perspectives on Family Ministry: 3 Views*, 2009, 150.

tick. If you are going to direct them in the ways of the Lord, according to Genesis 18, you must know them and their inclinations. You must strengthen your child's weak areas and encourage his/her strengths. Parents must teach their children that they are sinners by nature. Parents must also point them to the mercy and grace of God shown in Christ's life and death for sinners.

Unholy human anger may teach your children to fear you. It moves them away from God. Even if a child professes his/her faith in Christ, the parent still has to shepherd, train, instruct and discipline their children. The Pastor and leaders have to make a commitment to the family of the entire church. It has to be a partnership with the same goals of discipleship.

The family of God gets the reputation we live out in our homes. Children are prepared for their experience of the church family by their experience in our own families. That's why God uses familial terms to describe himself as a Father, Christ as the Son, us as his sons and daughters, Christ as our brother, the Church as Christ's bride, and fellow Christians as sisters and brothers.

6. Local Congregation

SAY: What role do you believe the local congregation should play in the family and individuals?

The local congregation must set the example of who and what is church according to God's design. There should be programs in place to provide training, intervention, or activities for families and individuals. The pastor and leadership should be teaching all biblical truths to the family and the individuals.

Components of the local church to its congregants are:

- Weekly worship and fellowship
- Communion
- Baptism
- Discipleship
- Bible study
- Men being trained to become spiritual fathers and leaders
- Women being trained
- Spiritual disciplines being trained and exercised
- Accountability
- Christian worldviews
- Learning how to worship, pray, fasting, giving, evangelizing, serving others, marriage, child training, mentoring, intercession, growing in the fruit of the Spirit, growing in ministry gifts, family worship, how to live, and how to minister to others.

A church that lines up with God's Word and it is lead biblically will experience His blessing, and a church that closely resembles what Jesus and the apostles expected the church to look like. The church is not a family of families but the family of God. Scriptures that explain that are 1 Cor.

12; 1 Pet. 4:17; 1 Tim. 3:15. The church is the partner with the families and individuals, where they are right now, to fulfill the mission of Jesus in the world.

7. A Child's Heart

So, you're a parent now with a child or children with their own God made design. A parent is a shepherd and instructor of their child's heart. Today some parents are frustrated and confused. Children just don't act like they should, and parents want to know why. You are a steward over them. Raise them God's way so when they leave, they will continue God's way. Amen.

The Bible is the constitution over our lives. It provides all for children, parents, family values, nurturing and discipline so you are equipped for parenting. You must not mirror the problems of the world as you raise children. God's ways must be applied and can be successful. So, the task of the parent is to be a kind authority, display love, live the lifestyle of a Christian, shepherd the child to understand themselves in God's Word, keep the gospel in clear view, so they can live as people of God.

As a parent you begin by shepherding the child's heart.

SAY: Let's discuss authority. We/you must live under the authority of God in the home, church, state, and business. The child must be directed on God's behalf for their own good. So, as you exercise your authority, it must be to empower them to be self-controlled that can live freely under God's authority. You must request the child to obey God because God requires them to obey and honor you. A child will not resist authority if it is truly kind and selfless, they are understood, they understand God and his ways, understands how the world works, and you are committed to them to be successful.

SAY: Next is shepherding, which is the activity of the parent to the child. It helps a child to understand himself in the world in which he or she lives. You must teach the child to know the "what and why" of their actions. They must know that they were made by and for God. They must be led to discover, shepherd their thoughts, help them to learn discernment and wisdom. Open and honest communication will help the child to understand the meaning and purpose of life, and the ways of God's wisdom.

SAY: Next is focus on the gospel by directing the attitudes of their hearts. Show them the "what" of their sin and failure and the "why". They must know that God works from the inside out. As they grow they will receive internal transformation and empowerment. Let's look at Ezekiel 36:25 (the fullness of the gospel); 36:26 (the grace of forgiveness); 36:27 (the grace of eternal change is found in the gospel). The gospel enables them to face the worst like sin, badness, weakness, and they will find hope because of grace.

SAY: Next is the child must internalize the gospel's message. They will examine what the gospel claims and will decide if they should accept or deny it. As a parent you want a result of your child telling you what it means to know God.

As a parent, you must instruct a child's heart through their mind. The Bible links the thought to the heart.

Parents, especially the fathers are to take personal responsibility for the Christian formation of their children. The Apostle Paul commanded fathers to train their children "in the training and instruction of the Lord" (Eph. 6:4).

As a parent you must also instruct a child's heart. "the heart is the wellspring of life" (Prov. 4:23). We impress the child's heart with the truth. Solid parenting skills are built on solid truth. As you instruct a child's heart, they can experience delighting in God and the goodness of his ways. First parents must remember that you are engaged in a battle inside of us (James 4:1) and outside of us (Eph. 6:12). Sometimes we house and feed the enemy. Know your spiritual enemies, identify the enemy's power, and influence. Second, apply biblical formative instruction as an offensive and defensive weapon against the enemy of your children's soul. Remember to put on the full armor of God daily (Eph. 6:10-17 and 1 Pet. 5:8).

The culture of the world will teach children that authority is something that they do not have to obey at school, at home, and at church. We know Monday through Friday that they are at school, around teachers and friends more than the home. Parents you only have the evenings and weekends, depending on work schedules. We must be teaching in and out of the home about behavior, love, what to believe, decision making, how to think from the Scriptures, and how to live. These types of deliberate teachings are called formative instruction which "forms" or "shapes" our children. It is a lifetime process from infancy to adulthood rooted in Scripture. (Prov. 22:6). Your life must also express God's Word as well. When we speak and live the words of God, we too speak and live with authority (1 Pet. 4:11).

Discipline is different than formative instruction because formative instruction should be happening all the time. Discipline should be applied only when behavior needs to be corrected. If you only instruct when the child needs discipline, the child will not listen to the instruction because of fear of the discipline. Formative instruction must teach that discipline is a part of God's way for the parent to provide protection, direction, safety, and blessing to children. Teach your children to love the Scriptures for the promises and the warnings. Teach your children the history of the Scriptures, how to develop Godly habits, how to apply scripture to their lives, modeling spiritual vitality, and grow into a mature relationship with your children.

8. Spiritual Disciplines

Spiritual disciplines are those practices found in Scripture that promote spiritual growth among believers in the gospel of Jesus Christ. The Spiritual disciplines which are for the purpose of godliness, are bible intake, prayer, worship, evangelism, serving, stewardship, fasting, silence and solitude, journaling, learning, and perseverance. Many of these disciplines we have already

Goal Nine: Discipleship: Disciples to Disciple Others

discussed, and they are all important for the purpose of godliness.

<u>SAY:</u> Where does discipline fit in if God wants us to be conformed to Christlikeness?

Answer: Without holiness, which is Christlikeness, or godliness-no one will see the Lord. We can stand before God only in the righteousness that's been earned by another, Jesus Christ. 1 Timothy 4:7 gives us the answer, "Discipline yourself for the purpose of godliness (NASB).

Let's start going through these spiritual disciplines.

1. **Bible** intake of reading and studying the Word of God is personal. Hearing the bible read and studying it with the church is interpersonal. Practice reading the Bible aloud or use an audio Bible (Rev. 1:3). Jesus went to pray alone (Matt. 4:1; 14:3; Mark 1:35; Luke 4:42) and Jesus went to the synagogue on the Sabbath Day (Luke 4:16). The purpose of bible intake is to "keep it" and do what God says and develop in Christlikeness. Read and study, meditate, memorize and apply the Word of God. Attend a Bible-believing church where the Word of God is faithfully preached.

2. **Prayer** is the will of God. Jesus expects us to pray (Matt. 6:5; 6:6, 6:7, 6:9; Luke 11:9; Luke 18:1). God's Word says, Colossians 4:2, "continue steadfastly in prayer.", 1 Thess. 5:17, "Pray without ceasing." Prayer is communication int the spiritual realm. Prayer is learned which means the best way to learn how to pray is to pray. Read the scripture, meditate on it by taking what God has said and think deeply on it, close it, and then shift to speaking to God about it in meaningful prayer. As you grow in prayer you will also go into confession, thanksgiving, supplication, or intercession and prayer for others.

3. **Worship** God expects us to worship. We worship God, which means we ascribe to the proper worth of God, we magnify His worthiness of praise. We also approach God as He is worthy. Our worship is focusing on responding to God. Revelation 4:8 tells us that God is holy, "Holy, holy, holy, is the Lord God Almighty, who was and is and is to come!" As we read the word of God, the Holy Spirit opens the eyes of our understanding, God is revealed in the Scripture and we respond in worship. If your revelation and focus on God is a small amount, it will result in a small amount of worship of God. Reading the Bible and meditation are the heart of private worship. Worship is God centered focus and it responds from the soul. We also worship in spirit and in truth. John 4:23-24 says, "23 But the hour is coming, and now is, when the true worshipers will worship the Father in spirit and truth; for the Father is seeking such to worship Him. 24 God is Spirit, and those who worship Him must worship in spirit and truth." You must have the Holy Spirit within you before you can worship in spirit and truth. To worship in truth is to worship according to the truth of the Scripture. Worship God as He is revealed in the Bible, not as we want. God is of mercy and justice, love, and wrath, who welcomes into heaven and condemns into hell. To worship according to the truth of the Scripture is to worship Gods in the ways He gave us His approval in the Scripture. You must worship in public and in private. Jesus said, "Worship the Lord your God' (Matthew 4:10).

Worship must be a daily discipline. Worship is a means to godliness, as we truly worship, we become like Him.

4. **Evangelism** God expects all Christians to evangelize. Evangelism is when one presents Jesus Christ in the power of the Holy Spirit to sinful people. It is presented so that they may come to put their trust in God through Him. Then they will receive Jesus as their Savior and to serve Him as their King. It can be presented to one person or to a crowd. Scriptures on evangelism, Matt. 28:19-20; Mark 16:15, Luke 24:46-47; John 20:21; and Acts 1:8. Yes, God gifts some to be evangelists, but God expects us all to be His witness. The power is the Holy Spirit which is the same Holy Spirit power that changed your life. Develop an obsession for souls to be saved, ask God for more people to be converted, and God will produce the fruit. If you are a believer living God's Word, then you have the most powerful Christian witness inside of you. Not sharing the gospel is disobedience. Remember you must be able to talk about what the Lord has done for you and what He means to you.

   How would you do? Answer these questions: Can you talk about how people have broken the law of God who created them and are under his condemnation because of sin? Can you explain how God sent His Son, Jesus who kept the law and to others the credit for His obedience? Can you talk about how Jesus was willing to die on the cross for us as a substitute for the sin? Can you explain the urgency of repentance? Can you ask them to believe that Jesus' life and death can make them right with God? Can you tell them that God can give eternal life? If yes, then you can evangelize to lost souls. Amen

5. **Serving** Service to God must become a priority. Sloth and pride loathe to serve. We must serve for the sake of Christ and His kingdom and the purpose of godliness. If you do not then you will serve every once in a while, when it's convenient or to self-serve. Hebrews 9:14 says, "14 how much more shall the blood of Christ, who through the eternal Spirit offered Himself without spot to God, cleanse your conscience from dead works to serve the living God?" You must serve the Lord because you want to obey Him. We sin when we refuse to serve God. Remember what it was like when you did not know Christ, to be without God, no hope, guilty, unforgiven, and on the way to hell? Be motivated to serve because of gratitude, gladness, not guilt, humility, and love. We are all gifted to serve (1 Peter 4:10). 1 Peter 4:10 tells us that we are all gifted with at least one spiritual gift, and it was given for the purpose that you serve with it for the kingdom. Yes, serving God and others is hard work. If serving costs nothing, then it will accomplish nothing.

6. **Stewardship** So, God has given you the gift of time and work to do during that time assigned to your lifespan. Do we know how much time we have? No. We must use the time wisely because the last days are evil. Prepare now for where you will spend eternity. The time is short and passing and the remaining time remains uncertain. Use this time to discipline yourself for godliness. You are accountable to God for your time, talent, and treasures (money) John 9:4; Romans 14:12; 1 Cor. 3:13-15; Hebrews 5:12; Matthew 25:14-30; Proverbs 26:13-14; Proverbs 24;33-34; 1Timothy 5:8. Remember God owns everything you own, we own nothing, and

we are His managers. You are temporary steward of the things that belong eternally to God. Stewards also give which is worship. Giving says you have faith in God's provision, you trust God. Ask yourself these questions: Prepared for the end time? Are you prepared for the end time? Are you using God's time wisely in all aspects of life? Are you doing the will of God when it should be done? Do I accept God's principles for giving? Do you give like you really mean it? Stewardship must be for godliness.

7. **Fasting** Fasting is when a Christian will abstain from food for a period of time for a spiritual purpose. The purpose must be God-centered. There are several fasts, such as, normal fast which is to abstain from all food, except water) (Matthew 4:2; Luke 4:2), partial fast (limitation of the food but not all food) (Daniel 1:2; Mathew 3:4), absolute fast (avoid all food and drink) (Ezra 10:6), supernatural fasts (Deut. 9:9; 1 Kings 19:8), private fast Matthew 6:16-18) congregational fasts (Joel 2:15-16; Acts 13:2), national fasts (2 Chronicles 20;3), regular fast (Leviticus 16:29-31), and occasional fasts (Matthew 9:15). Jesus gave us instructions on what to do and what not to do. Fasting should be done for biblical spiritual purposes, such as, to strengthen prayer, seek God's guidance, express grief, seek deliverance or protection, express repentance, return to God, humility before God, concern for the work of God, ministering to the needs of others, overcome temptation, dedicate oneself to God, express love and worship to God, and many more spiritual purposes. It is for godliness.

8. **Silence and Solitude** When you are silent you are abstaining from speaking so you can seek a spiritual goal. You focus your mind on God and rest your soul in him. Solitude is that you withdraw to privacy for spiritual purposes. It can be minutes or for days. You are alone with God and you just think. Silence and solitude are normally together. Jesus practiced silence and solitude (Matt. 4:1; 14:23; Mark 1:35; Luke 4:42). It helps to minimize distractions especially when you are praying. It helps to express worship to God, to express faith in God, seek the salvation of the Lord, physical and spiritual restoration, you regain spiritual perspective, you seek the will of God, and you control the tongue. You can seek solitude and silence daily by finding a quiet place, have a goal of a time, give up a responsibility to have that time. It is for godliness.

9. **Journaling** A journal or a diary can be a place to write your prayers, plans, desires, dreams, visions, praise reports, testimonies, strategies, study the Word and so much more. It is about God and your life. You can use it to chart your progress in your Christian daily walk. It can help you to understand and evaluate yourself, meditation, express thoughts, and feelings to the Lord, you remember what God has done, monitor goals and priorities, and maintain other spiritual disciplines. It is the purpose of godliness.

10. **Learning** Proverbs 10:14 tells us, "The wise lay up the knowledge". Wise and righteous people can never get enough wisdom or knowledge. The wise and righteous remain teachable. We are always lifetime learners, so always seize the opportunity to learn. Proverbs 18:15 says, "An Intelligent heart acquires knowledge, he or she "seeks" it". God is glorified when we use the mind He made to learn of him, His Word, His ways, and His world. Our life begins with

learning the gospel, about Him, and His message to the world. You must discipline yourself to become an intentional learner. Take the time to read and choose your books well that are about God and the Christian life and walk with God. The goal is Christlikeness because godly learning leads to godly living.

11. *Perseverance* Our daily life can be so busy, for example, work, school, children, family, parents, marriage, illness, conflict amongst family members, financial tension, and so much more. How do you persevere in the disciplines of godliness through it all? The role of the Holy Spirit in your life is very key to increasing your spirituality. You must submit to the Holy Spirit's transforming instruction and power in your life. Romans 8:29 tells us the Spirit of God will begin to carry out the will of God to make the child of God like the Son of God. There will be days when you want to quit and give up on the people of God, but you can't do it. What you must do is to allow the Holy Spirit to produce the desire and the power in you which leads to godliness. The Holy Spirit will cause you to persevere. Your spiritual maturity also includes your growth as you fellowship with other people of God. Ephesians 4:16 speaks about the mutual edification of the whole body being joined and held together. Fellowship is to exhort one another. As you seek to become like Jesus Christ you will experience struggle and the Holy Spirit will help you to persevere through it. Remember the devil is committed to your failure. The Holy Spirit preserves you in the grace of God as you take the struggle of your cross and follow Christ to become Christlike. 2 Peter 1:6 says, "in your self-control, perseverance, and in your perseverance, godliness" (NASB). It is for godliness.

9. Small Groups

A group needs to know what it exists for. Groups need to be spirit-led to last. Eventually you will be moving into a small group.

ASK: What are the components of a small group?

Puntam explains,

1. **"Shepherding:** A leader of a small group is a shepherd. The leader models shepherding, he seeks to teach the groups' members to become shepherds themselves in their families and in future groups that they may lead.

    Scripture: Ezek. 34:2-5. Ezekiel explains an example of lack of care for the people. People need spiritual water. 1 Peter 5:4, Christ is the primary shepherd for his people. Leaders in the church must feel the need to chase the strays. A leader must encourage all members of the group to become shepherds themselves. Leaders intentionally guide their small group members into caring for one another. A leader models what playing together as a team looks like and helps prep each person to play his or her part.

2. **Teaching:** In the small group is where real teaching takes place. There must be Q & A, modeling, and the Bible. The leader must help group members interact with the Word and

with others so that people are participating in whatever is discussed. Point the person to what the Bible says about it. As a leader, you want people to go to Christ, to abide in Christ and His Word.

3. **Authenticity and Accountability:** It is encouraged and modeled. Love is the foundation. People who sin will walk away from God because they feel unworthy. Sharing breaks the power of secrecy in people's lives. Encourage your group members, not to judge but to praise them for bringing things out of the darkness and into the light.

Scripture: Gal. 6:2 Encourages us to bear one another's burden. This is what a small group is about. You want to mourn with those who mourn and rejoice with those who rejoice. Listen first, be gentle and empathize, pray, be people who point others to God's Word. People need to plan, move forward, and grow. Set boundaries for what's appropriate."8

The small group is a biblical relational environment in which discipleship takes place.

Small group selections should be made by every disciple that went through this discipleship plan. Walking with Father, Son and the Holy Spirit is a daily Christian lifestyle. Learning about God is a daily teaching. Disciples cling to Christ with an ever-deepening desire to know Him better and to become as much like Him as possible. Genuine disciples of Jesus Christ pursue godliness. Decide to discipline yourself for the purpose of godliness. Don't delay! Begin now! Amen.

Retrieved from https://ordinariateexpats.files.wordpress.com/2015/01/unity-logo.gif

10. Closing

Reflection in Action by Connection

Answer the questions on the lines provided.

Question 1: How does a disciple grow in the four spheres of life?

A: _____

_____

_____

Answer: by relationship to God through the head, heart, and hands. By relationship with the church which is God's family, by relationship in the home life, and by relationship to the world.

Question 2: What are the spiritual disciplines?

A: _____

_____

_____

Answer: The disciplines are Bible intake, prayer, worship, evangelism, serving, stewardship, fasting, silence and solitude, journaling, learning, and perseverance.

Question 3: Do you have a specific discipline that needs improvement, and if so, how will you move forward for improvement?

A: _____

_____

_____

Note: Remember to discipline yourself for the purpose of godliness.

Question 4: There are fives stages that a disciple will go through for spiritual growth. What are those five stages?

A: _____

_____

Answer: Dead, Infant, Children, Young Adult, Parent

Question 5: What are the three stages of discipleship?

A: _____

_____

_____

Answer: Declaration, Development, Deployment SAY: The Saving of Souls Foundation thanks you for attending the Soul Discipleship Plan. Your next focus is to make a covenant and become a part of one of the small groups. It will take 8 complete commitment, Putman et al., DiscipleShift, faith, and a relationship 2013, 186, 188. with Jesus Christ, our Lord and Savior.

Questions and Answers

We are now open for questions and answers. Anything that is not answered today, will be answered in two weeks. Let's set a time to meet and hear each other's testimonies of what has happened since this training and the next step to move forward.

Prayer

We will pray corporately for everything that was taught and revealed. Each of you now knows your spiritual gifting and you must all seek God for the manifestation so you can get to work for the kingdom of God.

Let's pray.

Evaluation Measurement

Evaluation

Please help improve our discipleship plan by taking a few minutes and answering a few statements about your disciple training experience from Goal one to nine.

Date: _____

Name: _____

Presenter's Name:_____

Goal Topics:

1. Circumcision of the Heart
2. Gifts of the Spirit
3. The Bible
4. Weapons of Spiritual Warfare
5. Praise & Worship
6. Kingdom and Church
7. Mission & Missions
8. Evangelism
9. Discipleship: Disciple to Disciple Others

Goal Nine: Discipleship: Disciples to Disciple Others

	Strongly agree	Agree	Neutral	Disagree	Strongly disagree
Materials provided were helpful					
Length of training was sufficient					
Content was well organized					
Questions were encouraged					
Instructions were clear and understandable					
Training met my expectations					
The presenter and presentation were effective					
Spiritual gift was identified					

Statement_____

_____

REFERENCES

Anthony, Michael J, *Christian Education*. Grand Rapids, MI., Baker Academic, 2001.

www. ChristianBibleStudies.com, Theology 101, 2009.

Van Brummelen, H. *Walking with God in the classroom: Christian approaches to learning and teaching* (3rd ed.). Colorado Springs, CO: Purposeful Design (ACSI). 2009. ISBN: 9781583310984.

Earley & Dempsey, *Disciple Making Is…* Nashville, TN: B & H Publishing Company, 2013.

Earley & Wheeler, *Evangelism Is-How to Share Jesus with Passion and Confidence*. B & H Publishing Group. 2010. (digital)

Enns, Paul, *The Moody Handbook of Theology*. Chicago, IL: Moody Publishers, 2014.

Fay, William. *Share Jesus Without Fear*. B and H Publishing Group, 1999. (digital)

Fee, Gordon D. Stuart Douglas. *How to Read the Bible for All Its Worth*. Zondervan, Grand Rapids, Michigan 49530, 2003.

Groothius, 2011

Herzog, David. *The Courts of Heaven*. Glory Zone Publishing, 2013.

Johnson, Melissa A., *Serving First Ladies In Ministry*, Women on the Frontline Ministries, 2010.

Jr. Marzullo, Frank, *Spirits that Attach to Leaders and Attach to the Church*, 2013.

Jr. Marzullo, Frank, *Spiritual Warfare Now- Fighting for the Sons of Men*, 2013.

Köstenberger, Andreas, L. Scott Kellum, and Charles L. Quarles. *The Cradle, the Cross, and the Crown: An Introduction to the New Testament*. Nashville, TN: Broadman & Holman, 2009. ISBN: 9780805443653.

Lea & Black, *The New Testament: Its Background and Message*. Nashville, TN: B & H Publishing Group, 2003.

References

Malphurs, Aubrey. *Being Leaders: The Nature of Authentic Christian Leadership*. Grand Rapids: Baker Book House Co., 2003. ISBN: 9780801091438.

Maxwell, John C., *Developing the Leader Within You*, Nashville, TN: Thomas Nelson, Inc., 1993.

Merrill et al., *The World and the Word: An Introduction to the New Testament*. Nashville, TN: B & H Publishing Group, 2011.

McRaney, William. *The Art of Personal Evangelism*. Nashville, TN: B and H Publishing Group, 2003. (digital)

Moreau et al., *Introducing World Missions: A Biblical, Historical, and Practical Survey*. Grand Rapids, MI: Baker Academic, 2004.

Prince, Derek. *Blessings and Curses*, Biblical Truth Simply Explained, Grand Rapids, MI: Chosen Books, 2003.

Pipes, Jerry Dr., Lee, Victor. *Family to Family: Leaving a Lasting Legacy*. 1999. ISBN: 0-840085109.

Putman et al., *DiscipleShift*. Grand Rapids, MI: Zondervan, 2013.

Renfro, Paul, 2009. Liberty University Custom. *Perspectives on Family Ministry: 3 Views*. Nashville: Lifeway Church Resources, 2009. ISBN: 9781943965311.

Richards, Lawrence and Bredfelt, Gary. *Creative Bible Teaching*. Chicago, IL: Moody Publisher., 2009.

Sanders, Oswald J., *Spiritual Leadership: Principles of Excellence for Every Believer*. Chicago, IL: Moody Publishers, *2007*.

Scott, Kenneth, The Weapons of Our Warfare Volume I, 2002. ISBN: 978-0-9622009-2-3.

Stedman, Ray C. *Body Life: The book that Inspired a Return to the Church's Real Meaning and Mission*. Grand Rapids, MI: Discovery House, 1995. [212 pp.]. ISBN: 9781572930001.

Tozer, A. W. *Knowledge of the Holy*. New York: Harper One, 2009. [117 pp.]. ISBN: 9780060684129.

Tripp, Tedd, and Margy Tripp. *Instructing a Child's Heart*. Wapwallopen: Shepherd Press. 2008. ISBN: 9780981540009.

Tripp, Tedd. *Shepherding a Child's Heart*. Wapwallopen: Shepherd Press. 1998. ISBN: 9780966378603.

Webb-Mitchell, Brett P., *Christly Gestures: Learning to be Members of the Body of Christ*. Grand Rapids, MI: Wm. B. Edermans Publishing Co., 2003.

Whitney, Donald S. *Spiritual Disciplines for the Christian Life*. 2nd ed. Colorado Springs: Navpress, 2014. [304 pp.]. ISBN: 9781615216178.

Winter & Hawthorne, *Perspectives on the World Christian Movement: A Reader*. Pasadena, CA: William Carey Library, 2009.

Wray, Bruce, and Lynn Wray. *Charting a Course for Your Family's Future – A Purposeful Guide to Parenting*. 2013. (E-Book). ISBN: 9781935986676

Wright, Steve, and Chris Graves. *ApParent Privilege*. Nashville: InQuest Ministries, Inc. 2008. ISBN: 9781931548731.

Yount, William R., ed. *The Teaching Ministry of the Church*. 2nd ed. Nashville: B&H Publishing Group, 2008. ISBN: 9781943965427. (digital)

Zumpano, Ben, M.D., *Spiritual Warfare Prayers*, 1999. Digital

Dake Annotated Reference Bible, Thomas Nelson, Inc., 1982

The Woman's Study Bible, p 9, 126, 162, 228, 266, 392, 558, 652, 664, 686, 732, 736, 738, 748, 774, 868, 1014, 1446, 1450, 1461, 1464, 1483, 1488, 1524, 1528, 1531, 1538, 1559, 1569, 1635, 1655, 1670, 1683

From *Nelson's NKJV Study Bible*, copyright©1997 by Thomas Nelson, Inc., Used by permission

Retrieved July 18, 2016 from http://christianity.about.com/od/biblefactsandlists/qt/Bible-Numerology.htm

Retrieved from July 18, 2016, http://www.pojc.org

Retrieved on July 18, 2016 from http://www.joshuamediaministries.org/dreams/animals

Retrieved on August 13, 2016 from http://www.bibleuniverse.com/articles/keys-to-bible-symbols#sthash.qTHscvbD.dpuf

Retrieved on August 21, 2016 from http://www.bibleuniverse.com/articles/keys-to-bible-symbols#sthash.qTHscvbD.dpuf